IMAGES
of America
ATHENS COUNTY

On the Cover: This photograph shows the James B. Southerton home in Dover Township in 1905.

IMAGES
of America

ATHENS COUNTY

Ron Luce

ARCADIA
PUBLISHING

ISBN 978-0-7385-9383-8

Published by Arcadia Publishing
Charleston, South Carolina

Printed in the United States of America

Library of Congress Control Number: 2012930693

For all general information, please contact Arcadia Publishing:
Telephone 843-853-2070
Fax 843-853-0044
E-mail sales@arcadiapublishing.com
For customer service and orders:
Toll-Free 1-888-313-2665

Visit us on the Internet at www.arcadiapublishing.com

To John

Contents

Acknowledgments		6
Introduction		7
1.	Before There Was an Athens County, Ohio	9
2.	The Founding of Athens County and Early Pioneers	15
3.	Townships, Villages, Cities, and a Handful of Stories	25
4.	Athens County in Times of Trouble	113
5.	Select Images of Athens County's Past	119
Bibliography		127

ACKNOWLEDGMENTS

Many people have helped make this book possible. I thank the good people of the Athens County Historical Society and Museum for making the collection of pictures available to me and for supporting me in this endeavor. Staff members and volunteers helping with this project include Jessica Cyders, Laura Farrell, Sara Green, and student volunteers. A special thank you goes to "my sons" Cyrus Moore and Konrad Stump, who helped in researching numerous pieces of information that ended up in this book. I also thank the many people who have donated their precious artifacts and pictures to the Athens County Historical Society and Museum to make them available to the public far into the future. A special thank you is owed to my very good friend Mary Davis, who provided her entire collection of pictures for me to peruse and use. Brenda Ruth also provided pictures. Jeff Ruetsche, my editor at Arcadia Publishing, has been of immense help and is deeply appreciated. In particular, I thank John Cunningham, who makes it possible for me to do such projects with his endless support and encouragement.

Unless otherwise noted, all pictures are from the archives of the Athens County Historical Society and Museum. Those pictures referred to as being from "the Anastas Collection" are a special collection within the Athens County Historical Society donated by the late James Anastas of Athens.

Introduction

Athens County is the kind of place that some of us think of as magical. It is the kind of place that too few know about, but once they find their way here and experience it, they do not want to leave. This is clearly evident in the numerous people now living and working in Athens County who came here to go to Ohio University and then found that the city of Athens and the county as a whole had wrapped itself around them—they could not shake it and they just had to stay.

Perhaps it is the preponderance of rolling hills, great forests, open land, small towns, or rural life—or any of numerous possibilities—that initially catches us. For me, it was the hills. I came from upstate New York, near Lake Ontario, where flat land went on forever. When I first arrived in Athens County for graduate school, I was quickly mesmerized by the power of the hills to envelop me and to sing in my ears the ancient songs of the land and the laments of what has been done to it in the past by greedy developers who reaped its black diamonds and then left it struggling for survival. I am lulled by the voices of the men and women who came here from all over the world to work our mines and dream an American dream. As I learned of them, I became proud of the workers who stood their ground for their rights and for this place they love, even against formidable, much more powerful foes.

For me, there is a spirit in Athens County that knows the joys and nobility of life, as well as the sorrows, and holds them in harmony with one another. There are sacred places here: those of the ancients who lived here before the arrival of Europeans, those we have created from our experiences making this place home, those we share, and those we forever hold secret unto ourselves.

When I agreed to do this book, I was overwhelmed by the immensity of things to say—all the things I love about this place, the history, the experience, the spirit—and I knew that in the space of this small book, I could not give readers what I have gained over these past 30 years. The *History of Hocking Valley, Ohio*, goes almost 1,400 pages, Walker's *History of Athens County* is almost 600, and Beatty and Stone's book, *Getting to Know Athens County*, goes to almost 300 pages, and these are just the major writers who have told the stories of this place. Thousands of pages of supplemental information fill the file drawers and shelves of the Athens County Historical Society and Museum. What could I offer in this handful of pages that would be worth saying?

Clearly, it is not possible to share all the history of this great county in a single book, nor is it possible to express much about even a single portion in the space allotted here. Thus, I came to think of this book as an introductory history and a pictorial teaser that I hope evokes feelings of nostalgia if you are from here and to want more (even if you have not yet been here), to turn to books like those mentioned above and come to the Athens County Historical Society and Museum. In what follows, the reader is treated to a quick glimpse in words and pictures of a few of the county's outstanding places and a few bits of history that may engender further study.

For those who have not yet come to Athens County, I warn you to be careful looking at these images; you just might get hooked like I did. While you are "wetting your whistle" viewing these pages, I will be working on the much longer and in-depth versions of the history that I hope to share with you in the future. Enjoy!

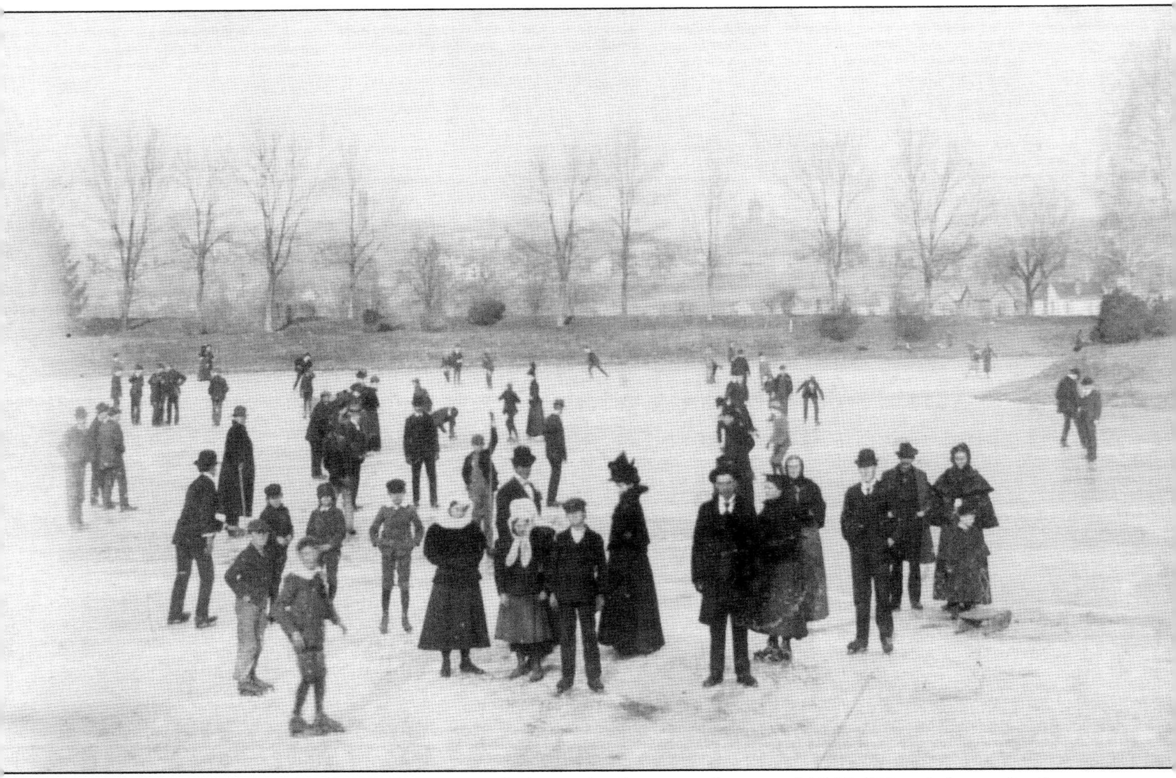

This image is of people ice-skating at Athens Asylum pond around 1900. The Athens Asylum was commonly used by town folk for picnics and get-togethers in the late spring, summer, and early fall. During the winter, the ponds provided a much safer environment for skating than the river.

One

Before There Was an Athens County, Ohio

It is fairly common for people who live in a place to be unaware of the history attached to that piece of land they too often come to take for granted. That place becomes like a favorite old pair of blue jeans, simply put on without thought and unconsciously loved but given little concern until they are finally worn too far. Then, the sense of loss becomes apparent. Athens County has changed significantly since it became known to Europeans and then East Coast Americans. Some of those changes have allowed people to prosper and to grow. On the other hand, some of those changes have forced the irremediable destruction of the past or reduced it to tidbits of information that historians, archaeologists, and paleontologists can only speculate upon. Thus, perspective is lost that might have helped people be more appreciative of the places now called home.

Some who live in Athens County are unaware of how special the county is as part of the Ohio and American adventures. However, residents are rich with stories to tell and much to appreciate; much that precedes Europeans landing on the shores of this great country. Much of what is now called Athens County was formed as a result of glacier movement during the Pleistocene epoch and is a result of the Illinoian and Wisconsin glaciations. The receding of these glaciers helped form the Hocking River, creeks and streams, floodplains, terraces, slopes, and ridgetops that are so much a part of today's landscape. Over eons, plant life, animal life, climate changes, and effects of time laid the foundations that served human beings as they came upon this remarkable place.

There are few pictorial remnants (in some cases, none) of small communities that have come and gone, and written records are limited. The towns and communities that continue to thrive and/or leave a pictorial and written record are Albany, Amesville, Athens, Buchtel, Canaanville, Chauncey, Coolville, Glouster, Guysville, Hockingport, Jacksonville, Millfield, Nelsonville, New Marshfield, Shade, Stewart, The Plains, and Trimble; these will be the central focus of the pictures and captions that follow. Though many interesting facts, details, and stories are omitted by not delving into the numerous areas of the county barely mentioned, the goal here is to present a sampling. A new and updated all-inclusive history that does justice to those communities and people not mentioned here needs to be done at some point in the future.

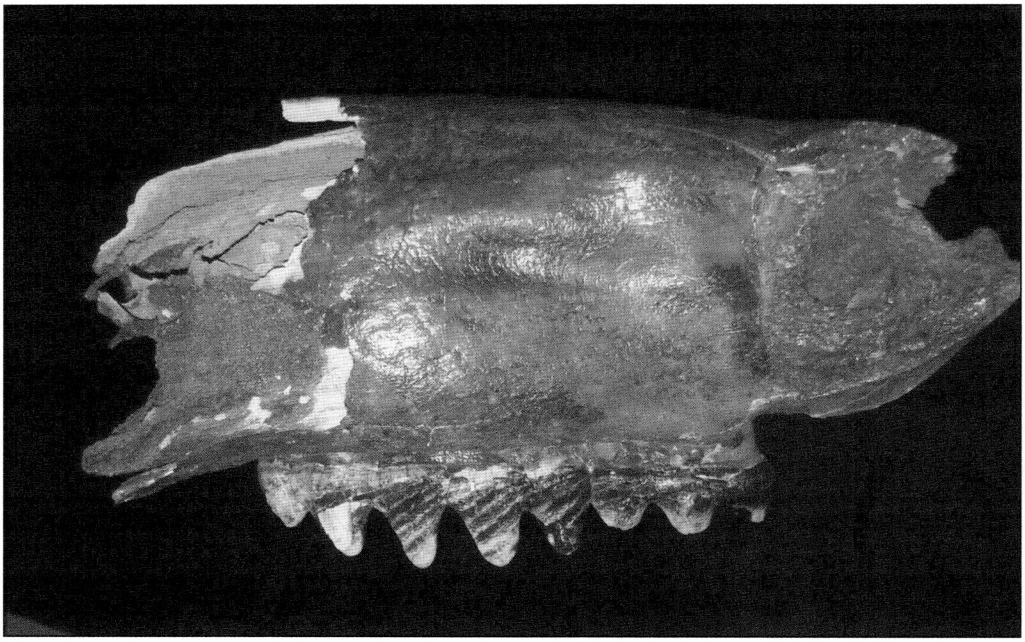

Before there was an Athens County, Ohio, or any other location that is now called a town, county, state, or country, there was just land, rivers, streams, flora, and fauna. Some early people moved freely among the treasures of this area using its land and resources to survive. They found an abundance of animals to hunt, plants that would produce food, clean water, a tolerable climate, and land that could be made to serve them. These pictures are of a mastodon jawbone that is housed in the Athens County Historical Society and Museum. (Both, author's collection.)

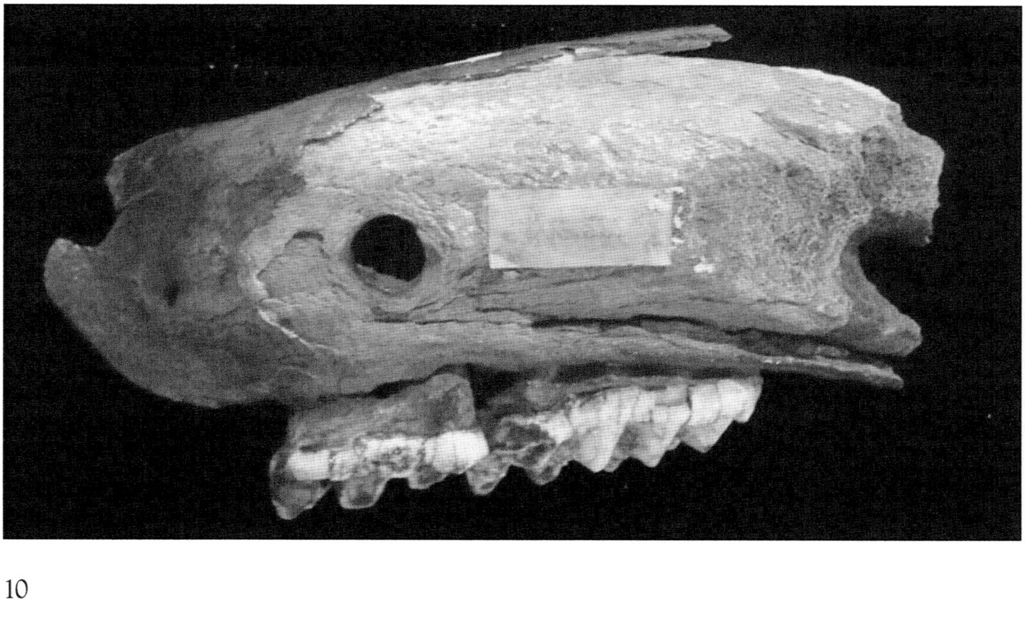

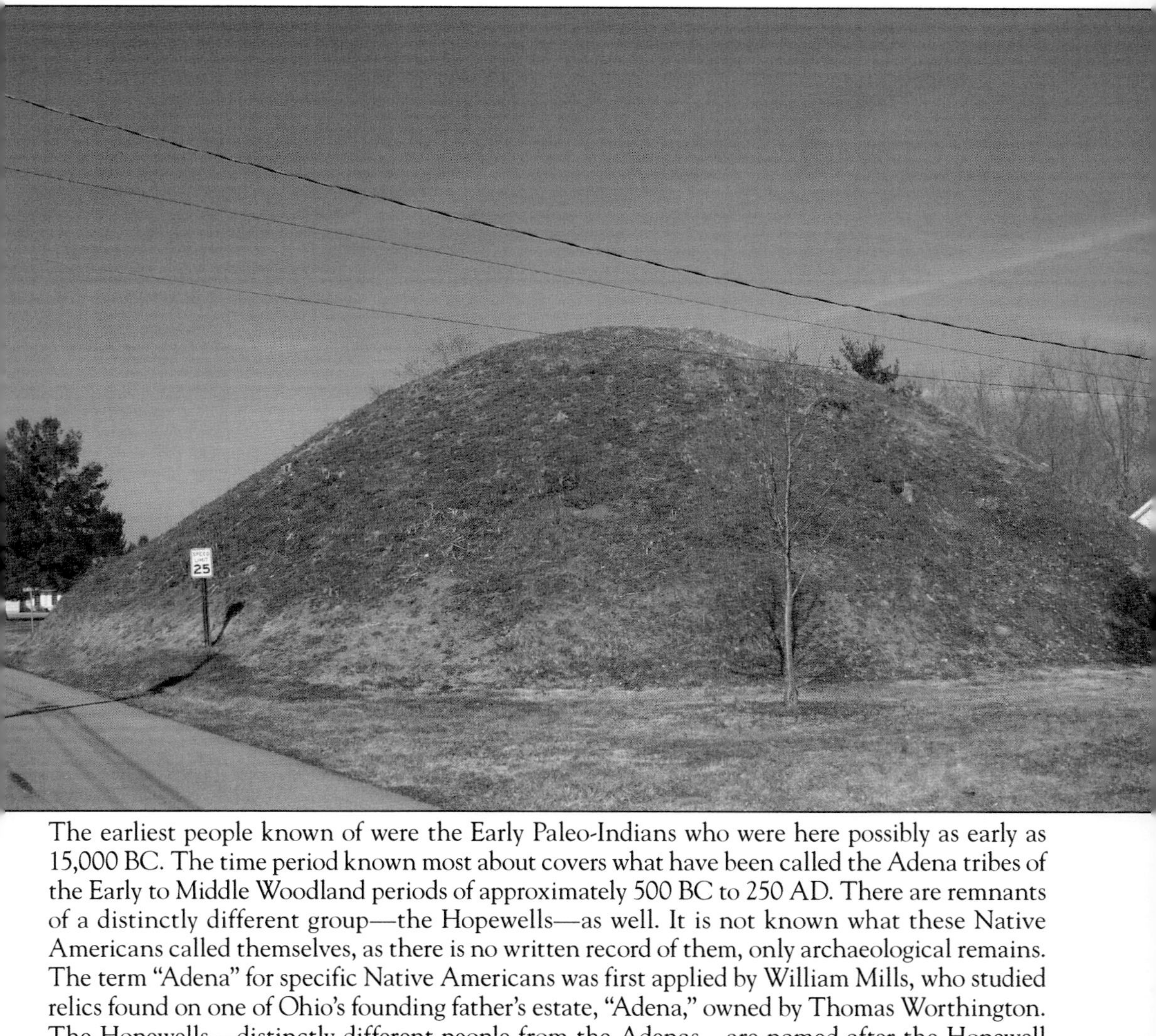

The earliest people known of were the Early Paleo-Indians who were here possibly as early as 15,000 BC. The time period known most about covers what have been called the Adena tribes of the Early to Middle Woodland periods of approximately 500 BC to 250 AD. There are remnants of a distinctly different group—the Hopewells—as well. It is not known what these Native Americans called themselves, as there is no written record of them, only archaeological remains. The term "Adena" for specific Native Americans was first applied by William Mills, who studied relics found on one of Ohio's founding father's estate, "Adena," owned by Thomas Worthington. The Hopewells—distinctly different people from the Adenas—are named after the Hopewell family whose land provided archaeological specimens for study. Pictured is the Hartman Mound in The Plains, Ohio. (Author's collection.)

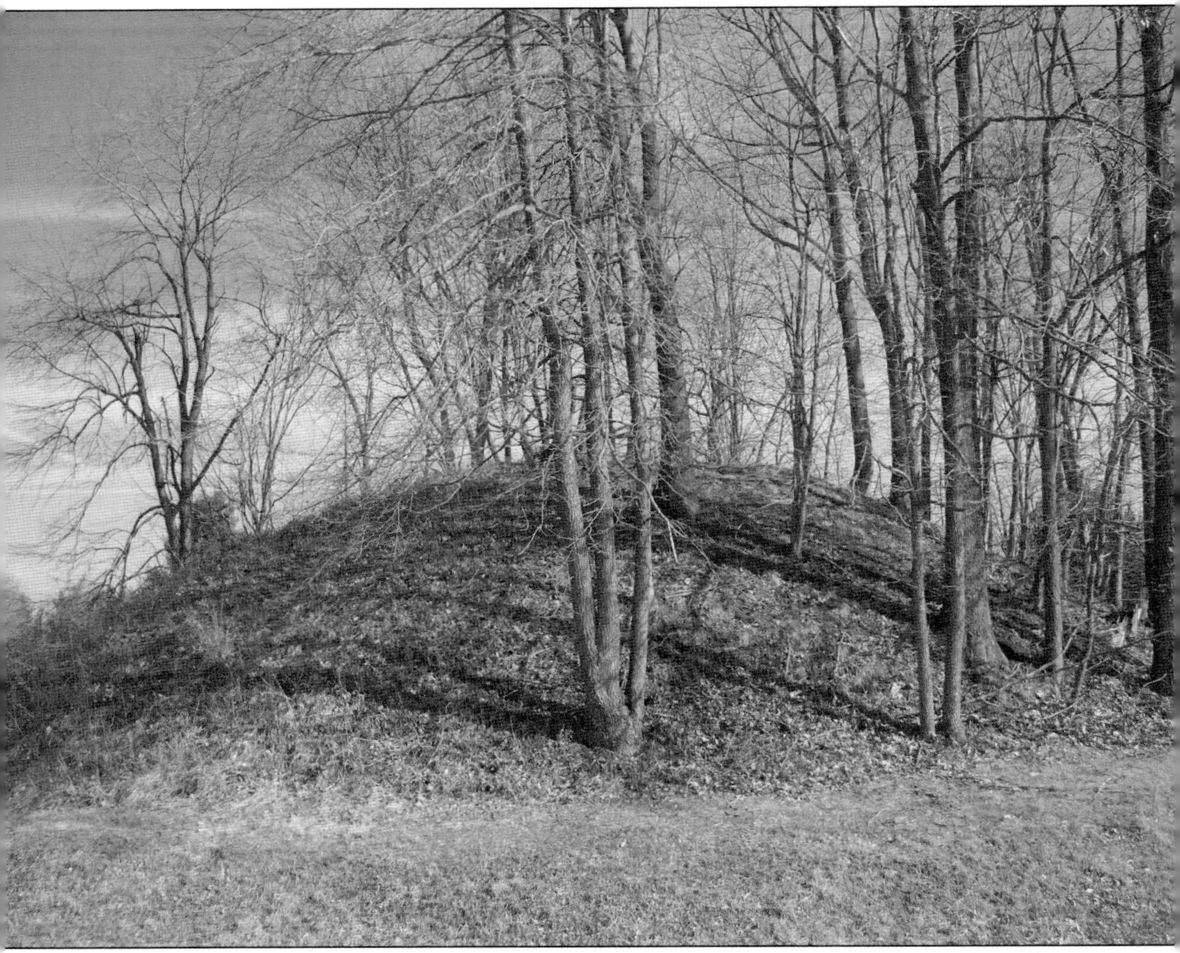

All around Athens County, there are reminders of the Adena and Hopewell past. Burial mounds dot the landscape, and there is at least one full ritual circle still intact. Petroglyphs have been found in Athens County as well. The Native Americans who built these structures and created these artworks were deeply involved in ceremonial rites; they built the mounds to bury and honor their dead and gathered in open ritual circles to enjoy a sense of community. This is the Connett No. 5 Mound in The Plains, Ohio. (Author's collection.)

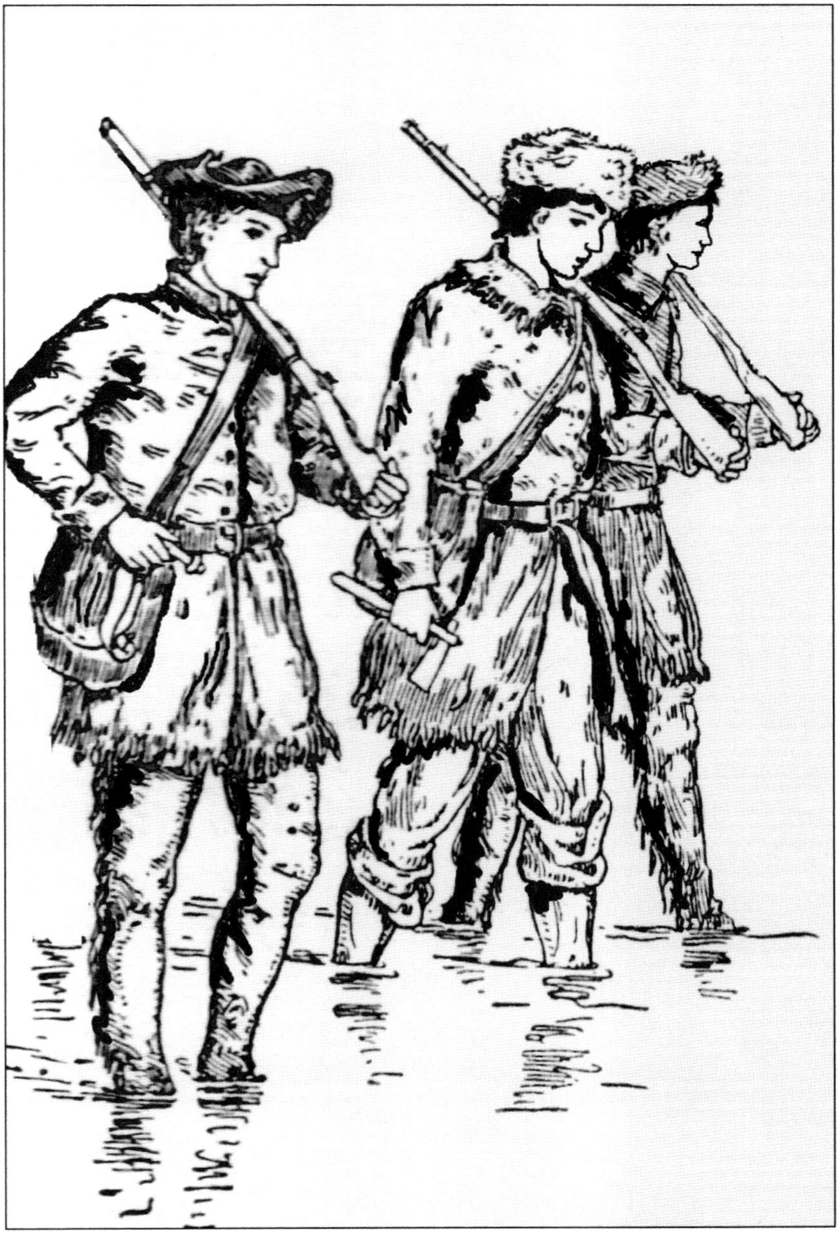

Europeans first came through what was to become Ohio in the late 1600s as they explored the land from Canada down the Mississippi and Ohio Valleys. The British and French—dominant countries at that time—fought for control through the French and Indian Wars. By 1749, the British had built a trading house on the Great Miami River. The French objected, attacked, carried off English survivors to Canada, and destroyed the property in 1752. Once the French and Indian Wars ended with the Treaty of Paris in 1763, the British reserved land beyond the Alleghenies for Native Americans; however, there were free spirits of European descent who ventured into the wilderness as squatters or as trappers and hunters. It was not until the defeat of the British in the War for Independence that a major push to the west began anew. Much of present-day Ohio was begun with the fledgling US government's Land Ordinance of 1785, which directed government-sponsored surveyors to map the territory and lay out districts.

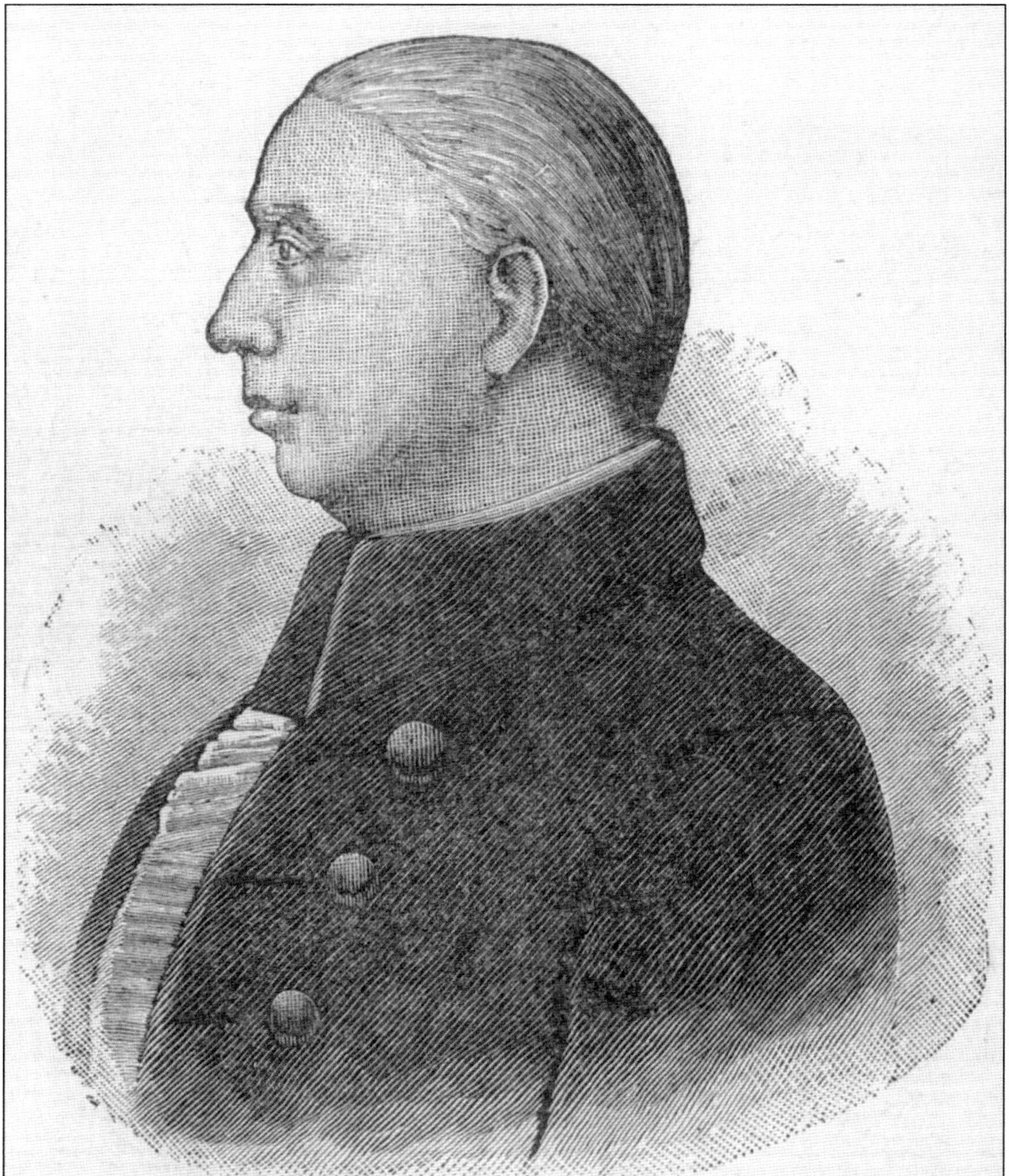

Rufus Putnam, pictured, was first offered the job of surveyor in the Northwest Territory in the 1780s. Due to a conflict, Putnam was unable to accept the offer and asked Benjamin Tupper to complete the survey. Unfortunately, Tupper met with Indian hostilities and returned to Massachusetts after getting only as far as present-day Pittsburgh, Pennsylvania. Despite Tupper's failed expedition, his stories of the land fired an interest in others to organize a land speculation agreement organized under the Ohio Company of Associates and promote expansion into the territory. Putnam promoted the potential for settlement from the early 1780s and ultimately led the first official settlers of Ohio into Marietta.

Two

The Founding of Athens County and Early Pioneers

Rufus Putnam had seen the opportunities for land speculation as early as 1782–1783 and encouraged his friend George Washington to pressure legislators to open up the territory for settlement. Putnam knew that, due to the high costs of the war against Britain, the new United States was struggling financially and that the Articles of Confederation made it difficult to tax citizens. The new government would ultimately have to turn to selling land as a way to increase its wealth and overcome its huge burden of debt. To protect its lands from foreign foes and Native Americans attempting to keep the settlers from the East out, as well as from manipulation by the individual states that held colonial claims on the lands, the government had to establish control. Negotiations began in earnest. It was during this negotiation and control phase that the US government established the Land Ordinance of 1784. This was followed by an ordinance in 1785 that provided a means for laying out the territory. Putnam and others watched and waited for their opportunity.

Putnam, Benjamin Tupper, and nine others, anticipating the government's need for income, met on March 1, 1786, at the Bunch of Grapes Tavern in Boston and formed the Ohio Company of Associates. Their goal was to buy huge parcels of land from the government at the earliest opportunity and sell the land to settlers at a profit. To accomplish their scheme, they needed assurances (which did not come to fruition with the Land Ordinance of 1784) that some form of government would be in place to provide at least minimal safety for settlers. Without such assurances, it would be difficult to encourage potential buyers of land to purchase, move their families, and make the territory a profitable enterprise.

On July 13, 1787, the famous Northwest Ordinance provided for governance. The Ohio Company completed a contract with the government during that fall. An expedition was launched the following spring, and on April 7, 1788, settlers, including Rufus Putnam, stepped from boats that brought them down the Ohio River to the mouth of the Muskingum River and what is now the city of Marietta. They erected a blockhouse there to protect them from the Native Americans who posed a significant threat. It would not be until 1795 and the Treaty of Greenville that the Indian threat would be diminished and a major move inland could take place.

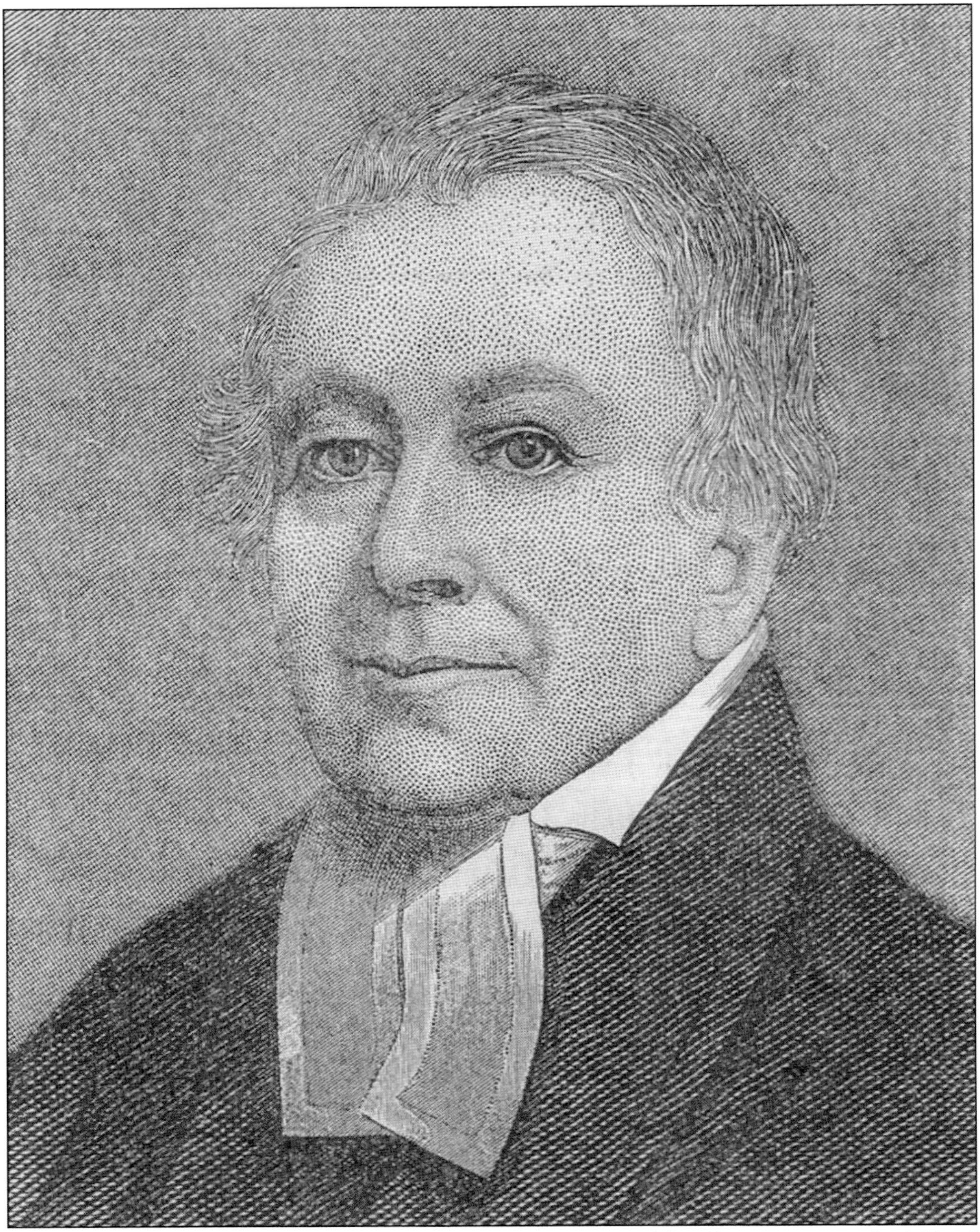

Pictured is Rev. Manasseh Cutler. Cutler was the representative of the Ohio Company who lobbied Congress for the acceptance of a contract whereby the government would sell the Ohio Company land in the Northwest Territory, which could then be resold to settlers at a profit. As a result of his political maneuvering, on October 27, 1787, a contract was signed between the Ohio Company and the Continental Congress's Board of Treasury. Today, the names of these earliest people who helped shape the county are still heard and seen, though many modern dwellers may not recognize their significance: Putnam Hall (named after Rufus Putnam), Cutler Hall (named after Manasseh Cutler), Tupper Hall (named after Benjamin Tupper), and the Bingham House (named after Silas Bingham, one of the earliest settlers) all reside on the Ohio University campus.

Prior to statehood, Rufus Putnam and colleagues surveyed vast areas of land in Ohio. What is now Athens County, shown here, was carved out of what they had mapped as a much larger Washington County. Because of growth, politics, and special interests, it took many years to settle county and township boundaries. The majority of land that came to be Athens County was officially separated from Washington County on March 1, 1805. At one time, Athens County included parts of what are now Hocking, Meigs, Morgan, and Vinton Counties, and its present borders were not finally established until March 23, 1850.

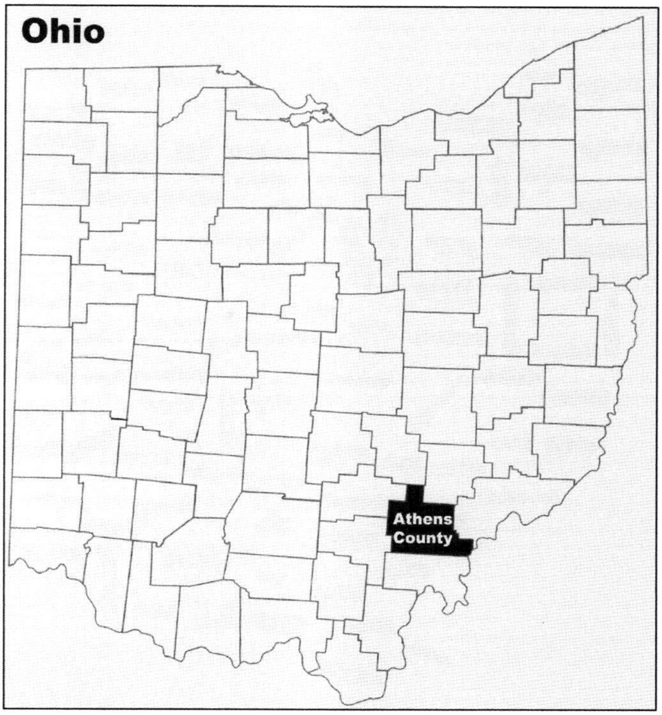

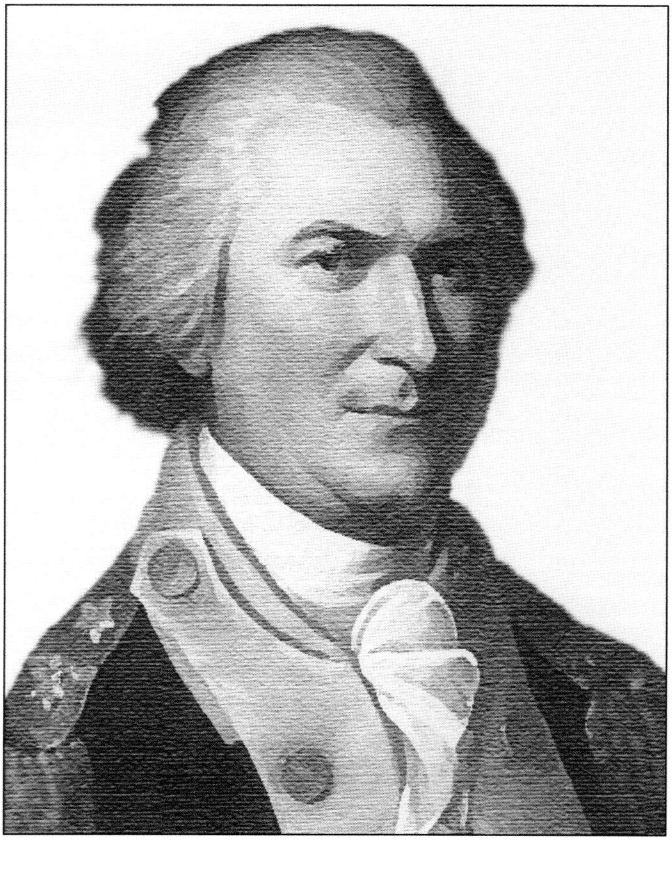

Pictured is territorial governor Arthur St. Clair. From 1788 until 1803, government was firmly in his grasp. He ruled absolutely and apparently envisioned a long period of time with the Northwest Territory under his control—and was not eager to give up power. He resisted Ohio's statehood until the sheer force of numbers and power of men willing to take their case to Congress prevailed.

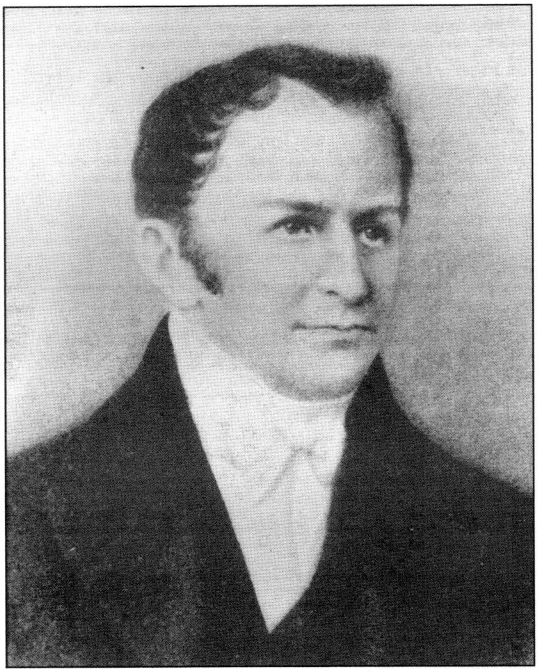

Thomas Worthington (at left) has been referred to as the "Father of Ohio Statehood" because he was the spokesman who met with Pres. Thomas Jefferson and members of the Congress to make the case for the removal of Arthur St. Clair and for Ohio's statehood. Worthington served as one of the first two state senators for Ohio and went on to become Ohio's sixth governor. Prior to statehood, Worthington played a major role in the writing of the state's first constitution of 1802. Through efforts of territorial leaders like Worthington, Edward Tiffin (below), Michael Baldwin of Chillicothe, and numerous others who were committed to statehood and willing to challenge Governor St. Clair, the state of Ohio became a reality in 1803, and St. Clair was removed. Law and order fell to the new state government centered in Chillicothe and headed by Tiffin, the first governor.

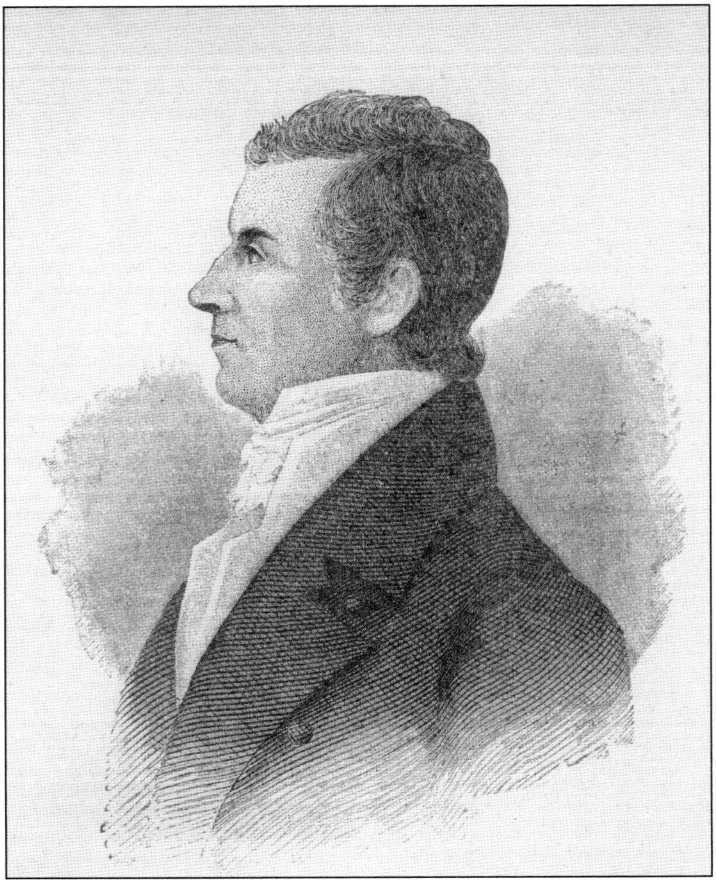

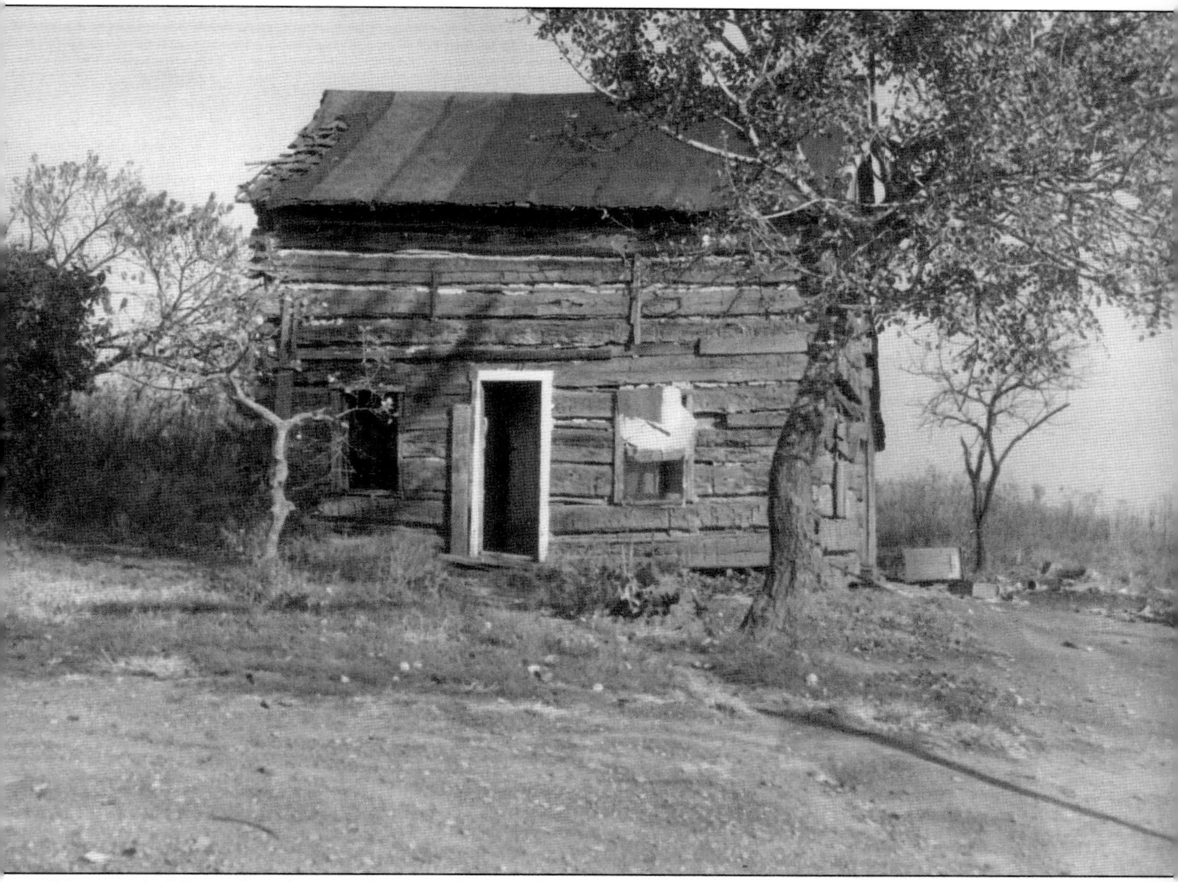

Wives, children, family members, and friends often remained in the East or at the Marietta area settlements until the first male settlers had done the preliminary work of clearing land and building shelters. The men came at first in small numbers but had the skills and courage to tackle the wilderness and create sturdy log cabins and begin planting crops in what is now the city of Athens and in other areas of what is present-day Athens County. Families and friends soon followed, sometimes walking from Marietta and sometimes making long treks over mountains and down rivers to get here. Soon, more people followed to help shape whole new communities, such as Albany, Amesville, Broadwell, Canaanville, Chauncey, Coolville, Guysville, Kilvert, Hockingport, Nelsonville, New Marshfield, Stewart, The Plains, and many others, some of which no longer exist. (Courtesy of the Anastas Collection.)

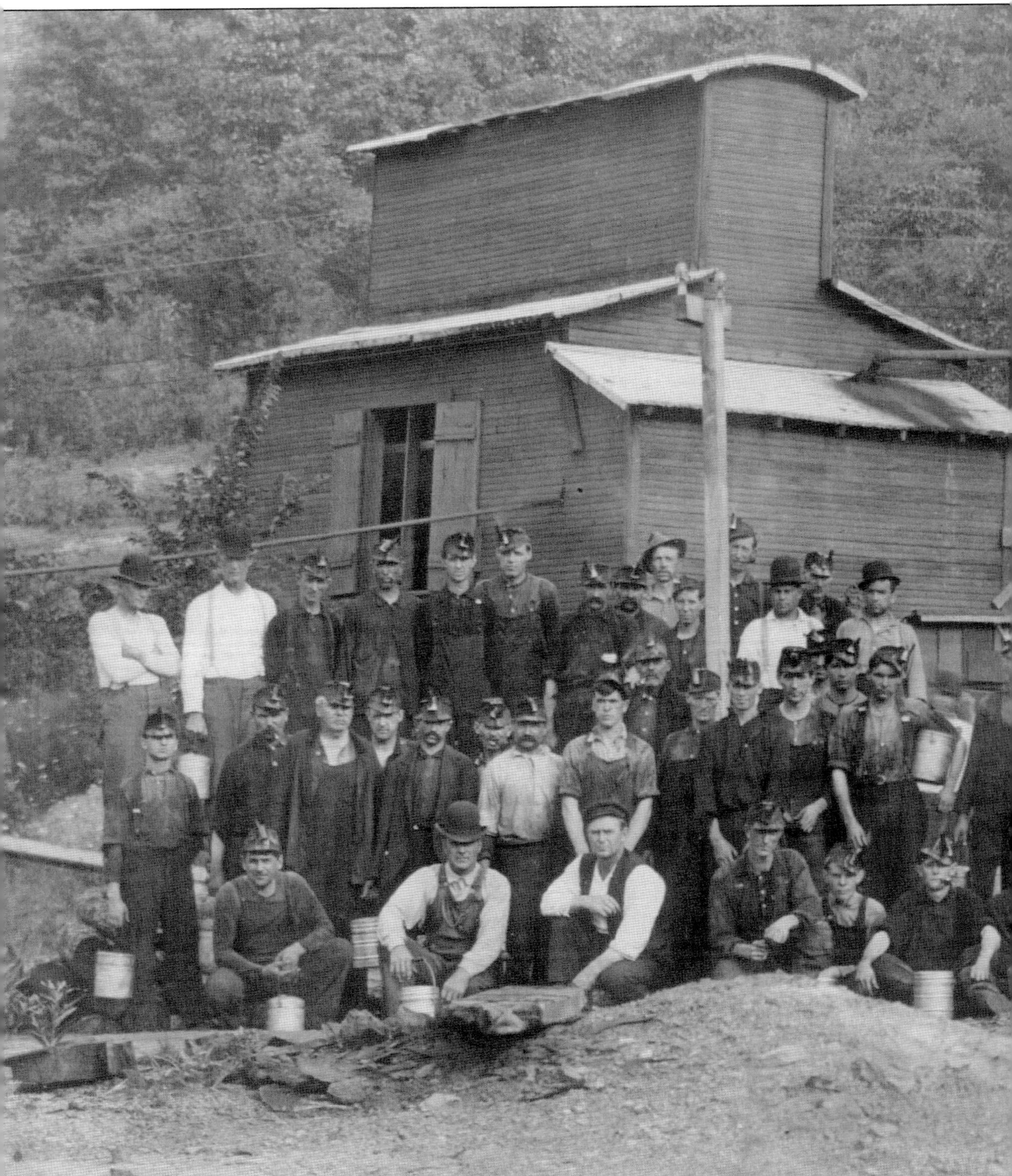

Rich deposits of salt, clay, and coal—and the profits to be made from them—later led to the creation of more communities that dotted the county from the late 1700s well into the 20th century. The first salt furnace in the county was built by Resolved Fuller Sr. between 1838 and 1840 and flourished around areas then called Armitage and Salinas and the still extant town of Chauncey. Clay for brick making and other ceramic products was discovered early and written about in the 1830s; the brick business thrived from the late 1800s into the 1900s. Coal was first

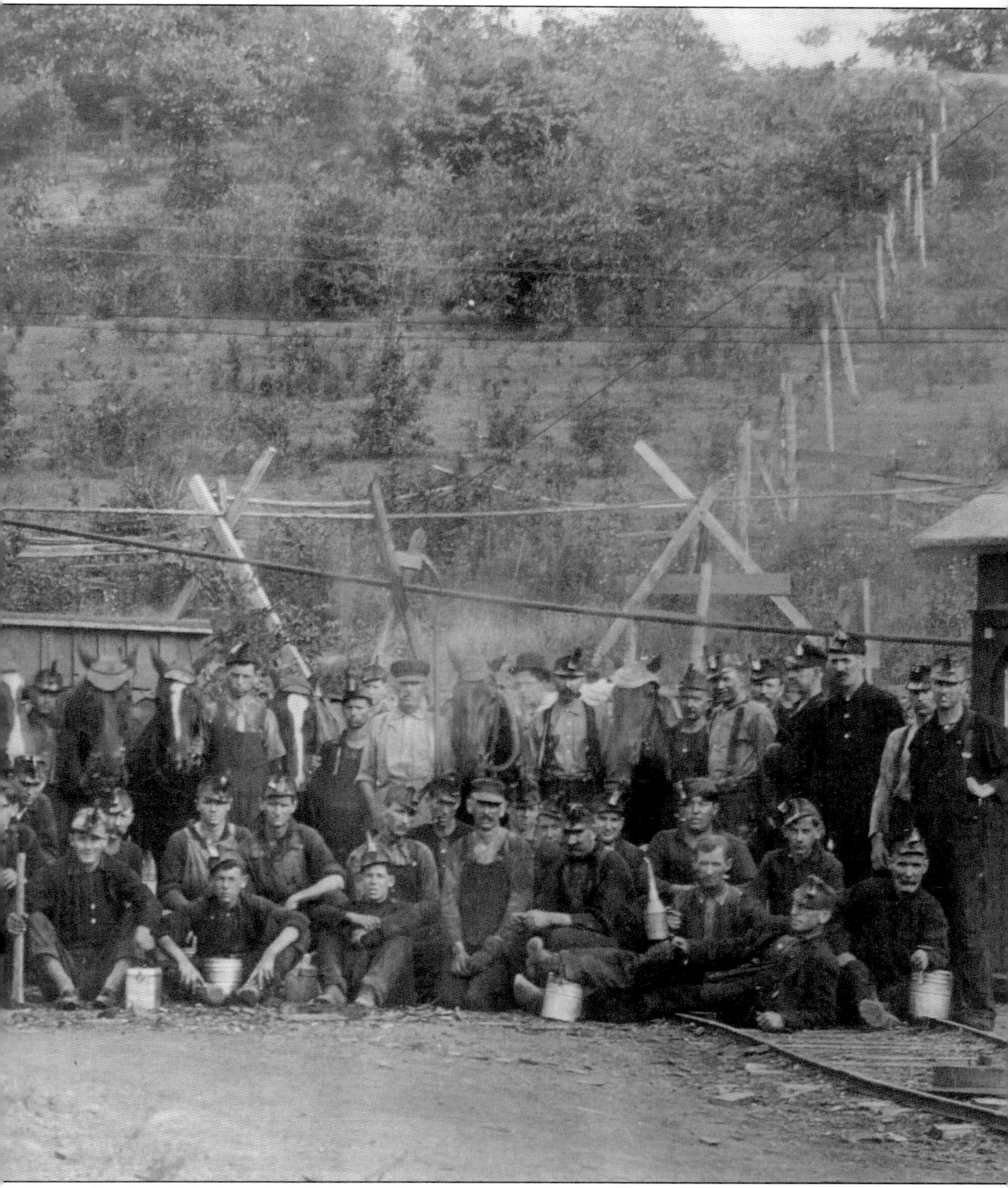

mined in Athens County in the 1830s for commercial use; prior to that, it was used for home or small-business operations. The plentiful supplies of wood provided the average homeowners and businesses with the heat needed without the unpleasantness of going underground; however, with the advent of the canal and then the railroads, coal became a highly marketable product. Also produced in the county were coke, iron, sandstone, and limestone. Pictured here is Chauncey Mine No. 275.

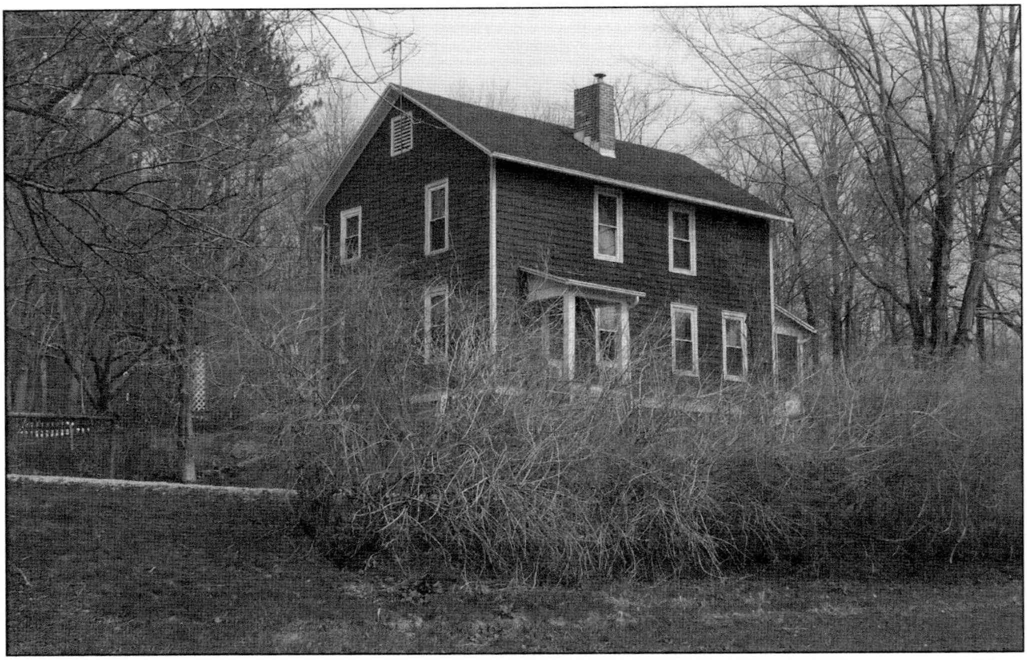

One of Athens County's earliest and most rugged settlers was Moses Hewitt, who came to Ohio from Massachusetts in 1790. He lived on the land shown here in Waterloo Township in 1802. The land was owned by the Hewitt family long after Moses Hewitt's demise.

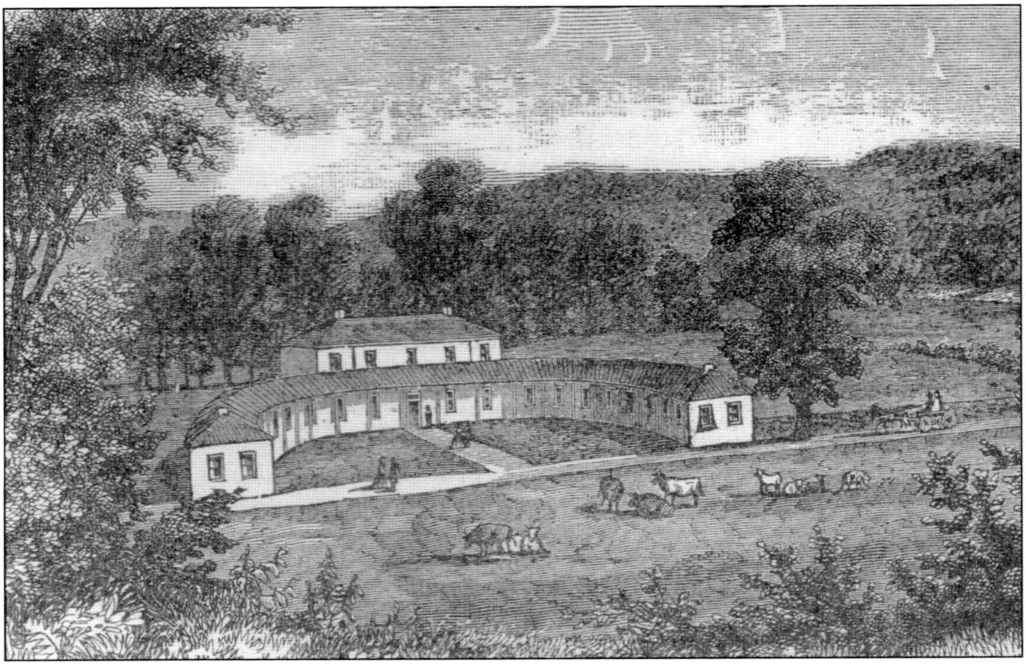

Shortly after his arrival in Ohio, Hewitt lived briefly on what is now Blennerhassett Island. Unfortunately, Native Americans presented significant threats, thus he and his family took refuge in "Neil's Station" on the Little Kanawha. This picture is of the Blennerhassett Mansion where Aaron Burr and Harman Blennerhassett were accused of treason against the United States; the land this mansion is on would have been a total wilderness in Hewitt's day.

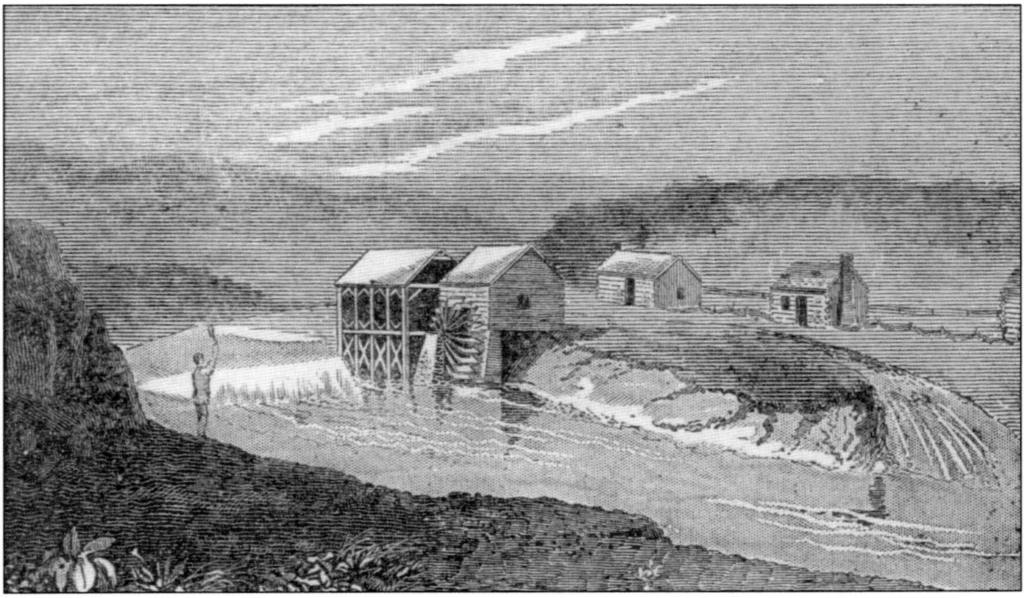

In 1792, Moses Hewitt left the Neil's Station garrison to find a stray horse and was taken captive by Indians. He was tied at night and constantly surrounded during the day. One day, the captors went hunting, leaving Hewitt alone, bound by rawhide strips; he broke free and ran off. After nine days of walking barefoot, naked, starving, and exhausted, he came upon the garrison on the Muskingum River near Wolf Creek mills. The mills are shown here in 1789.

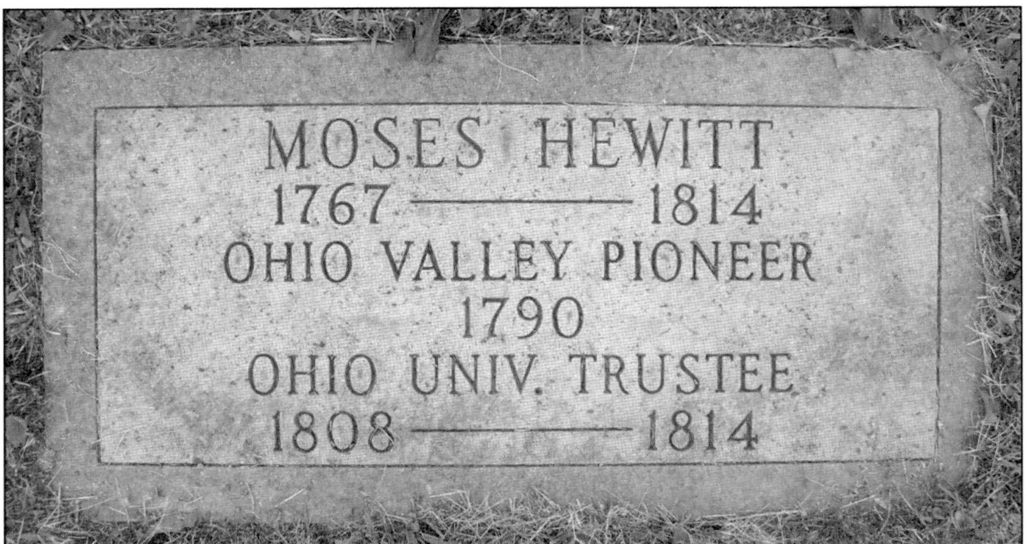

In 1797, Hewitt moved to Margaret Creek near the future Athens, and he purchased land in 1802 in what would become Waterloo Township. Shortly thereafter, he became a trustee of the university. As stated in *History of Athens County, Ohio: And Incidentally of the Ohio Land Company and the First Settlement of the State at Marietta*, "He was well fitted, and his judgment and good sense were of real value to the institution." At some point before his death in 1814 of typhus, Hewitt returned to Athens. He is buried in the West State Street Cemetery. (Author's collection.)

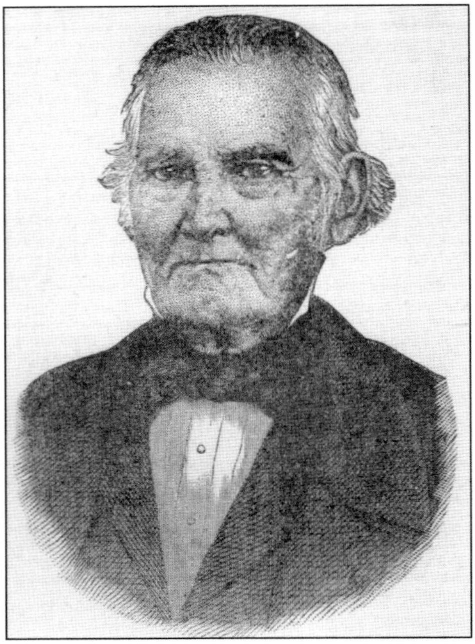

Ephraim Cutler and his family left Massachusetts in 1795 for the Ohio Territory, traveling by wagons over mountains to the Ohio River and by flatboat to Marietta. During the three-month trek to Marietta, two of his daughters died. In 1799, he moved to Ames Township. He was a judge and a representative to the territorial legislature. He is credited with saving Ohio from becoming a slave state.

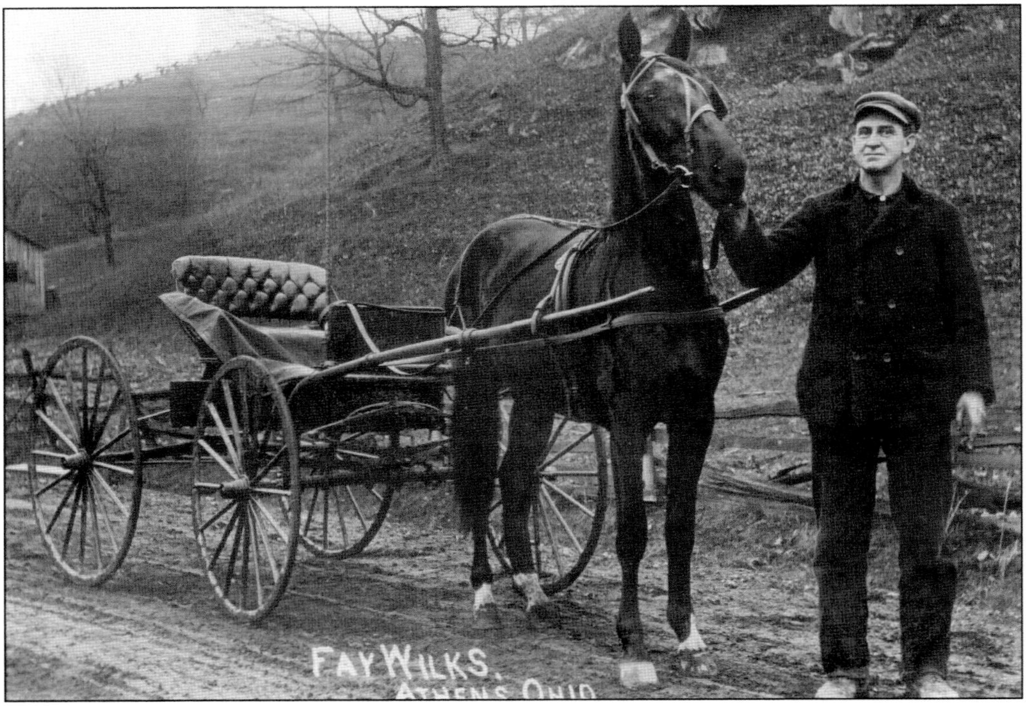

After a year in Ohio, Elijah Hatch returned to New York in 1801 to retrieve his family members, household goods, and animals. According to *History of Athens County, Ohio: And Incidentally of the Ohio Land Company and the First Settlement of the State at Marietta*, he was "the first man who ever drove a team, with a wagon, through the woods, from the mouth of little Hocking to the big Hockhocking." He became a judge in 1805, served nine terms in the state legislature, and was a trustee of Ohio University. Pictured is Athens County resident Fay Wilks on a road considered significantly better than the rutted roads of Hatch's time.

Three

Townships, Villages, Cities, and a Handful of Stories

Among the first known settlers in Athens County were Silas and Alvan Bingham; Isaac and Michael Barker; John Chandler; Barak, Edmund, and William Dorr; William Harper; Jonathan Watkins; John Wilkins; Solomon and Othniel Tuttle; Robert Ross; Henry Bartlett; Christopher Stevens; Robert Linzee; John and Moses Hewitt; Joseph Snowden; John Simonton; Robert Ross; the Brooks family; and the Haning family. Many settled in what is now the city of Athens, while others in what would become Ames and Alexander Townships; however, they were not necessarily the first to arrive. It is likely there were squatters—early settlers unconcerned with "legal rights" to property—on land prior to the formal settlements who were probably encouraged to move on once the legal owners showed up.

Spouses, family members, and friends followed the first settlers; with the influx of people, new communities came into being, like Nelsonville, Coolville, Chauncey, Trimble, Albany, and others. Many towns developed around the rich resources to be found. Salt, clay, and coal—and the profits to be made from these resources—created many communities that dotted the county from the early 1800s well into the 20th century. Coal, in particular, created numerous towns out of wilderness to accommodate mine workers. Some early named communities remain and thrive, some changed their names, some barely remain, and others are lost. However much of the past lingers in the landscape and historical records and artifacts.

In April 1805, Silas Dean, William Howlett, and John Corey agreed to divide the county into four townships: Alexander, Ames, Athens, and Troy. Alexander had been surveyed as early as 1795 and was inhabited by 1805. In its initial form, it contained land that later became parts of Meigs and Vinton Counties, as well as parts of Lee and Lodi Townships. Ames Township originally included what are now Marion and Homer Townships in Morgan County; it also included what are now Ward, Green, and Starr Townships in Hocking County and Trimble, York, Dover, and Bern Townships in current Athens County. Athens Township was surveyed between 1795 and 1796 and subdivided into Athens, Canaan, and Waterloo Townships. Troy was divided into Troy and Rome Townships in 1811 and later divided further to establish what became Meigs County.

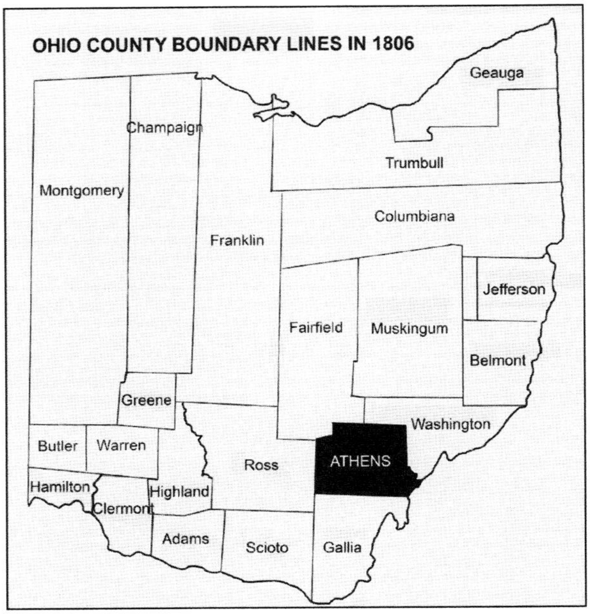

Early on, Athens County was considerably different from its formation today. This map shows the county as it existed in 1806, shortly after its creation. The author created the map based on the work of Randolph C. Downes.

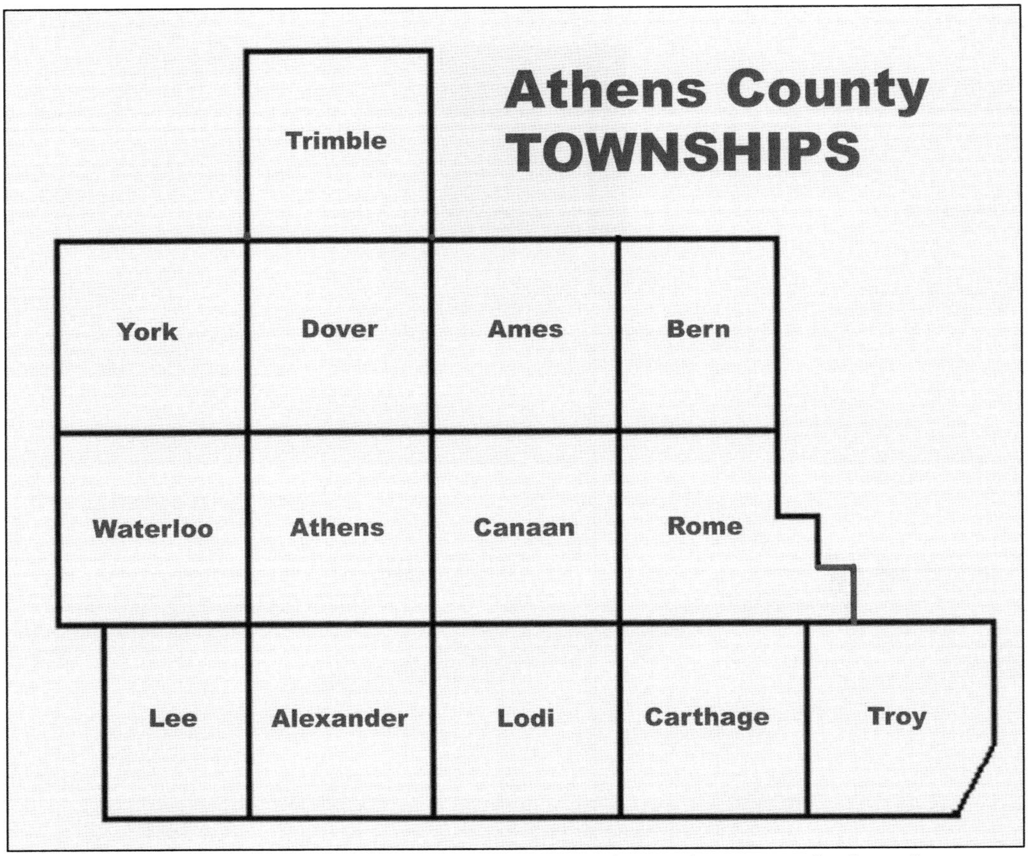

This map shows Athens County today with its 14 townships. The present-day boundaries were not finally realized until 1850. The following page shows the changes that created the current boundaries in chronological order.

Changes in the Original Four Townships
(Athens, Ames, Alexander, and Troy)
That Created the Current Boundaries of Athens County

1811: Dover Township was originally part of Ames Township until it was declared a separate township on Thursday, April 4, 1811.

1811: Rome Township was removed from Troy Township and declared a separate township on Thursday, April 4, 1811.

1814: Sections of Washington County were added to Rome Township.

1814: Sections of Athens County were detached and added back into Washington County.

1816: Jackson County was created and a portion of Athens County was taken.

1818: York Township had been part of Ames Township until 1811 when land was separated as Dover Township. York was then separated from Dover and organized as a township in June of 1818.

1818: Creation of Hocking County took part of what had been Athens County.

1819: Canaan Township was originally a part of Athens Township and was organized as a separate entity in 1819; it was named by Judge Walker of Ames Township, who was one of the County Commissioners at the time.

1819: Carthage Township was originally a part of Troy Township and was established as its own township on November 10, 1819.

1819: Lee Township was carved out of Alexander Township in November 1819.

1826: Lodi was created from part of Alexander Township and part of Carthage Township; though it was organized in 1819, it was not "detached" until 1826.

1826: Waterloo Township was originally a part of Athens Township and did not separate until April 1826.

1827: Trimble Township formed and separated from Ames Township in April 1827.

1828: Bern Township was separated from Ames Township on March 3, 1828.

1845: Homer and Marion Townships were taken from Athens County and added to Morgan County.

1850: The development of Vinton County took a portion of Athens County land, and Ward Township was given to Hocking County.

This is a chronological listing of changes in Athens County from its beginning up to 1850, when the county was finally formed to its current boundaries.

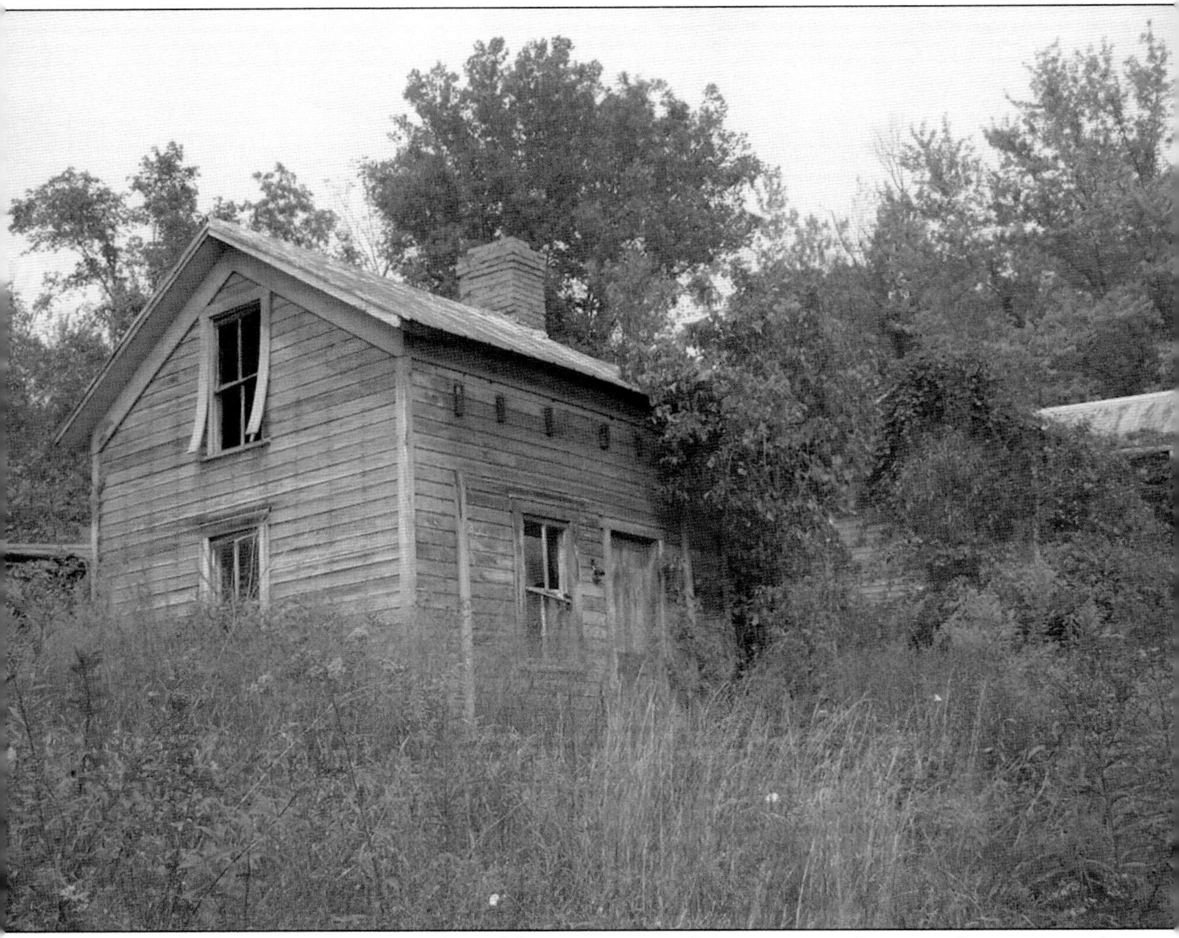

Many of the towns that once thrived here came out of the mining industry and some from the agricultural age. Coal operators and brick manufacturers often built houses, churches, and schools to provide their workers with basics for a community life and as a way to make sure they were readily available for work. In other cases, workers built their own homes in clusters. Some of the communities that have come and gone, been renamed, or are almost gone include the following: 210 Row, Anthony, Armadale, Armitage, Beaumont, Beebe, Bessemer, Big Run, Bretland, Broadwell, Brookville, Burr Oak, Carbondale, Carseytown, Chase, Circle Hill, Cole, Connett, Coolville Station, Detroit, Doanville, East Clayton, East Millfield, Elliotsville, Evansville, Federal (one in Bern Township and one in Ames Township), Federalton, Fisher, Five Points, Floodwood, Frost, Glen Ebon, Green's Run, Grosvenor, Grosvenor's Crossing, Hamley Run, Happy Hollow, Hartleyville, Hixson, Hebbardsville, Hickory Glades, Hocking, Hollister, Hull, Hunterdon, Imperial, Ireland, Judson, Kilvert, Kimberly, King Switch/Station, Lathrop, Liar's Corner, Lick Run Station, Lottridge, Luhrig, Lysander, Marshallville, Mechanicsburg, McDougal, McLeish, Mineral (Mineral City), Modoc, Morristown, New Bern, New England, New Floodwood, Newton, Nyo, Oakdale, Palos, Pigeon Roost, Plantville, Pleasanton, Pleasant Valley, Poston (209 Hollow), Pratt's Fork, Redtown, Salina, Sand Rock, Sharpsburg, Snow Fork, Stringtown, Tablertown, The Garden, Torch, Truetown, Tyler, Utley, Vanderhoof, Warren Station, Woodyards, Youba, and probably others long since forgotten. A once thriving community in Bern Township, Broadwell is all but gone with the exception of a few inhabitants and a number of rotting buildings, as seen here.

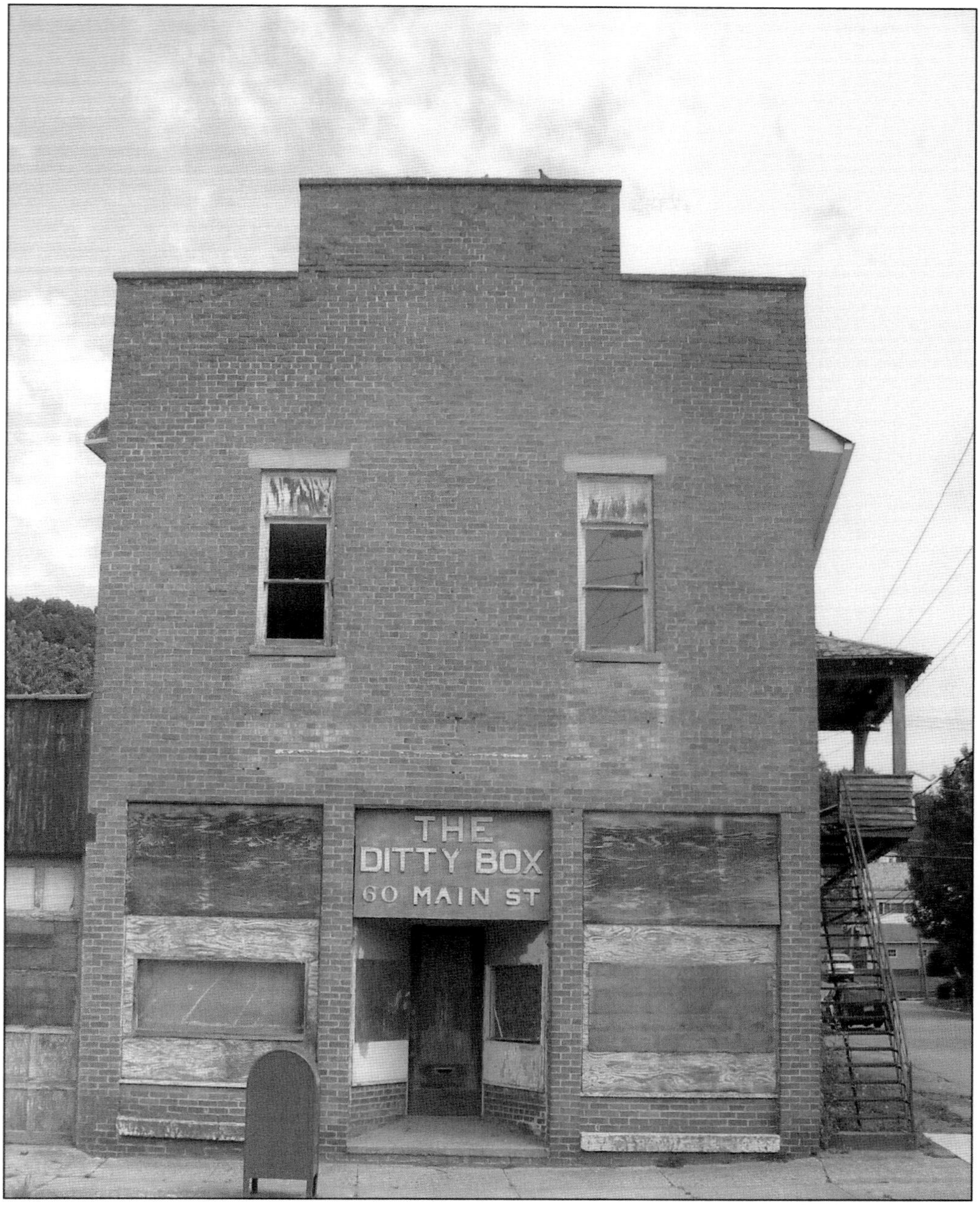

Some small communities struggle to survive the changes that have taken place in the past 70 years since mining, brick making, and saltworks left the area and agrarian workers ceased to work the land that provided a meager living; however, other communities manage to change with the times to be successful. Pictured is a building in Glouster in 2011. (Courtesy of Cyrus Moore.)

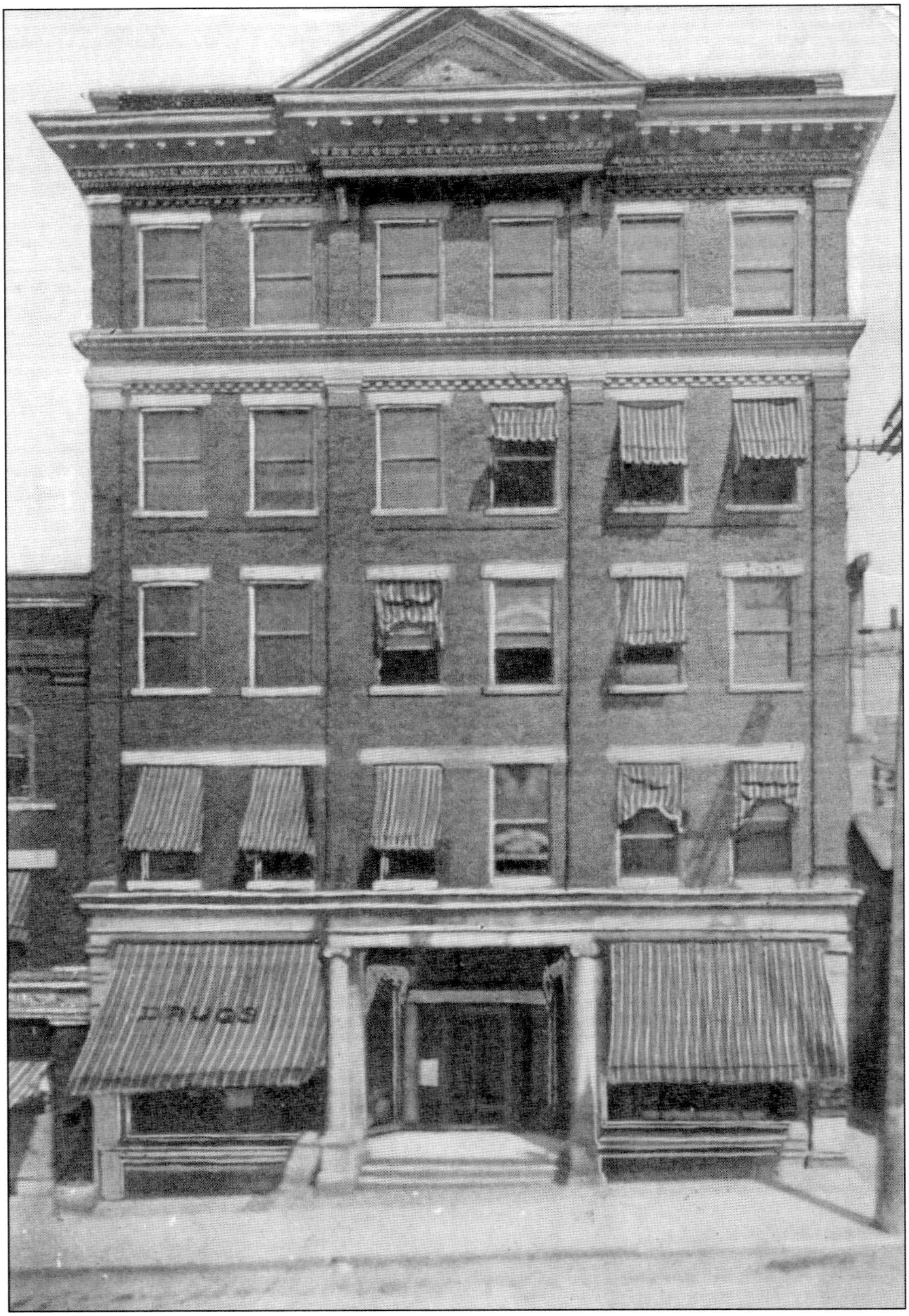

Athens County is moving toward becoming a tourist attraction as people become aware of the great history of the area. The scenic beauty and relative peace and quiet of the county attract many who seek a place to retire, raise families, or just relax. Pictured is the former First National Bank Building on Court Street, in Athens, in 1912. The building still stands alongside other grand structures on Court Street.

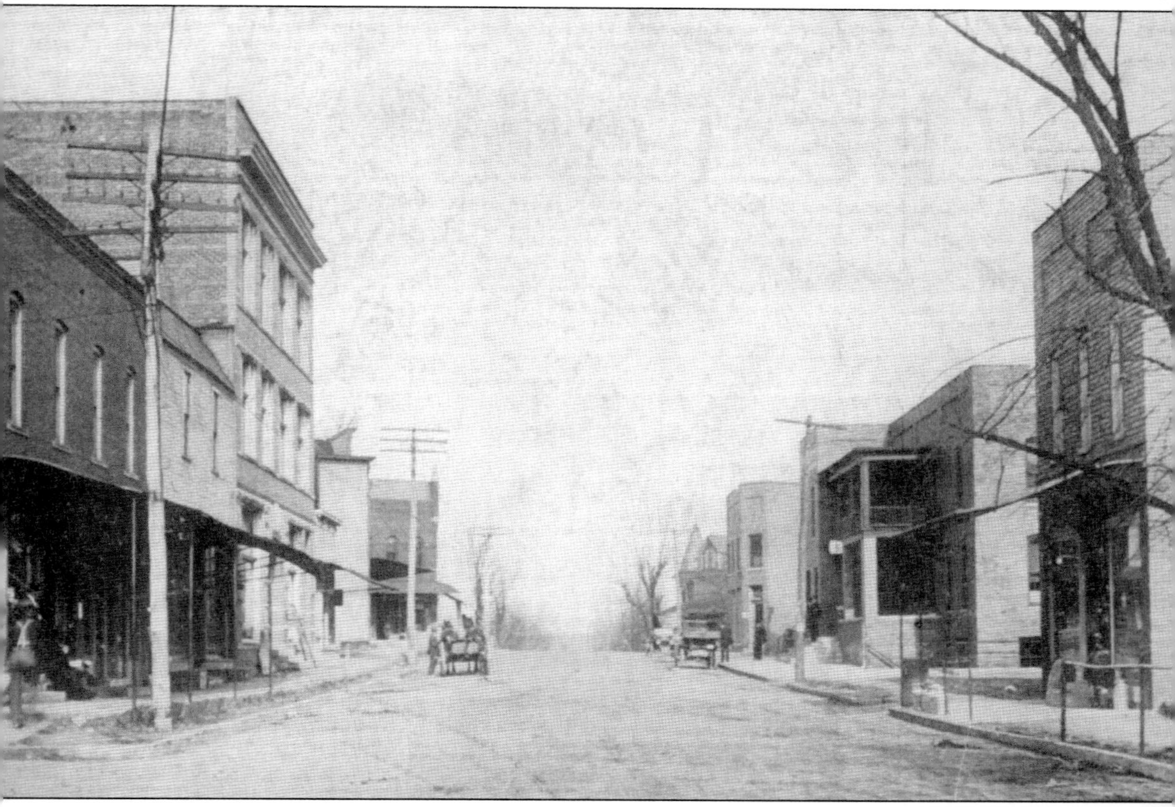

ALBANY. Albany is located in Lee Township and was incorporated in 1844. Historian W.E. Peters states that the town was named by William Graham for Albany, New York, and was laid out in 1838. According to Charles Manning Walker, town lots were established in 1832 or 1833*, and "the first house in the village was built by Lucius R. Beckley." A post office for Lee Township was established in 1829, located northwest of present-day Albany, so it is clear that the area had numerous people prior to the development of the village itself. This picture was taken prior to 1916.

(*This is one of several cases where historians disagree on information. It is the goal of the author to bring these issues to the reader's awareness to clarify that not all facts about the county have yet been solidified.)

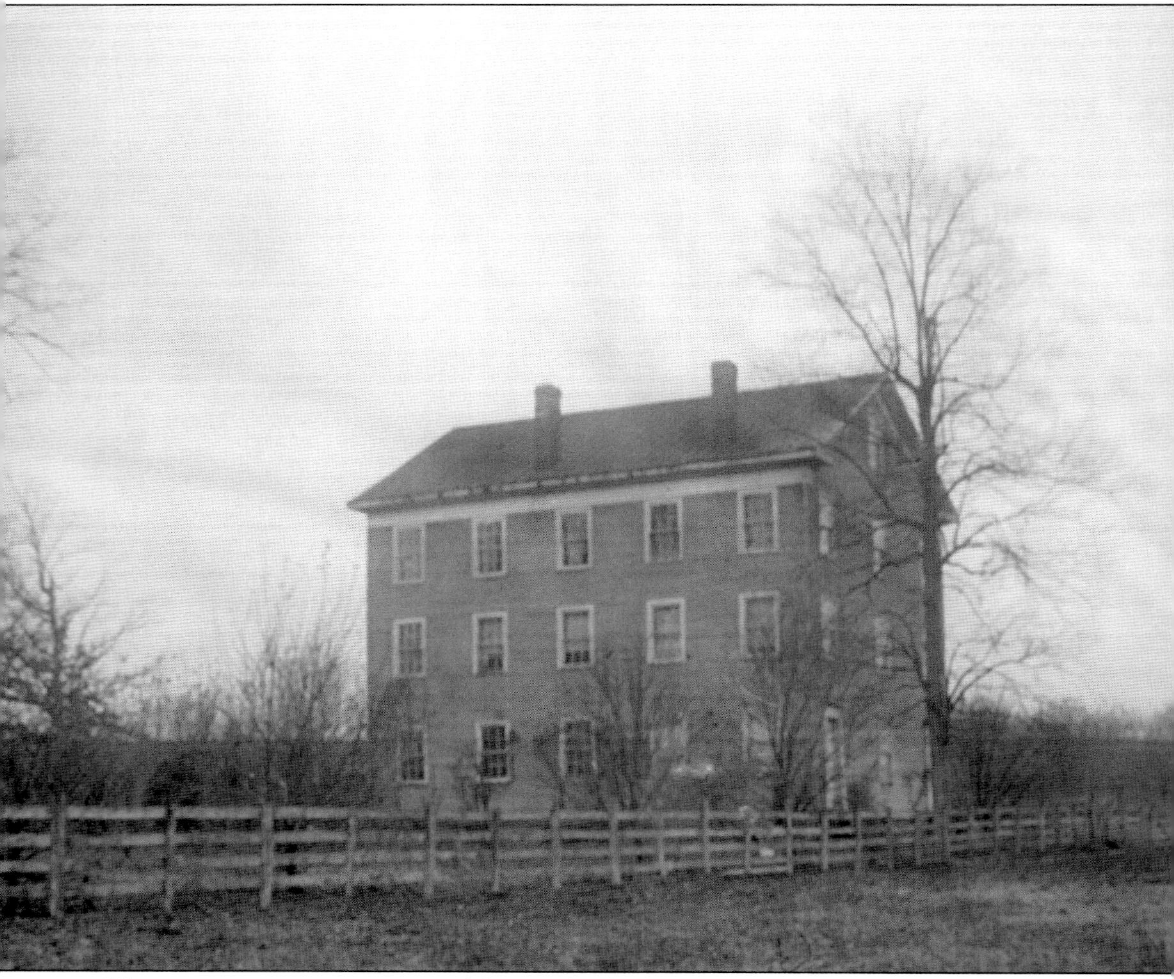

Education was a serious concern of the people of Albany as is expressed in the development of the Atwood Institute and later the Enterprise Institute. The *History of Hocking Valley, Ohio,* tells the story. The Albany Manual Labor University pictured here (later called the Atwood Institute) was established in 1848 when William S. Lewis, inspired by his daughter Lamira, who was a teacher, built a house to be used as a school. Interestingly, "students were admitted to this school regardless of color, caste or sex." The Labor University quickly became popular and was soon too small to support the numbers of students wanting an education. It was expanded over time and finally replaced in 1857 with the building shown here. By 1862, the school was burdened with debt and was taken over by the Disciples of Christ, Christian Church, which excluded students of color. At some point after another transition of ownership to the Free Will Baptists, Nehemiah Atwood donated $3,500, and the name of the institution changed to the Atwood Institute. (Courtesy of Mary Davis.)

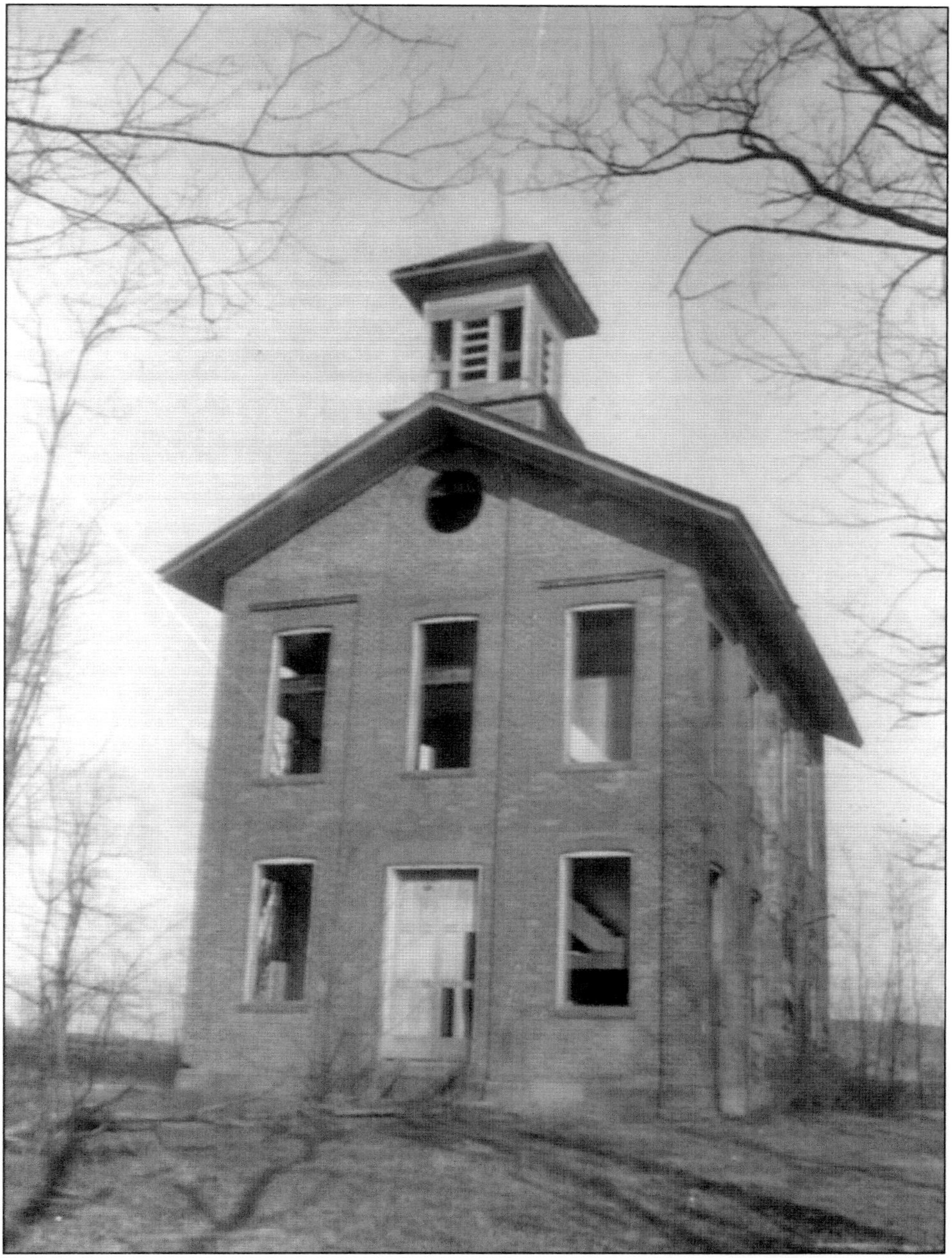

The Enterprise Institute was established as a reaction to the exclusion of people of color by the Atwood Institute after 1862. People of color organized and solicited donations from wealthy people both locally and in other states. The organizers obtained $3,000 worth of real estate from Thomas Carleton of Syracuse, Illinois, and $2,000 from the Freedmen's Bureau, as well as numerous other smaller donations. People of color of both sexes were admitted to the institution. Among the students of the Enterprise Academy were Olivia Davidson, the second wife of Booker T. Washington, and Milton Holland, a highly celebrated soldier of the Civil War. Holland was one of the first African American Congressional Medal of Honor recipients. He went on to success in politics, business, and education. Unfortunately, enrollment declined over the next 20 years, and the academy closed in 1886. (Courtesy of Mary Davis.)

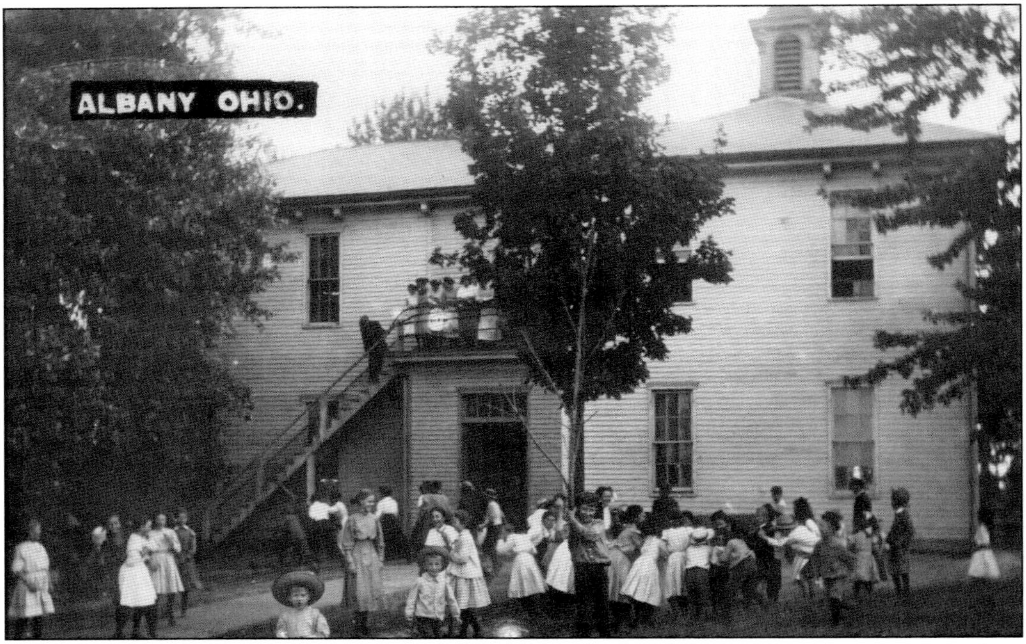

The Underground Railroad was a part of the county's history, but it was nowhere stronger than in Albany. Helping slaves was dangerous for those who chose to help. Slavery laws backed by government enforcement could lead to severe punishments. Despite the danger, many people risked arrest to help move fugitives north to Canada. The community's early stance on slavery and commitment to education of *all* of its citizens are sources of great pride.

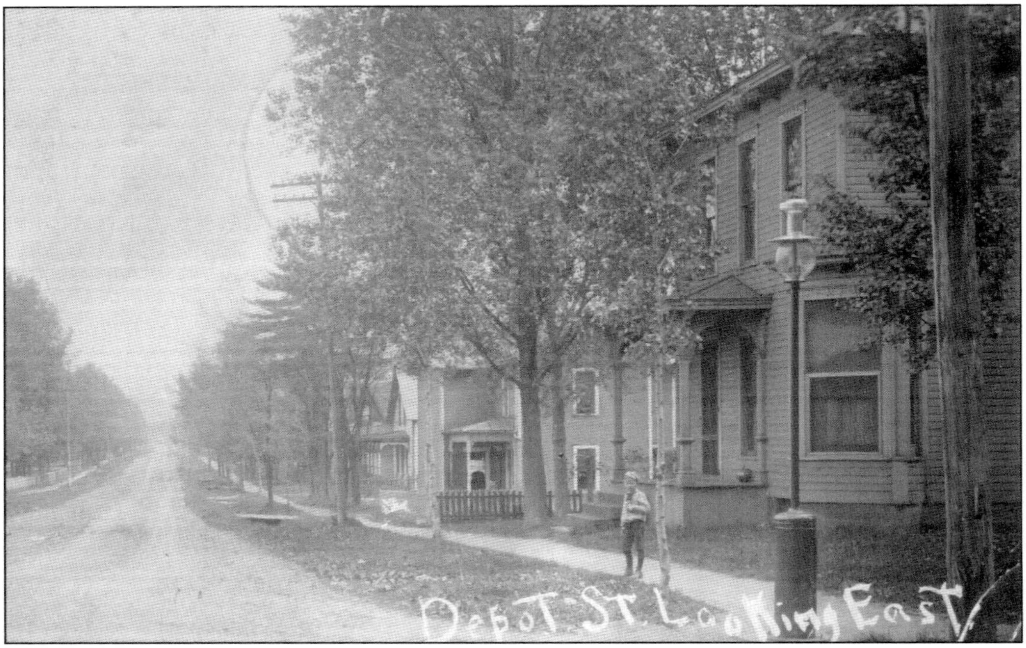

This c. 1908 picture of Depot Street is one of serenity; however, it is easy to surmise that life was very busy at the actual depot. Like many of the towns in Athens County, the connection to the railroad was an important factor in Albany for moving goods in and out of the community.

The Wells Library was created upon the death of Henry Wells when he left $1,000 as "a perpetual fund, the interest to be expended in books, and the further sum of two hundred and fifty dollars for an immediate purchase." Mary Weethee bequeathed the building to the town in 1868. (Courtesy of the Anastas Collection.)

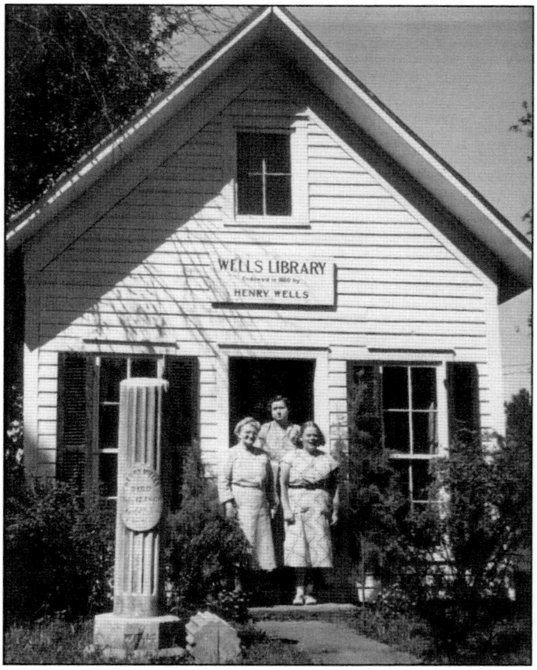

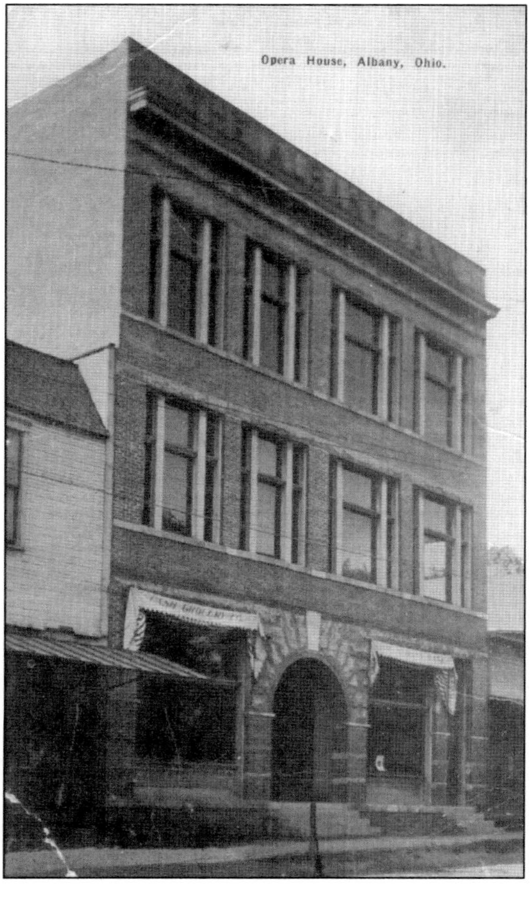

This picture is of the Albany Opera House in 1912. Opera houses were common in many towns in southeastern Ohio. They provided meeting spaces, venues for debates, locations for school graduations, and so on. In the days before television and movies, the opera house provided a place for traveling musicians, actors, minstrels, and others to entertain the public.

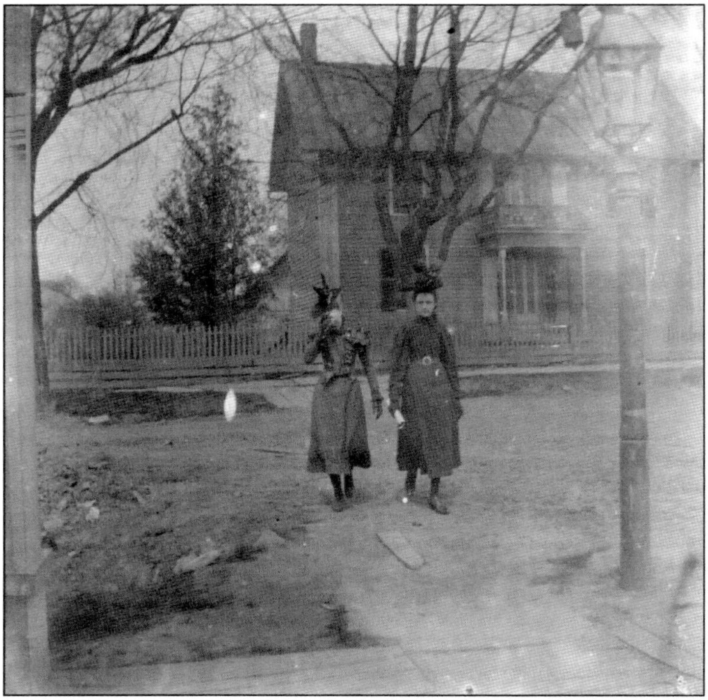

The John Howard Cline residence was on Washington Street, in Albany, in the early 20th century. Cline lived there with his wife, Della, and daughters, Martha and Louise. John went to the Atwood School before serving as a teacher and farmer. In the early 1900s, he moved his family to Albany and operated the Cline Mercantile business and drugstore in Albany for approximately 29 years before his death in 1934.

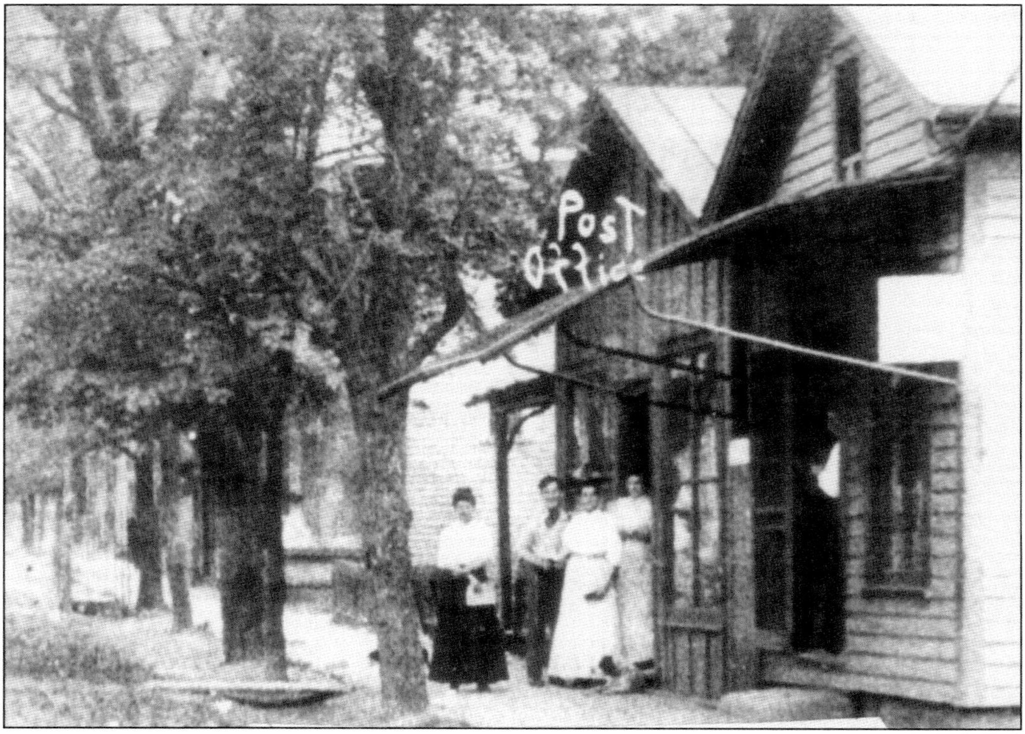

At the corner of Washington and State Streets were the post office and telephone company. The post office was a central meeting point for many citizens since they would have to come there to pick up mail prior to rural delivery. With the advent of the telephone, switchboard operators were needed to make manual connections between callers and individual homes.

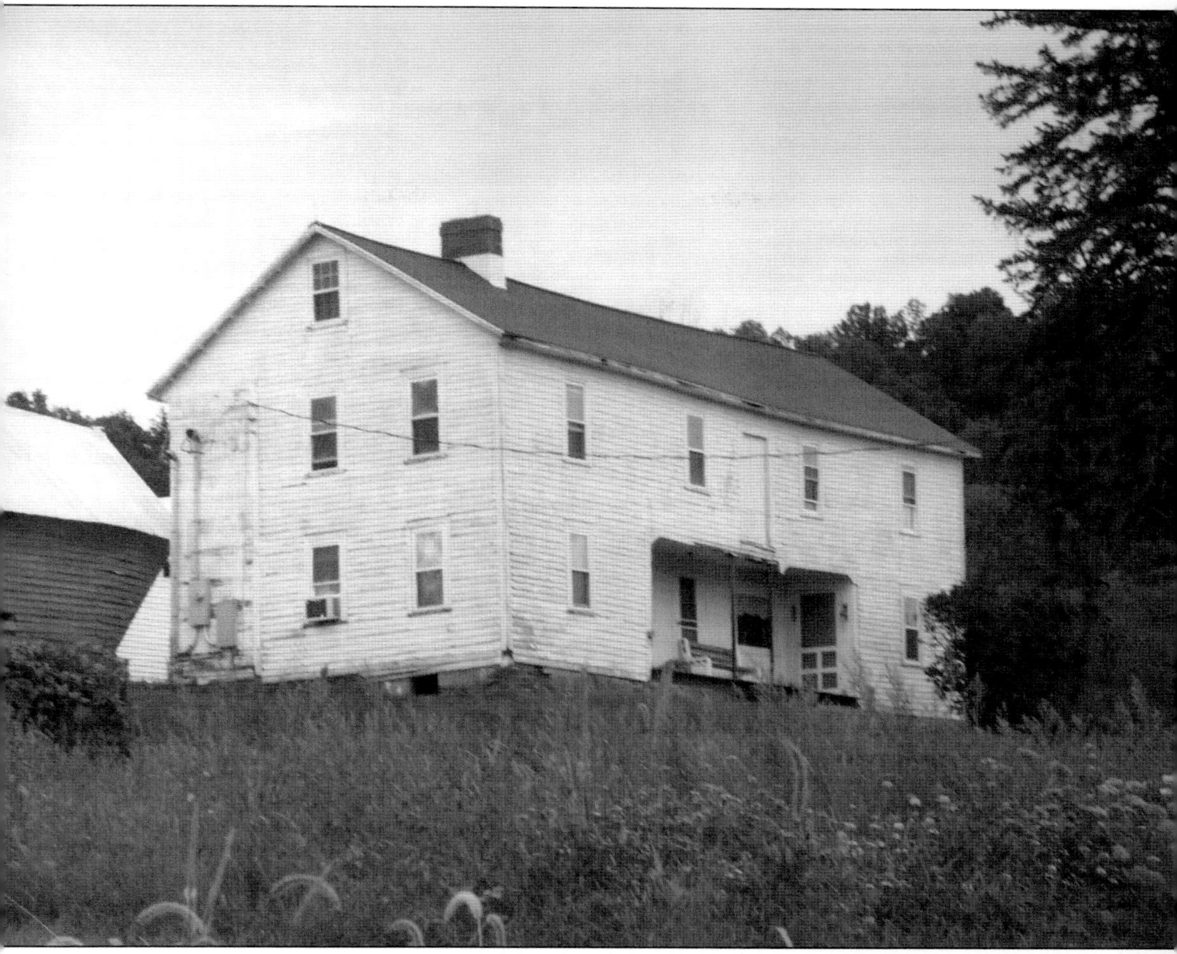

AMESVILLE. Lt. George Ewing and Judge Ephraim Cutler first visited what was to become Ames Township in 1797. Ewing built the first residence in March 1798. Cutler and Benjamin Brown soon built homes as well. The township rapidly became a destination for many families from the East that would play major roles in the development of the entire county. Amesville was laid out in 1839 by Hiram Cable and is the principle community in Ames Township. According to *Athens County, Ohio*, Cable named the town "in honor of Fisher Ames, a delegate from Massachusetts who was influential in establishing the Ohio Company in this Northwest territory." This 2011 picture is of the original Cutler house, which is still standing on Route 329, approximately a mile outside of Amesville. One of Amesville's favorite sons is Thomas Ewing, a first graduate of the Ohio University, who went on to fame and fortune as a businessman and politician. (Author's collection.)

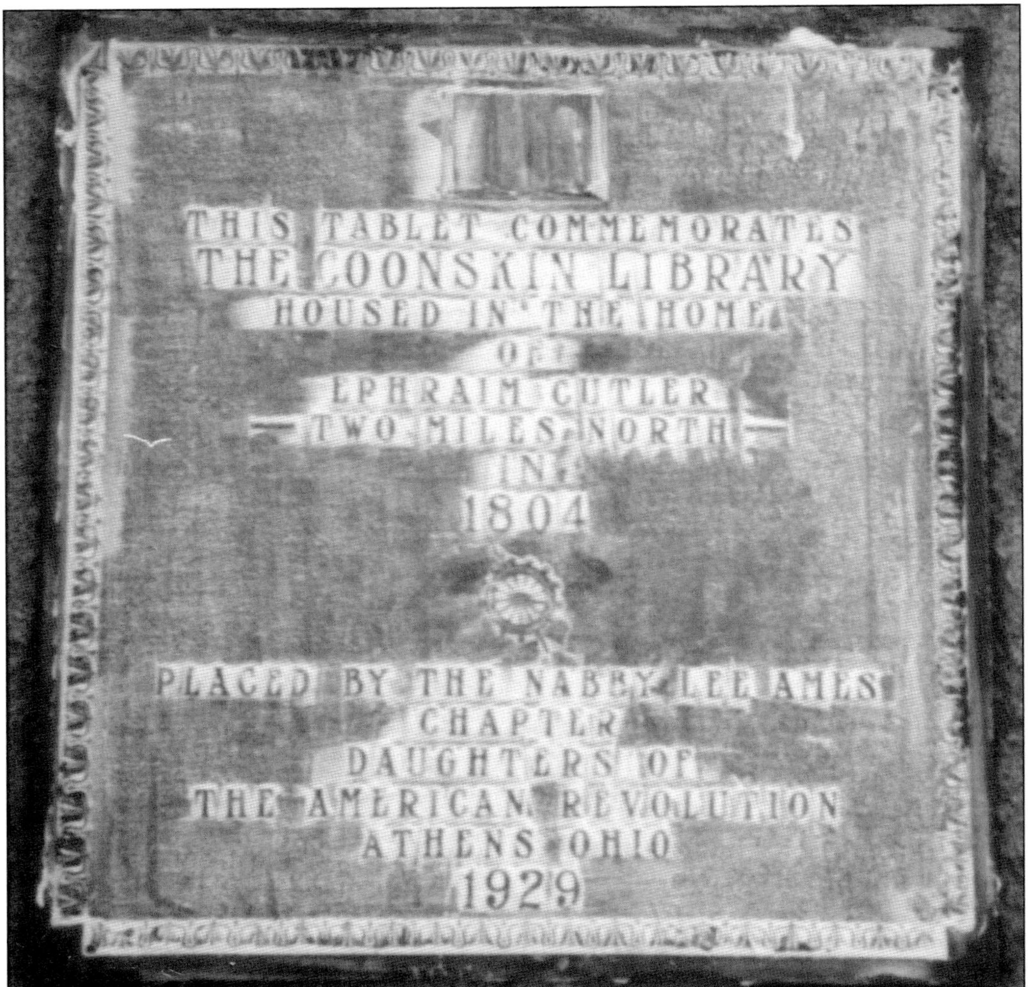

Among its many contributions to Athens County's history, Amesville is noted as the home of the first library formed in the Northwest Territory, the "Coonskin Library." Though there was a great deal of support for education, money to purchase books was problematic since people were "rich" with land, not cash. Many citizens were, by necessity, hunters. Because there was a cash market in the East for furs and skins, they determined to take furs to sell in Boston and purchase the first installation of books. Furs included bearskins and other pelts, but the concept of a "coonskin" (perhaps named such as a joke or source of derision) stuck as the expression of exchanging furs for money and, then, money for books. The citizens who launched the project probably did not call it by that name. Once purchased, the newly formed Western Library Association of the town of Ames managed the books. The marker reads as follows: "This tablet commemorates / the Coonskin Library / housed in the home / of / Ephraim Cutler / —two miles north— / in / 1804 / Placed by the Nabby Lee Ames / Chapter / Daughters of / the American Revolution / Athens, Ohio / 1929."

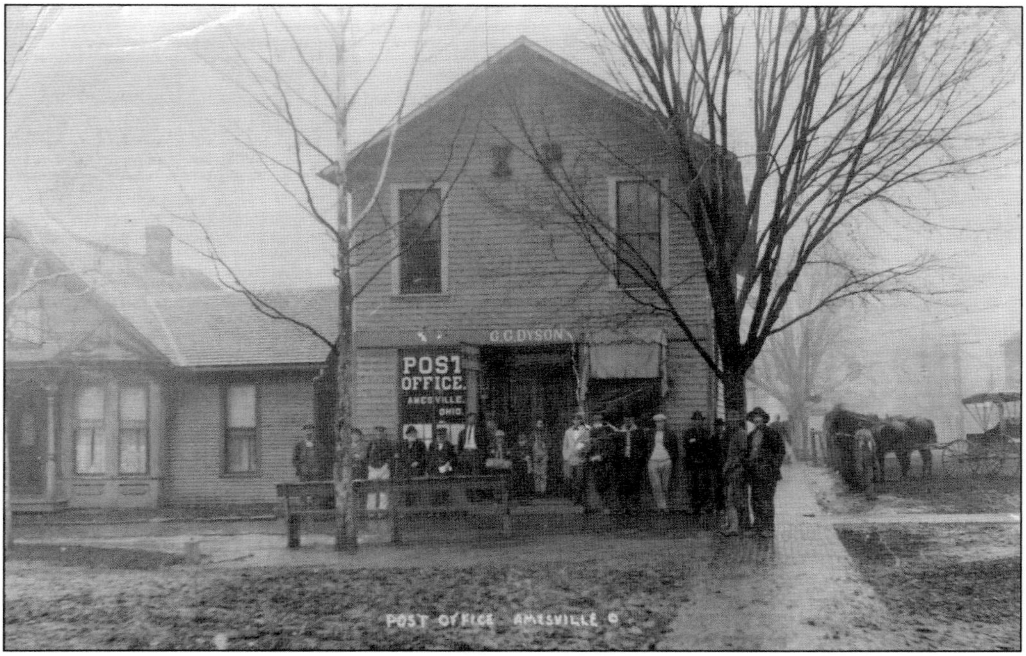

This picture, taken prior to 1914, is of the Amesville Post Office, the second post office established in Athens County. The first postmaster of Amesville was Loring B. Glazier, who served from 1821 to 1829. The town post office was a common meeting place for the public to engage with one another and converse about the topics of the day.

Three well-dressed women of Amesville are pictured here in 1908; obviously, they were at the height of fashion for winter weather in the town. In 1908, it was common for women of prominence to dress formally for ventures out into public, whether for church, shopping, or even a visit to call upon friends and neighbors.

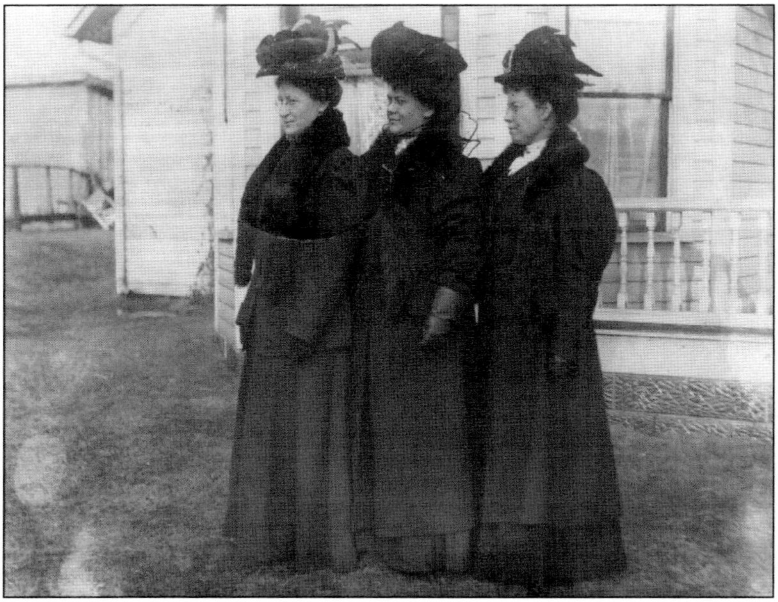

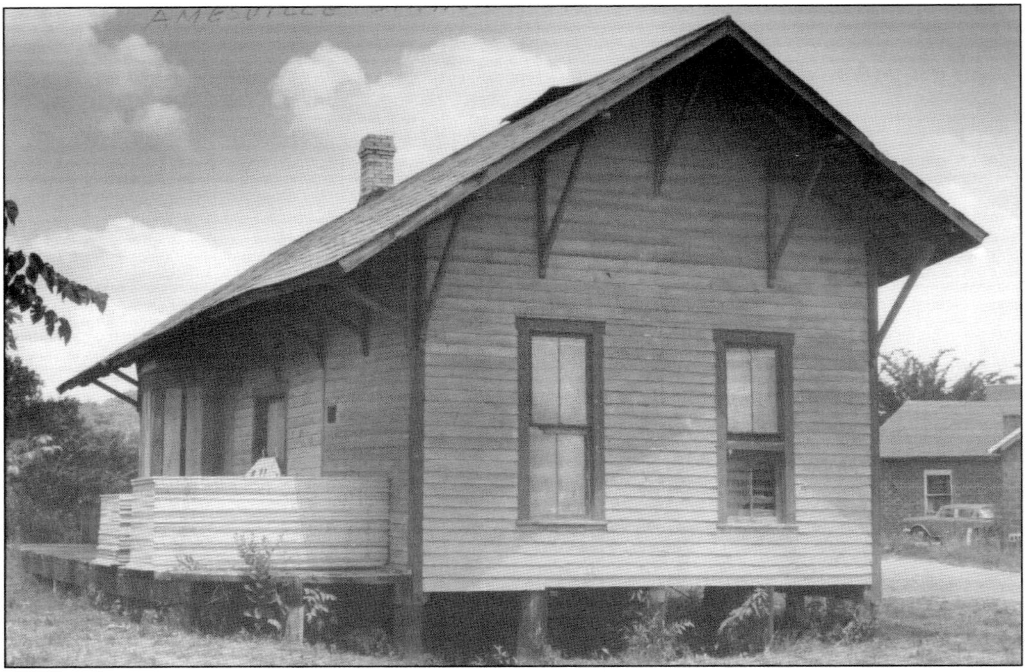

Pictured is Amesville's Marietta & Cincinnati Railroad station. The Marietta & Cincinnati Railroad provided an east-west route for moving goods through Athens County to lucrative markets. The railroad operated as the M&C until 1883, when it was renamed the Cincinnati, Washington & Baltimore Railway Company. (Courtesy of the Anastas Collection.)

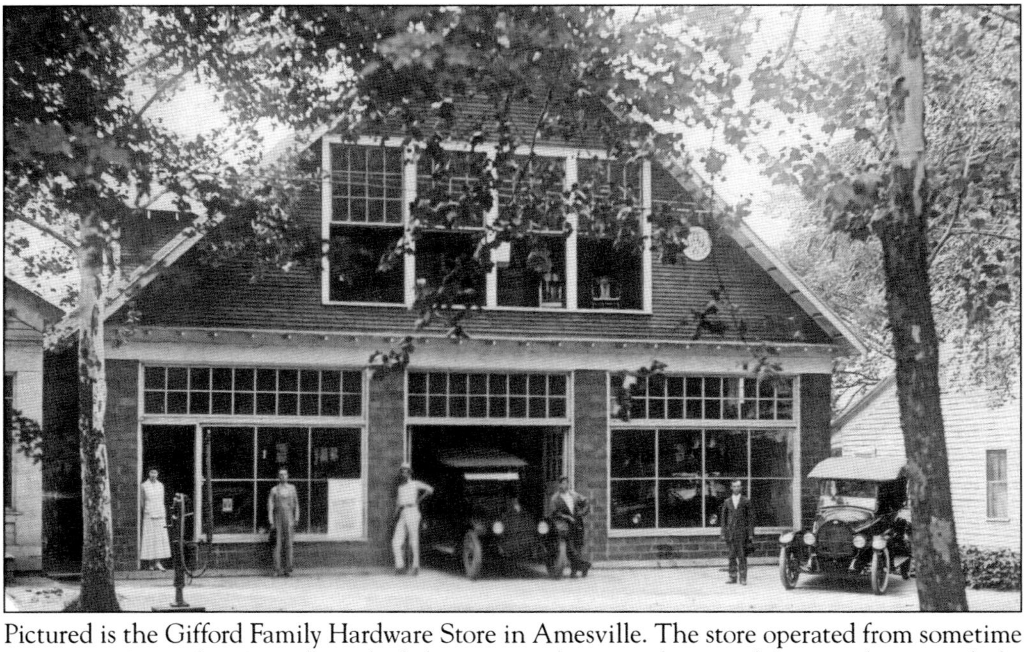

Pictured is the Gifford Family Hardware Store in Amesville. The store operated from sometime prior to 1950 until 1968 and supplied the town and surrounding rural areas with materials for maintaining homes and businesses. Until the advent of modern roads, most communities like Amesville provided for the day-to-day needs of their citizens through local businesses. Trips to Athens or other cities were often perceived as major excursions.

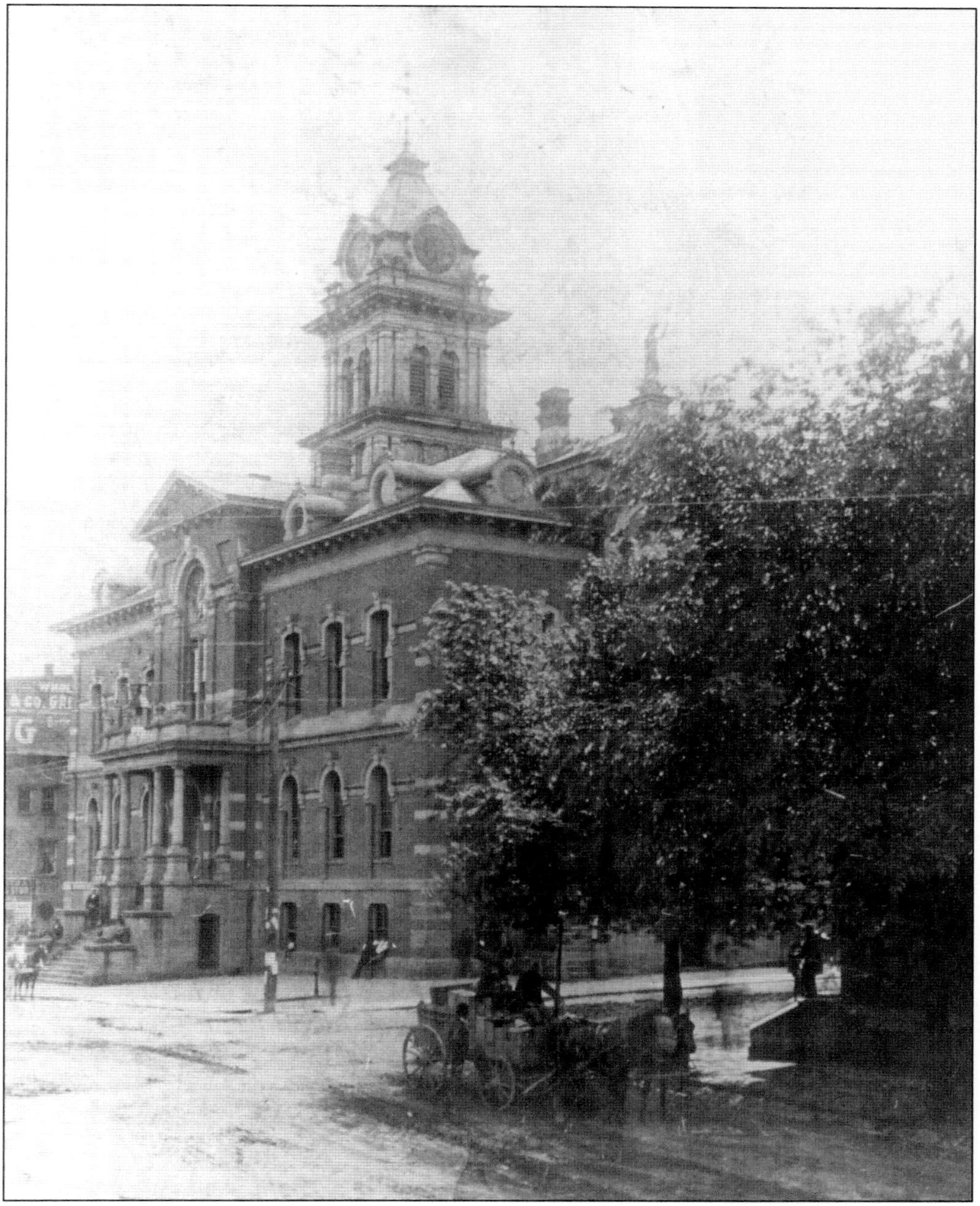

Athens. The city of Athens is the county seat of Athens County and is the home of Ohio University. What is now the city of Athens has the distinction of being the first permanent settlement within the county's borders. Settlers first appeared in 1797 shortly after the Indian threat was reduced by the 1795 Treaty of Greenville. The area was originally known as "Middleton" or "Middletown" for being half way between Marietta (Washington County's first settlement) and Chillicothe, which would become the first state capital (1803–1816). A December 1800 act confirming and establishing the town of Athens in the county of Washington is unique in that it focused on the development of a university that would actually own the town and lease town properties to individuals for homes and businesses. Pictured is the Athens County Courthouse around 1900.

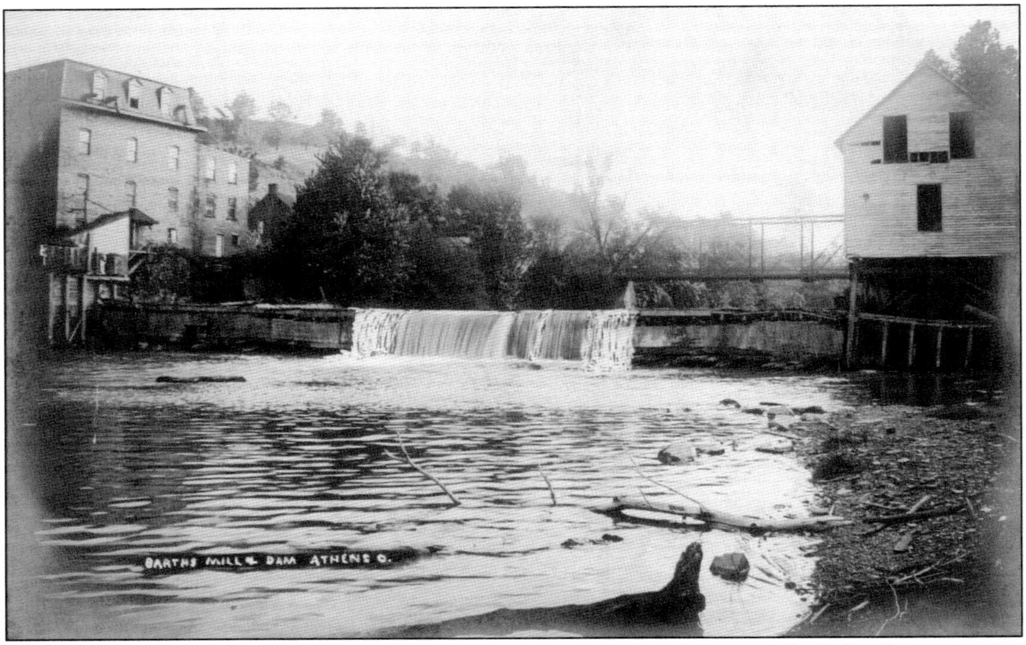

Ohio University was anticipated as early as 1787 in the contract between the federal government and potential purchasers of property of the Western Territory. It would not be until 1808 that building of the university got underway. In the meantime, mills, farming, and business of all kinds had begun. Pictured here is Barth's Mill and Dam.

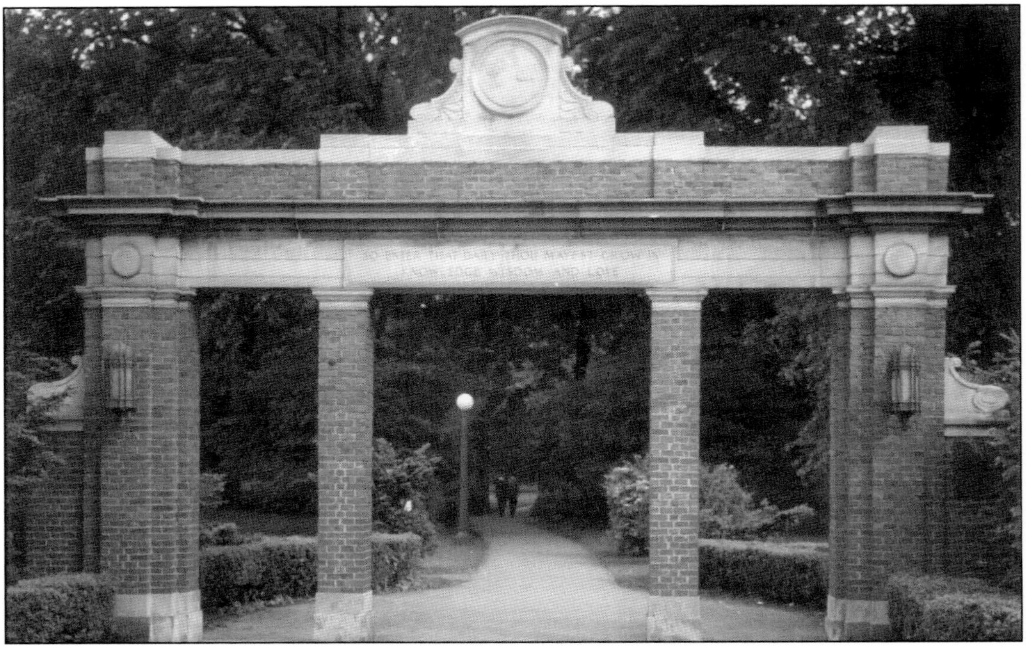

Though the year 1804 is normally attributed as the founding date of Ohio University, it was actually another four years before classes began. Jehiel Gregory was hired for $500 to build the structure just south of the current Memorial Auditorium (approximately where Galbraith Chapel now stands) referred to as "the Athens Academy," and it was advertised to open on the first Monday in October 1808. The school opened with three students. This image is of the Alumni Gate.

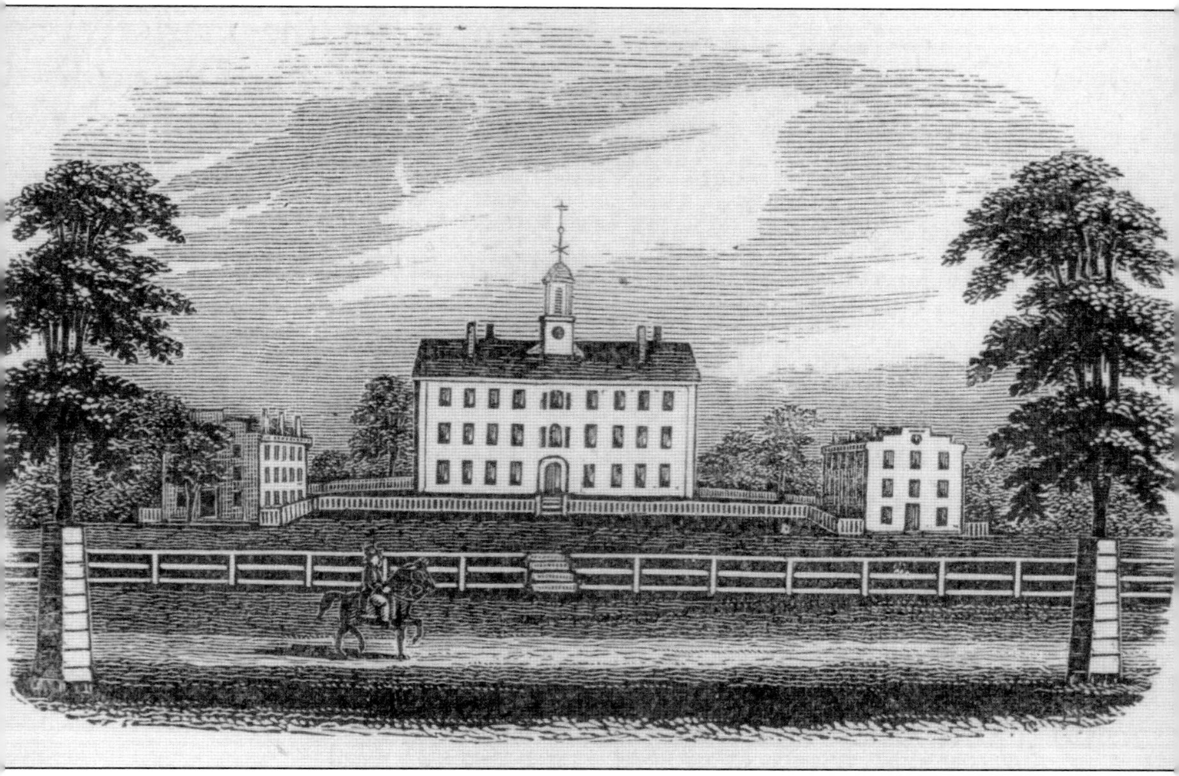

The original academy stood on the campus for approximately 10 years before Cutler Hall came into being. Construction for Cutler Hall was started in 1816 and completed by 1819. Once Cutler Hall was built, the academy continued as a preparatory school, then as a private school, and was torn down in 1841. Cutler Hall is today the "oldest standing academic building west of the Allegheny Mountains" according to local historians Elizabeth Beatty and Marjorie Stone. The Reverend Jacob Lindley was the first teacher hired. The first students were John Perkins, Brewster Higley, and Joel Abbot, none of whom completed his studies. Though Thomas Ewing and John Hunter were later awarded bachelor of arts and science degrees "in the Seminary" in 1815, it would not be until 1819 that courses equal to college level were offered on a regular basis. Henry Howe drew this early picture of Ohio University.

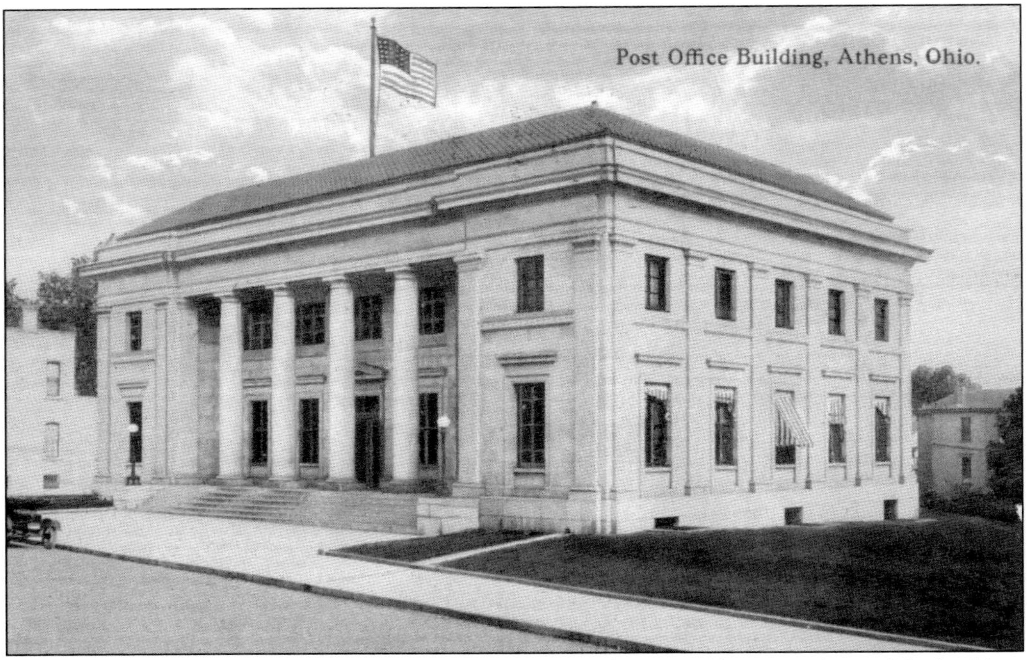

The Athens Post Office Building was built in 1916. After the post office moved out of the building that housed it for more public access and parking, the building was bought by the university and used as part of its engineering program. The structure is located on the corner of West Union Street and Richland Avenue.

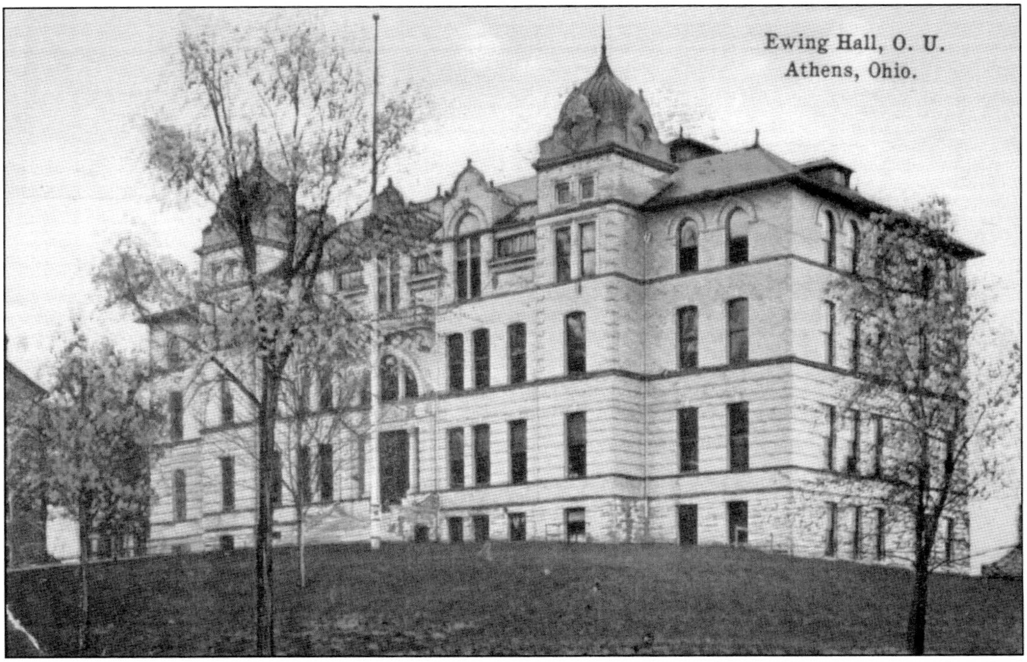

This picture is of the old Ewing Hall. According to Betty Hollow, the building was completed in 1898 and contained a 1,200-seat auditorium, classrooms, offices (including the president's office), a faculty room, a chemistry lab, an art room, and a gymnasium. The once elegant building was razed in the 1970s. (Courtesy of the Anastas Collection.)

The chapel, built in 1881, stood for many years on the campus of Ohio University on the west of the "West Wing." When Ewing Hall was to be built, the space where the chapel sat was needed. Rather than demolish the old building, it was picked up and moved. (Courtesy of the Anastas Collection.)

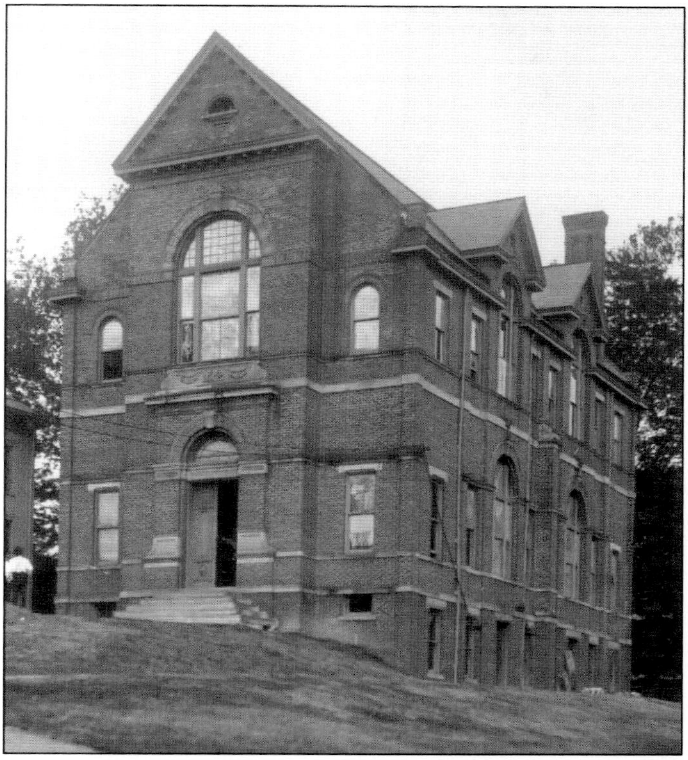

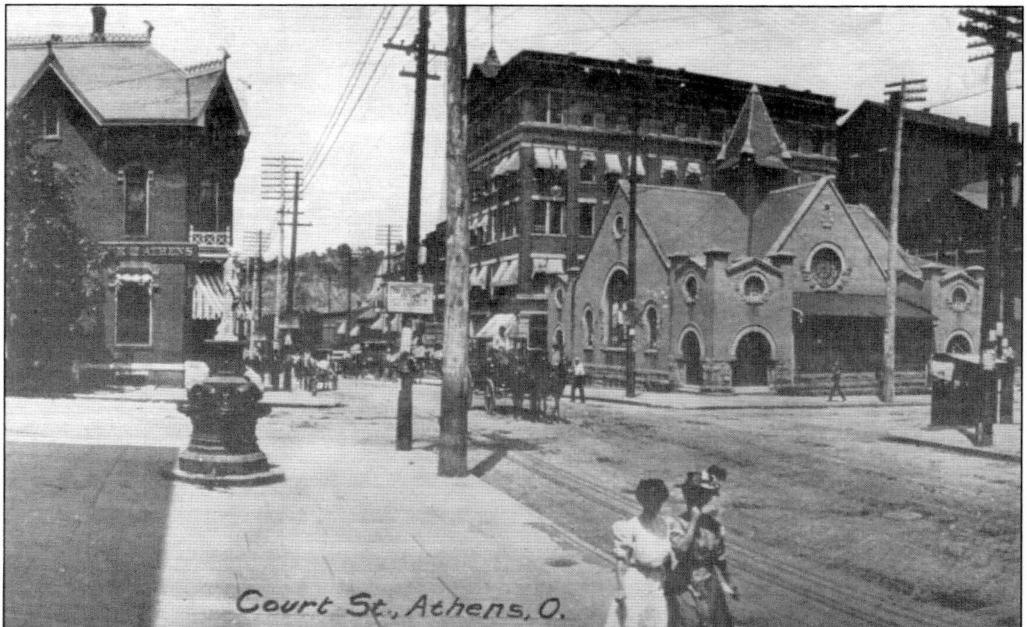

Of course, there is much more to the city of Athens than Ohio University. Development of businesses and cultural events, politics, religion, crimes, and so on could fill numerous books (and such books have been written and are available). Court Street is the main street of uptown Athens. Current buildings on the street range from the mid-1800s to the present. Pictured here is Court Street in the early 1900s. The viewpoint is from the south and looking north.

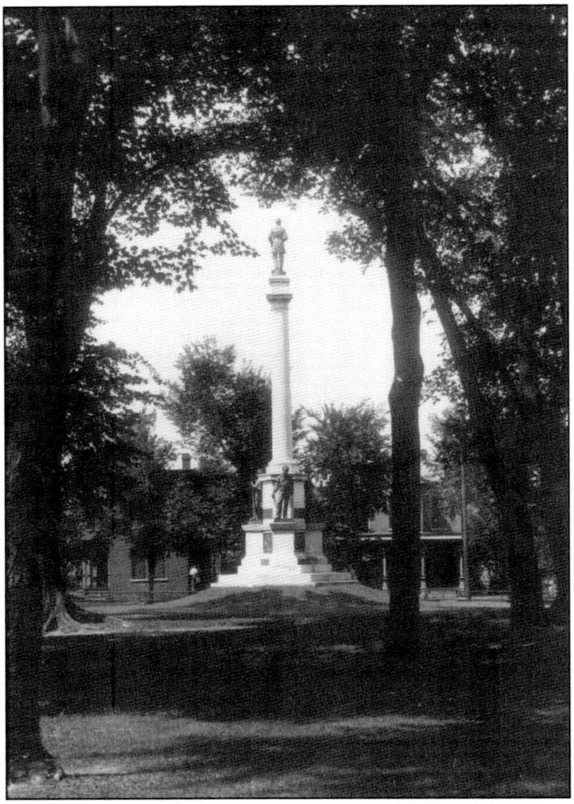

The Soldiers and Sailors (Civil War) Monument stands on the Ohio University College Green. The Athens County Monument Association chose this location, and the monument itself was dedicated on July 4, 1893; over 7,000 people attended. The sentry at the top extends the total height to 45 feet. On the lower base are an infantryman, a cavalryman, and a sailor. (Courtesy of the Anastas Collection.)

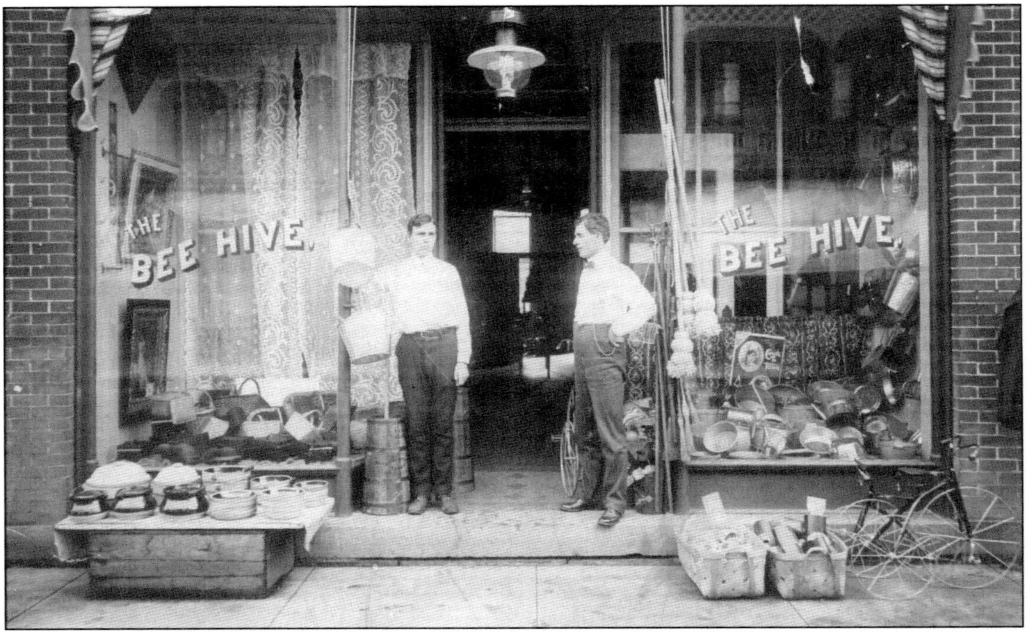

Shown here is Woods Bee Hive at 30 South Court Street. This storefront is similar to many of the early 20th century. Notice the large windows for light and display purposes and the door set back under the building to provide a natural cover from the elements. (Courtesy of the Anastas Collection.)

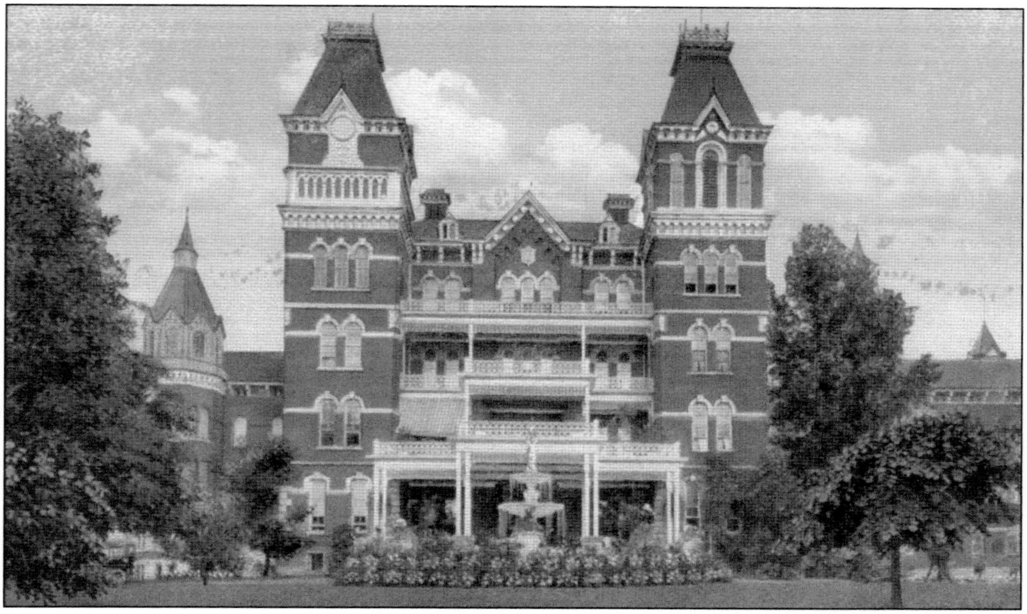

The Athens Lunatic Asylum was located on "the Ridges" across the Hocking River from the city of Athens on 150 acres of land. Construction began in 1868, and the buildings opened for patients in 1874. The asylum operated for many years but ceased in the early 1980s. Land was then sold to Ohio University, which now uses it for office spaces and the Kennedy Museum of Art.

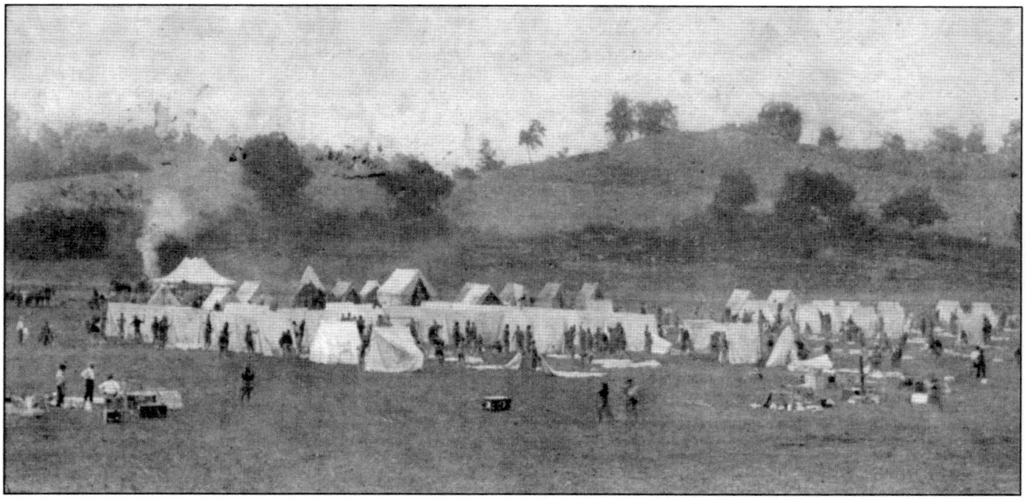

Though usually a peaceful and welcoming place, Athens history shows that the city has had its problems, too. One of the more interesting stories is of the 1904 "war" that took place on Friday, August 19. US Army soldiers and Ohio National Guardsmen camped on the outskirts of Athens clashed in downtown Athens. According to an *Athens Messenger* article, a Private Kelly of the US Army was arrested for drunkenness in an Athens saloon by a National Guard provost, but not until he emptied his revolver (not shooting anyone in the process) and was clubbed into insensibility. He was bound hand and foot and taken to the jail. Apparently, Kelly's friends had a plan in mind to release him. Approximately 100 of them (very likely under the influence of alcohol) met in the school yard, formed a column, and marched down Court Street six abreast to denigrate any National Guardsmen in hearing distance and to free their comrade. Numerous civilians were on the streets and had no idea of the danger they faced.

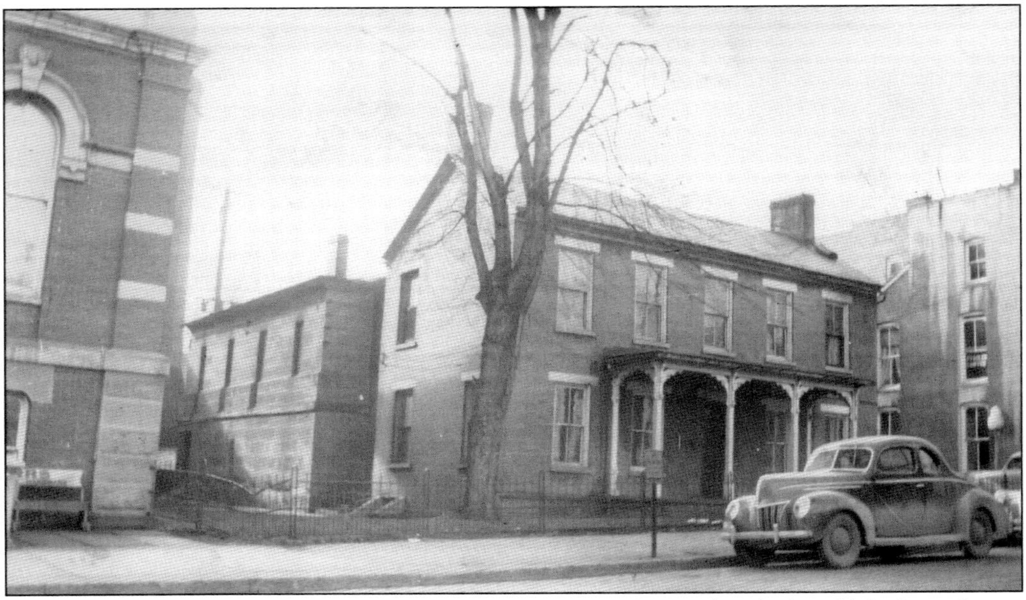

At the sheriff's office, Corporal Clark of the Ohio National Guard and a handful of guardsmen (under orders to do so) confronted the marchers. Almost immediately, shots were fired. Clark was killed, and Sergeant Blessing, Corporal Heald, and Private Ohl were wounded. The whole affair lasted only a few minutes. The crowds scattered—civilians for any form of cover and soldiers for their encampments. Military leaders and the sheriff quickly shut down saloons, called in special guards to watch over the town, and began seeking and arresting those involved. The image above is of the sheriff's office and jail. The image below is of the Bank of Athens, which sat on the corner of Court and Washington opposite the courthouse; the building to the left was directly opposite the sheriff's office. (Above, courtesy of the Anastas Collection.)

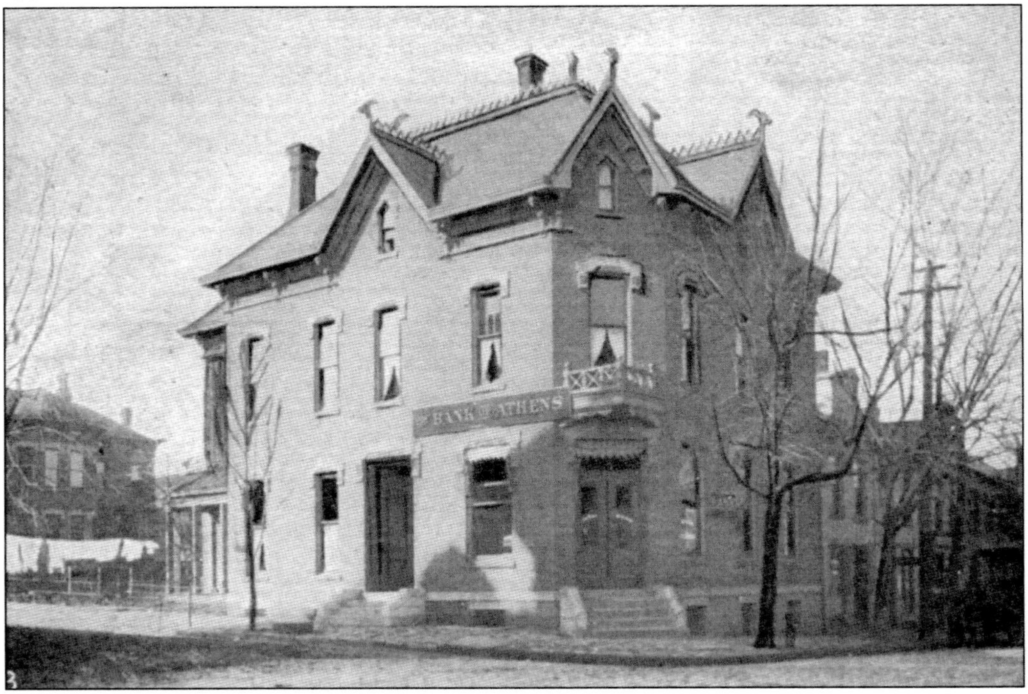

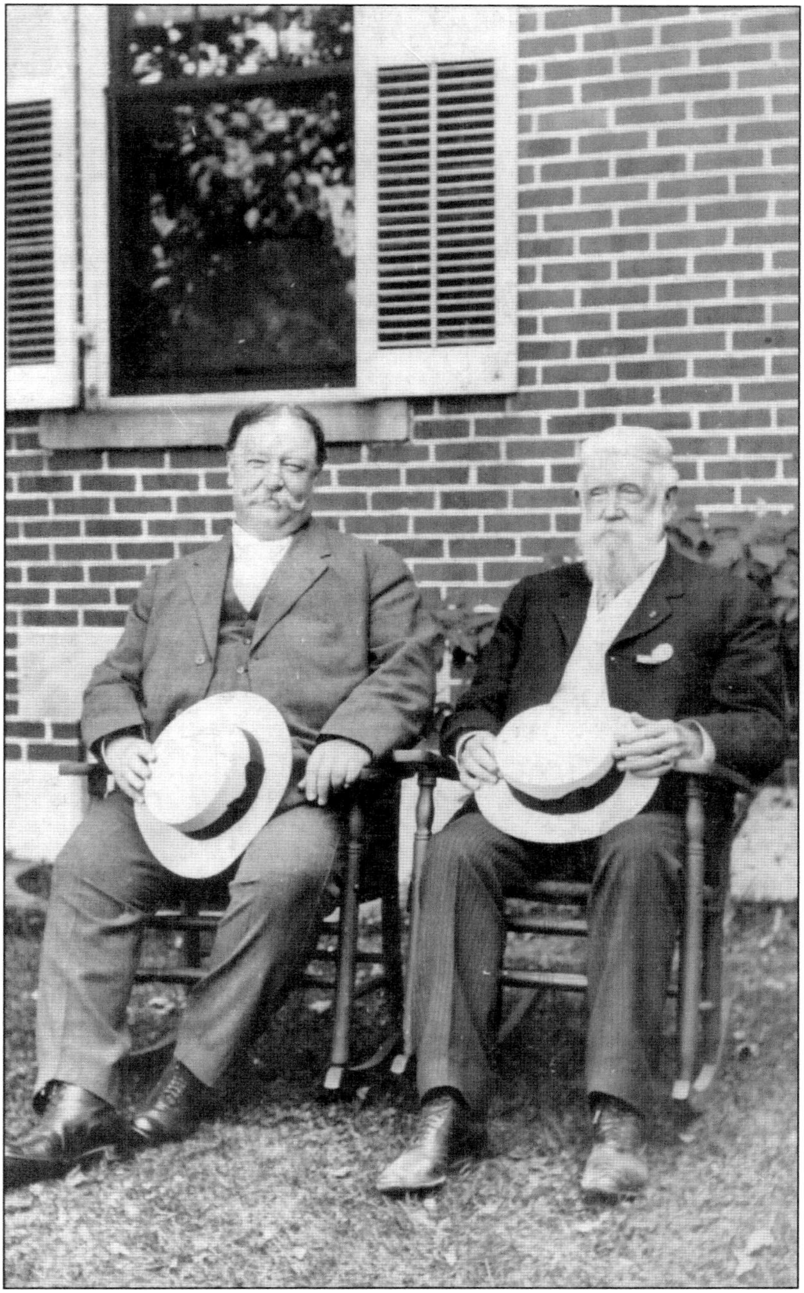

Five artillerymen and seven others were arrested and charged with the murder of Clark and the wounding of the other soldiers. In September, General Grosvenor, a Civil War veteran, former US representative, and prominent citizen of Athens, led the prosecution. Ultimately, some of those accused were released for lack of evidence, and no one was proven the murderer. John Lott was found guilty of assault with intent to kill and sentenced to one year in prison for his efforts to beat Walter Ohl with a pistol. Others were sentenced to 30 days in the Columbus Workhouse and fined $500 and the costs of prosecution, all small prices for a man's life and pain inflicted on others guilty of nothing but doing their jobs. This picture is of William Howard Taft (left) and General Grosvenor on the lawn of Grosvenor's home.

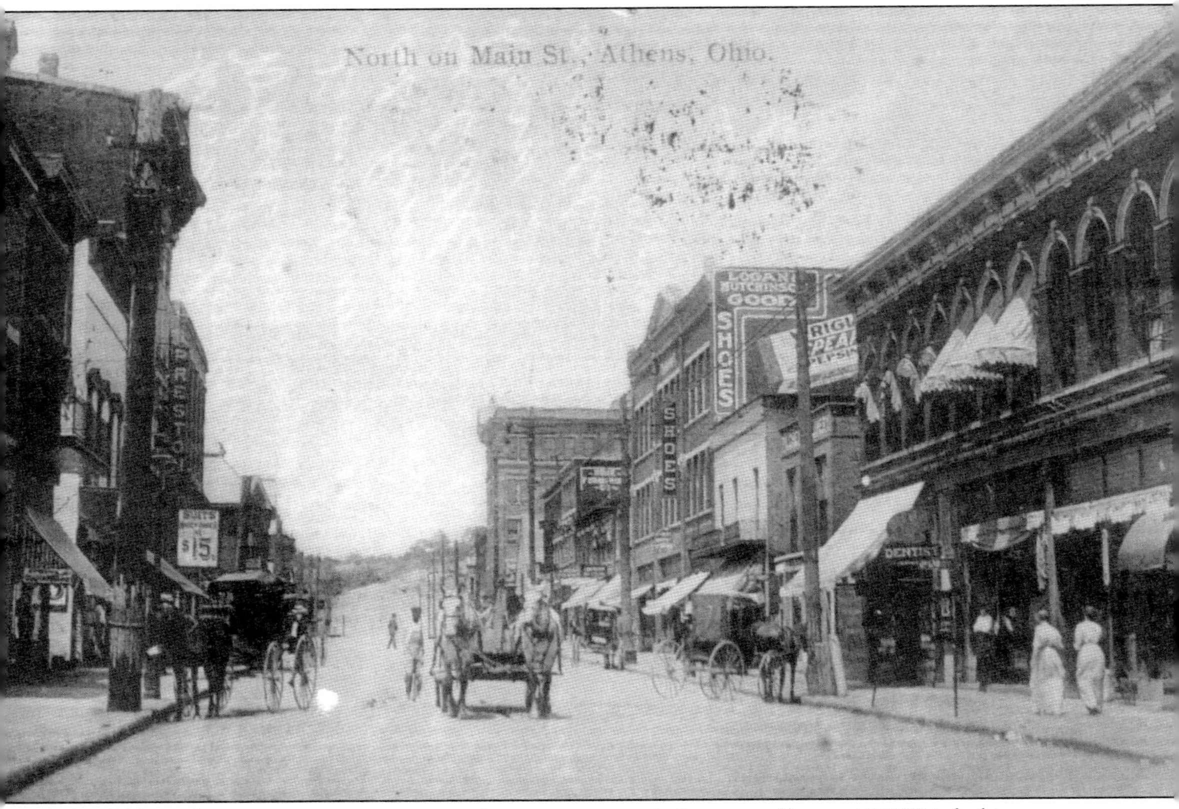

When the university is in session, the town currently boasts well over 40,000 inhabitants, many from all over the world. It is universally perceived as a great place to get an education, live, work, and raise families. As the county seat, the city of Athens contains numerous government offices and provides work for many city and county workers. Stores and shops of all kinds have been integral to the area since the beginning of its history. Industry over the years has included everything from saltworks to brick making to printing to medical testing operations to solar power manufacturing, and much more. The city of Athens is today a blend of a historical district—comprised of original buildings and brick streets—and modern accommodations and businesses. Ohio University continues to thrive and is a resource for creative community members who bring many cultures and cultural events to the region. Pictured is Court Street looking from south to north in 1916.

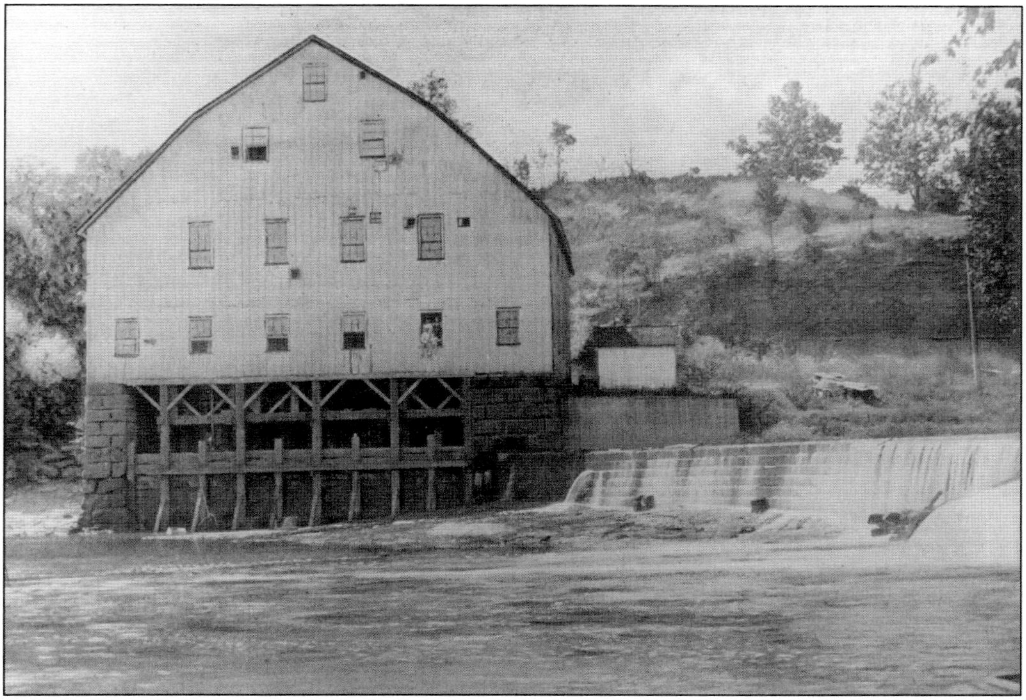

Herrold's Mill was built by Joseph Herrold in 1806 and rebuilt in 1826, and it operated until 1912. According to the *History of Hocking Valley, Ohio*, "Judge Pruden connected with it the first carding machine and cloth-dressing establishment started in the township." Henry Herrold sold the mill in 1911 to Edward S. White, who overhauled it only to have it burn down two months later. White's Mill now sits on the property. The current building was moved from Meigs County to the site.

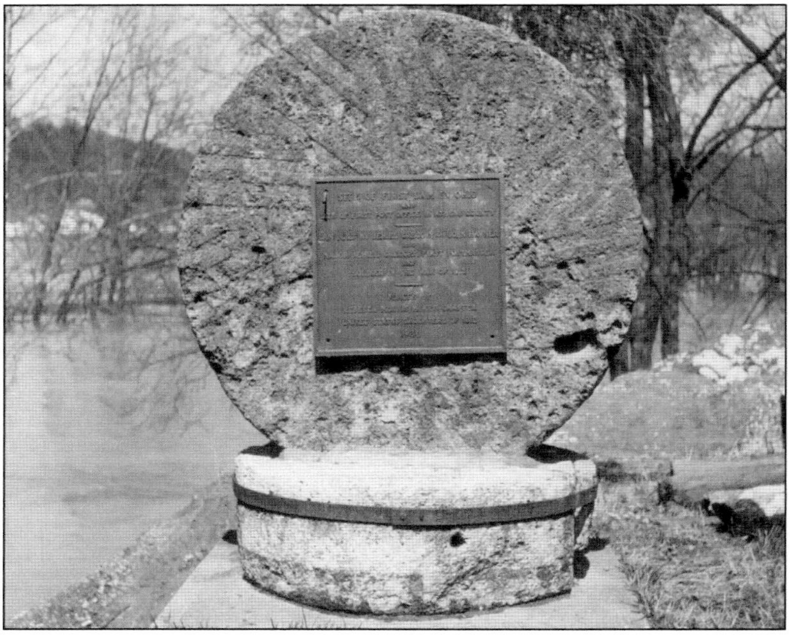

This stone marks the location of the first post office and dam in Athens County. The first post office was established in January 1804. The first postmaster was Jehiel Gregory, who kept the office at his house. In the spring of that year, Dr. Eliphaz Perkins was appointed postmaster and kept the office on State Street.

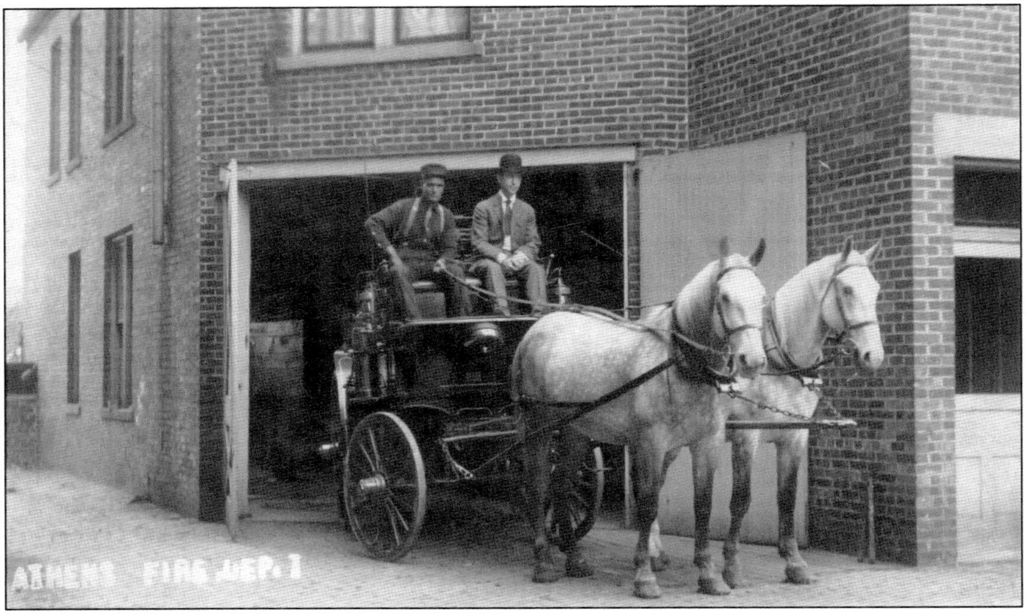

Hugh Meighn (left) and Ben Conert are shown on a horse-drawn wagon belonging to the Athens Fire Department. Numerous fires occurred over the years in the city of Athens, including the Herrold Mill, the Cline Building, Taylor's Eagle Hotel, the Theiss Mill, and the great fire of December 1877 that burned much of the east side of Court Street. There have been many other blazes in Athens and throughout the county.

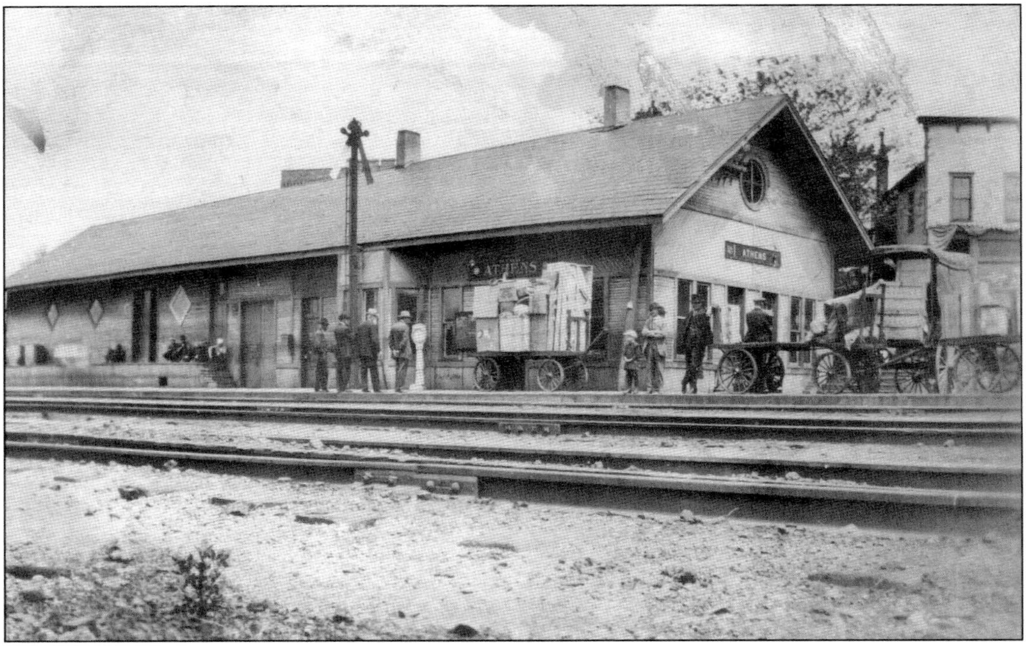

Pictured is the Athens Train Depot on May 11, 1914. The last tracks between Chillicothe and Athens for the M&C Railroad were laid on April 28, 1856; however, the railroad had numerous problems and was not trusted by many Atheneans. In 1870, the Hocking Valley Railroad provided passenger and freight service between Athens and Columbus and opened possibilities for travelers as well as business people wishing to move products to consumers.

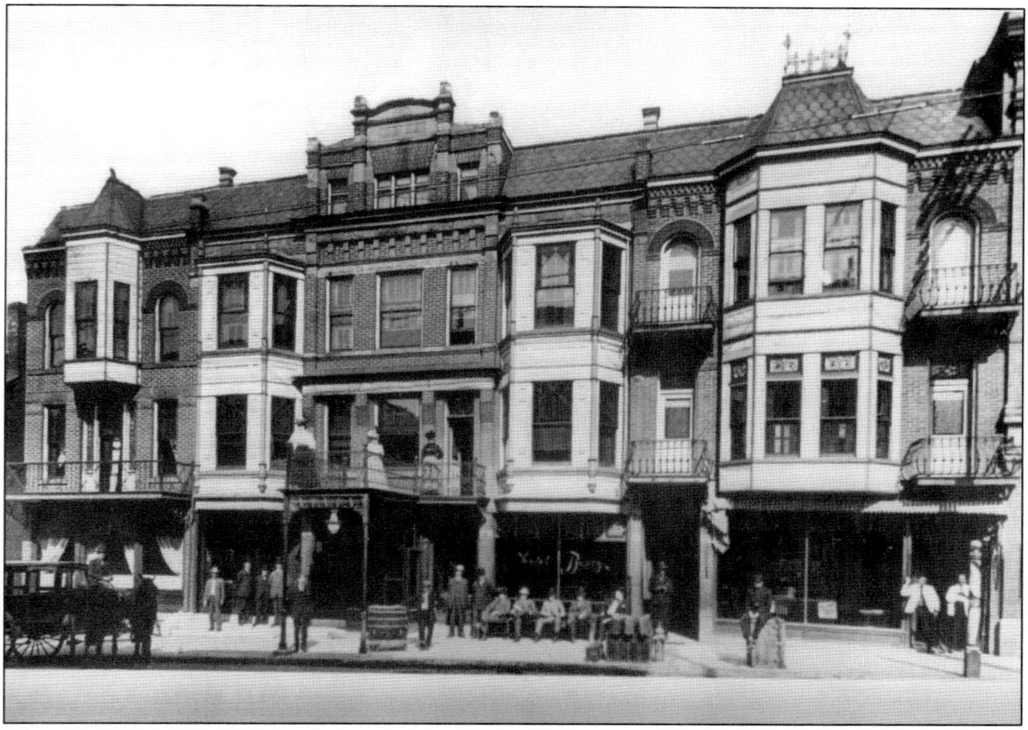

The Hotel Berry served for many years as the premier hotel in Athens and was known far and wide. It was owned and operated by an African American couple, Edward and Mattie Berry. The two were prominent in the community, and the service and food they provided were highly praised. Ironically, after they sold the hotel, blacks were not allowed in. The hotel went through years of deterioration and was torn down in the 1960s.

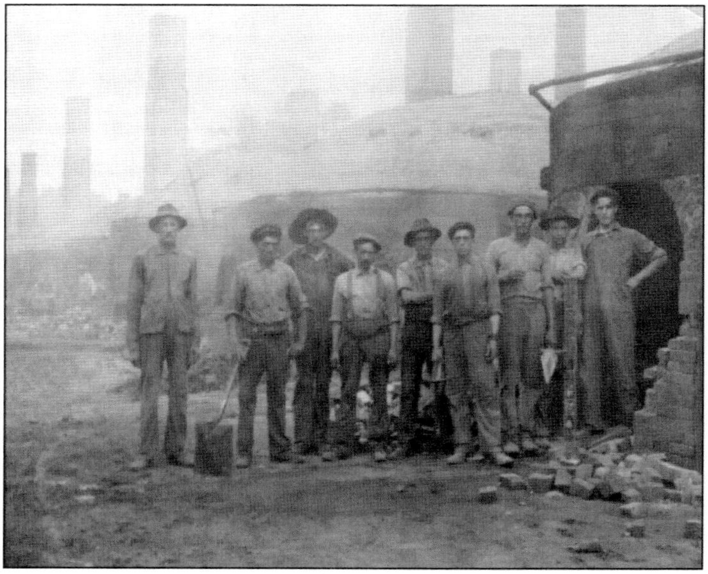

The Athens Brick Plant, started in 1893, was a supplier of paving brick for Athens and cities across the country. Located near what is now Stimson Avenue, the plant began producing 50,000 bricks per day almost from its beginning with a labor force of less than 100 men. Unfortunately, over the next 20 years, competition and the development of concrete and asphalt building materials caused the business to close. (Courtesy of the Anastas Collection.)

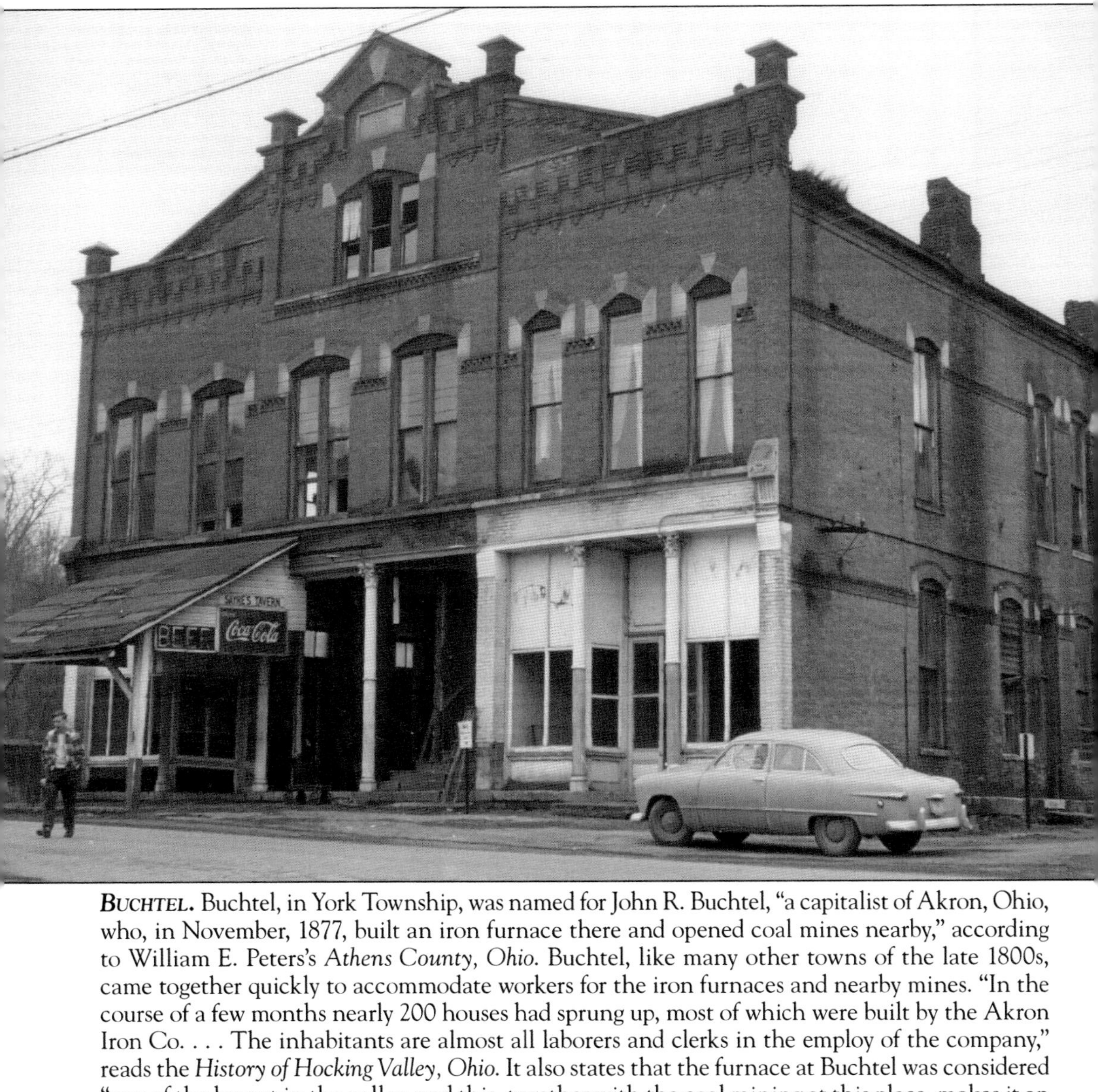

BUCHTEL. Buchtel, in York Township, was named for John R. Buchtel, "a capitalist of Akron, Ohio, who, in November, 1877, built an iron furnace there and opened coal mines nearby," according to William E. Peters's *Athens County, Ohio*. Buchtel, like many other towns of the late 1800s, came together quickly to accommodate workers for the iron furnaces and nearby mines. "In the course of a few months nearly 200 houses had sprung up, most of which were built by the Akron Iron Co. . . . The inhabitants are almost all laborers and clerks in the employ of the company," reads the *History of Hocking Valley, Ohio*. It also states that the furnace at Buchtel was considered "one of the largest in the valley, and this, together with the coal mining at this place, makes it an important mining center." Ivan M. Tribe describes Buchtel as a company town, but clarifies that its owner, John R. Buchtel, was a "somewhat benevolent though paternalistic corporate leader." Buchtel supported and helped pay for a school, gave land for a union hall, and did not demand that all businesses in town be owned by the company. This is a picture of the Buchtel store and opera house. (Courtesy of the Anastas Collection.)

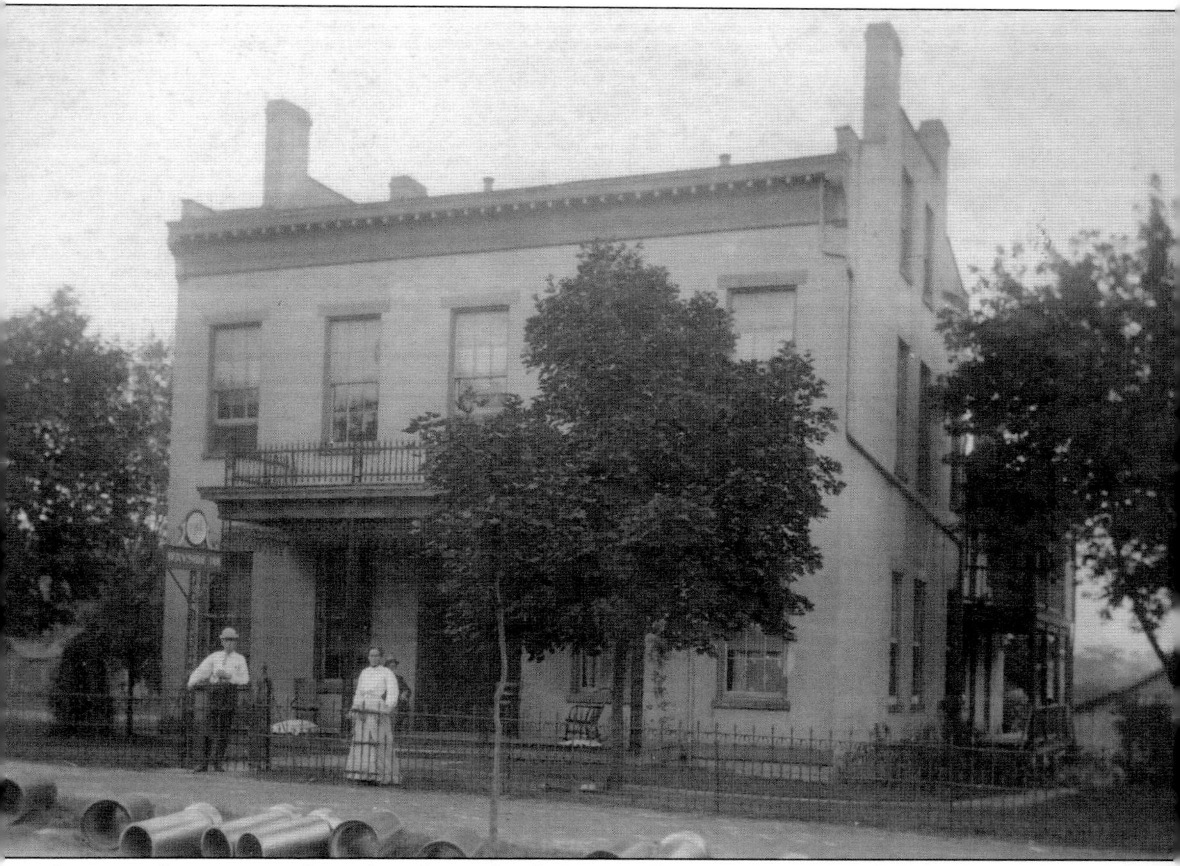

Some confusion exists about the relationship between a former town and Buchtel. Some people, even in Athens County, still think that Bessemer and Buchtel are synonymous. "Bessemer" was officially its own separate town on the west side of the hill that separated the two communities. It never lived up to its promise and essentially withered. For whatever reason, some people in what became Buchtel referred to themselves as being in Bessemer, perhaps because the former town had been the site of an earlier post office designation. However, they were not on the same plot of land and are two separate towns, one largely on paper and the other in reality. Buchtel currently serves as the home of the Nelsonville-York High School and draws numerous people to engage in programs and athletic events at the school. It is also home to the vicinity's Catholic church since the former church in Nelsonville and Buchtel united as one. This picture is of Buchtel's Wayside Inn around 1900.

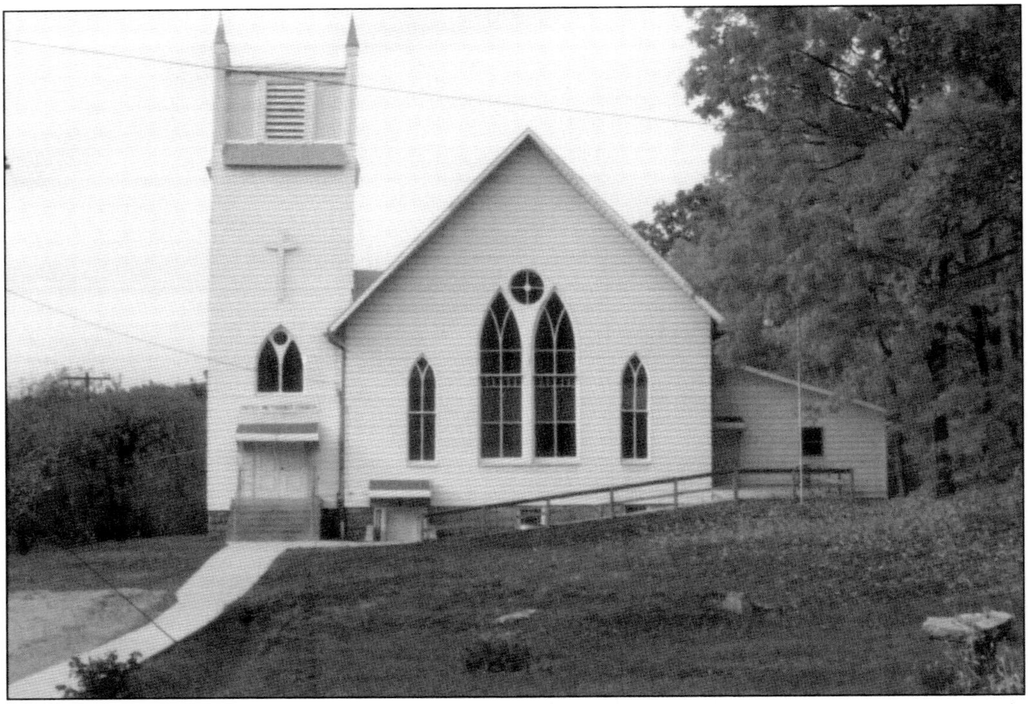

Buchtel's United Methodist church is shown here. Buchtel in 1883 had two physicians, approximately 1,500 inhabitants, two churches being built (one of them the Methodist church shown here), and what has been referred to as "the most extensive mercantile establishment in the Hocking Valley."

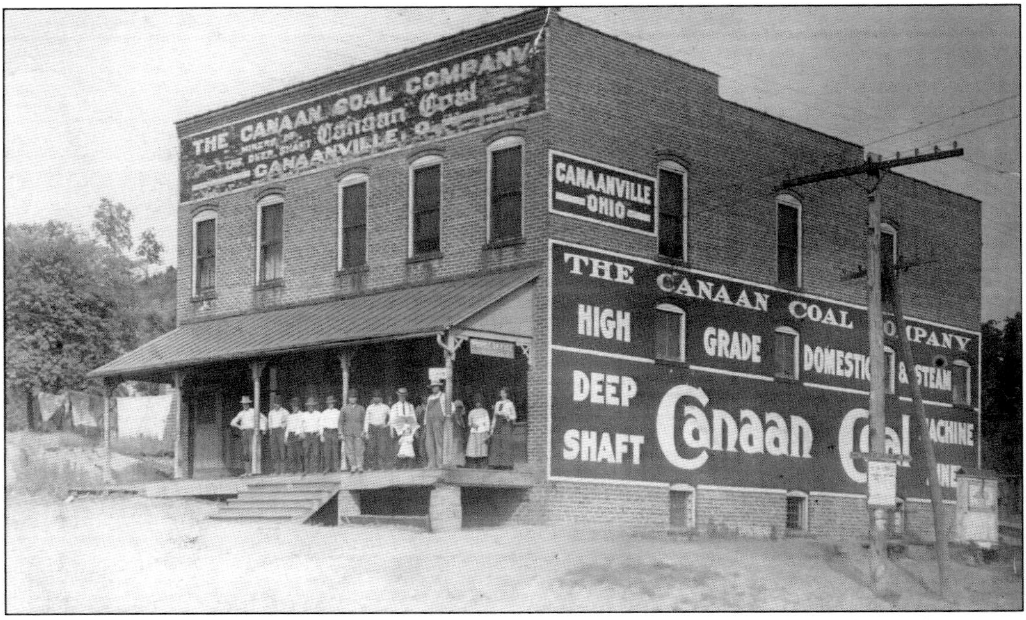

CANAANVILLE. Canaanville is east of Athens in Canaan Township. It was established in 1834, largely in service to the work of farming, but never achieved the status of a thriving community; however, it did have a flouring mill, blacksmith shop, and a hotel at one time. It served early on as a railroad shipping station for lumber and later as a mine site. The Canaan Coal Company Store, shown here, is still intact and readily observable from Route 50.

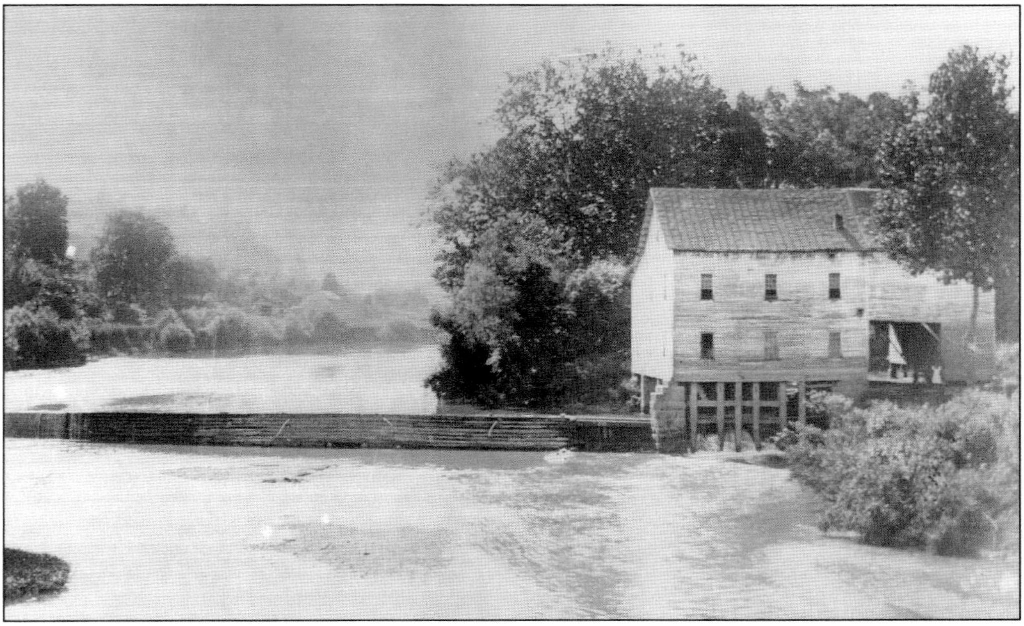

Webster's flouring mill, shown here, was built in 1824 by Ephraim Young and Henry Barrow. It was rebuilt by C.D.B. Webster in 1872. It was removed in 1905, and the dam was dynamited around 1917. It was the only manufactory in Canaanville at the time of the writing of the *History of Hocking Valley, Ohio*, published in 1883. That book proclaims the area was dedicated to farming but had one store and a post office.

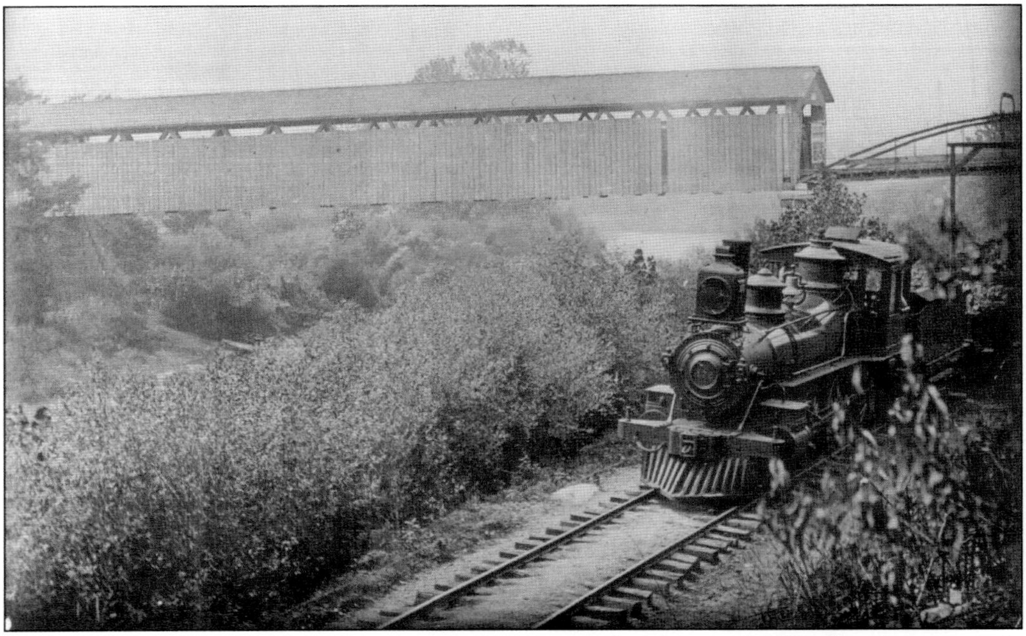

At one time, the Marietta & Cincinnati Railroad, completed around 1857, played a major role in opening travel across the state. It passed through Athens, Canaanville, Stewart, Qualey, New England, Cutler, and many other communities before reaching Harmer on Scott's Landing. Thus, as "railroad communities," Canaanville and surrounding towns faced the inevitable problems that existed with that phase of American history. (Courtesy of the Anastas Collection.)

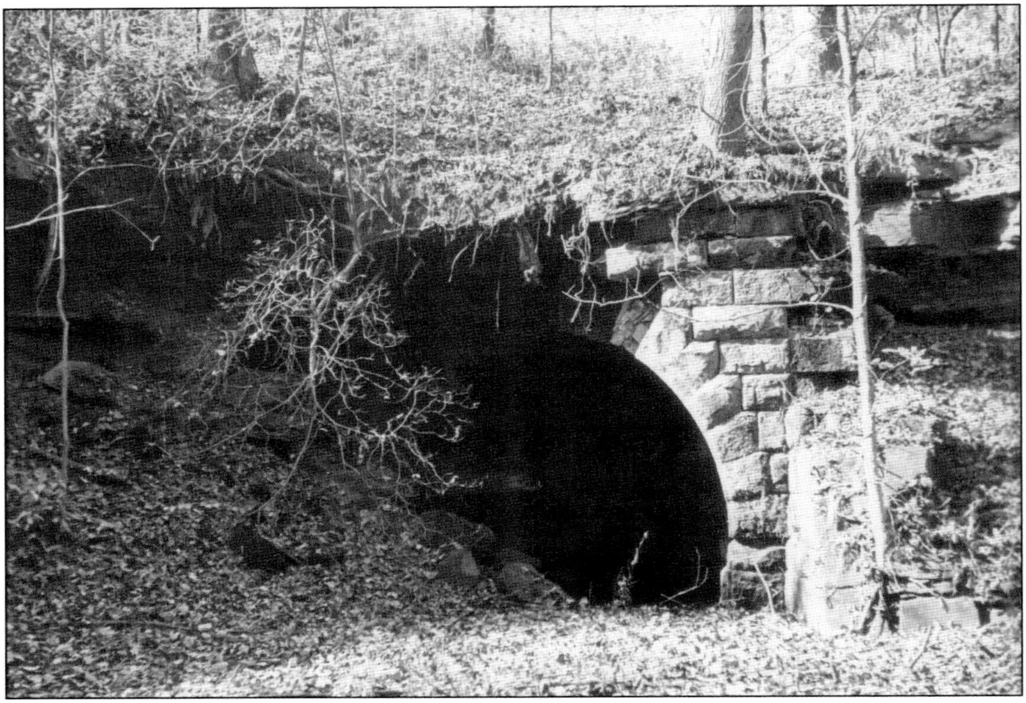

On Monday, September 21, 1868, near Canaanville, an accident occurred. Two handcars loaded with trackmen collided with a train, causing the Pilcher Tunnel to catch on fire. Five men were killed, and two others suffered serious injuries. Pictured is the Pilcher Tunnel long after its collapse. (Courtesy of the Anastas Collection.)

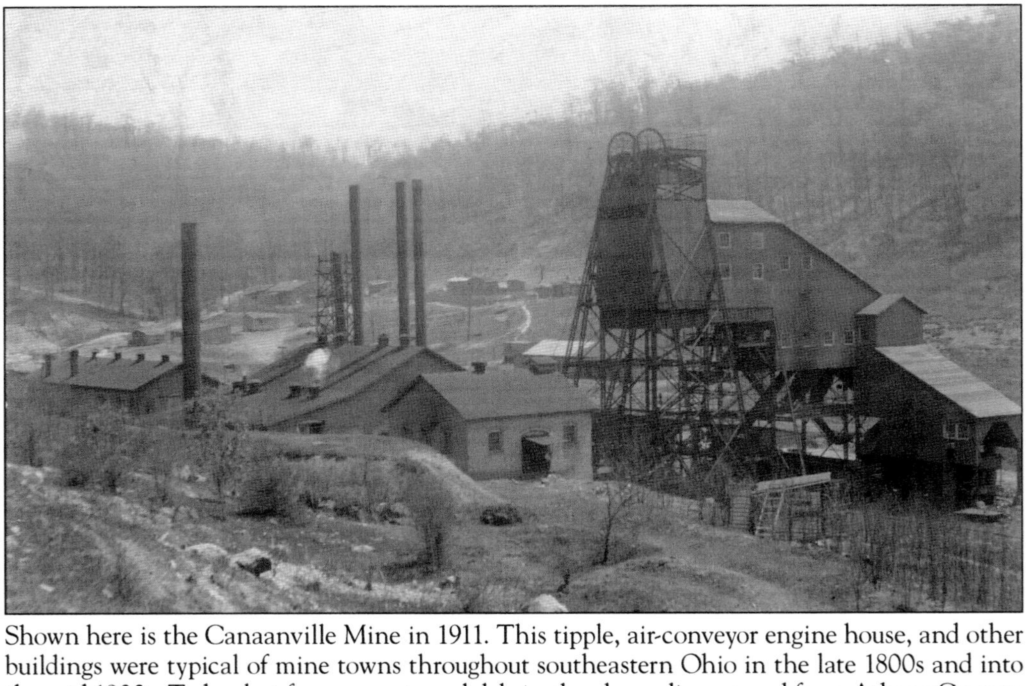

Shown here is the Canaanville Mine in 1911. This tipple, air-conveyor engine house, and other buildings were typical of mine towns throughout southeastern Ohio in the late 1800s and into the mid-1900s. Today, but for remnants and debris, they have disappeared from Athens County. (Courtesy of the Anastas Collection.)

Pictured here are homes in Canaanville in the early 1900s. The almost identical look of the buildings suggests that they were most likely built to accommodate miners' families. Interestingly, they are two stories as opposed to the square, one-story coal houses built all over Athens County. Typical of many "company-built" housing units for miners, there is little or no landscaping. Such houses were put up quickly with few frills.

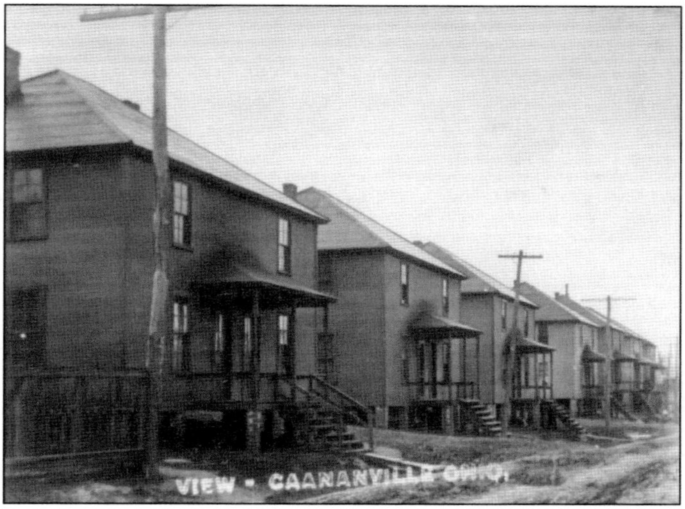

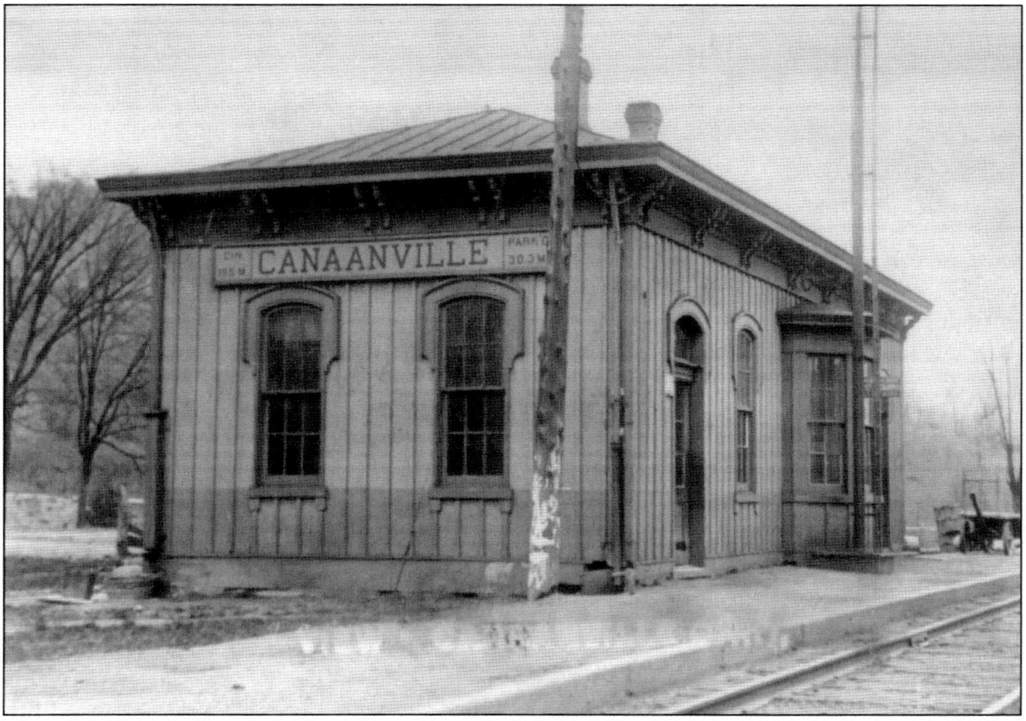

This depot was referred to in the *History of Hocking Valley, Ohio*, as the "Warren depot" and sat approximately midway in Canaan Township. Access to the depot gave farmers opportunities for shipping their goods, as none of them had to go much more than three miles to reach the building.

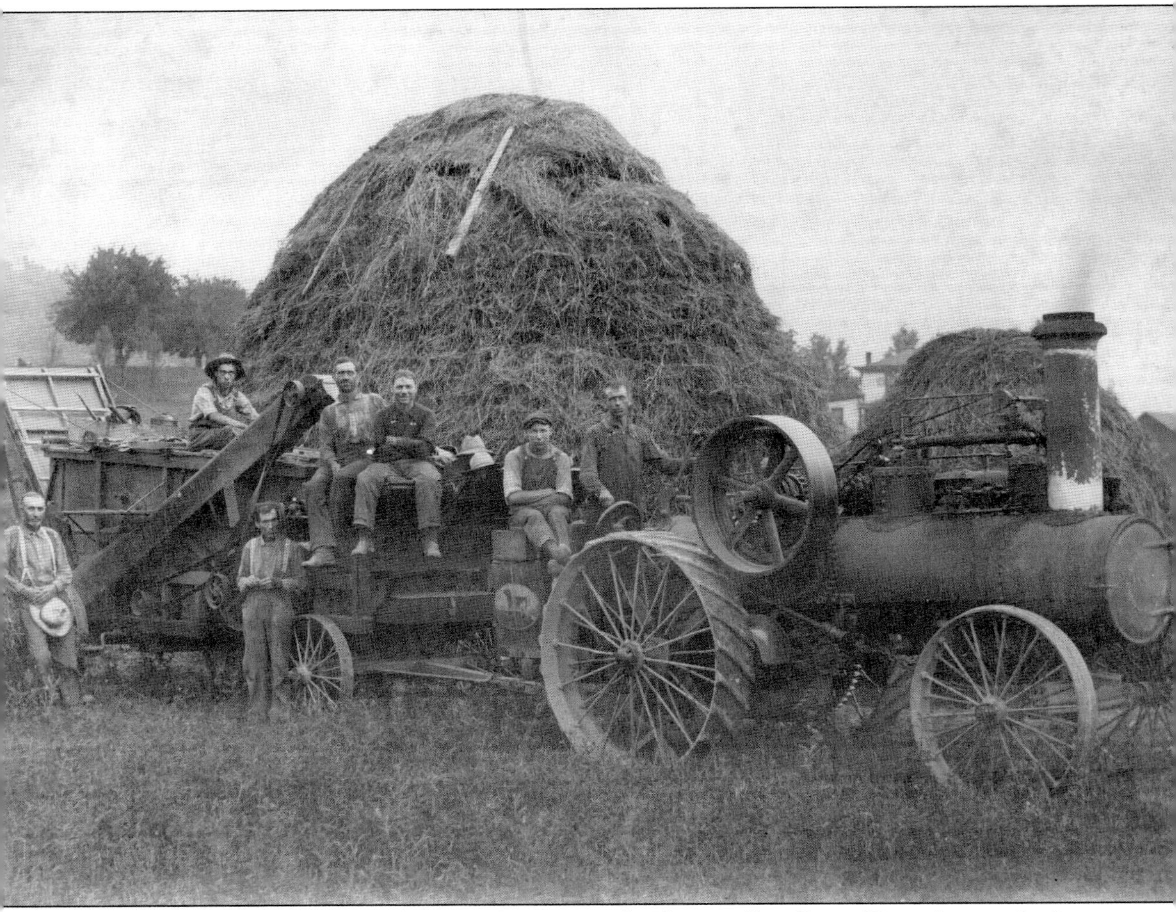

CHAUNCEY. The village of Chauncey (pronounced "Chan-see") in Dover Township was laid out in 1839. Prior to that date, it was largely the location of farmlands; however, the area was known as a potential salt producer. In 1831, farmer Resolved Fuller created a salt well on his property and set about the task of manufacturing salt for sale. Two years later, he sold his farm to Calvary Morris and Norman Root, who expanded the business. In 1838, they sold the land at a significant profit to a group of capitalists from Philadelphia, including Elihu Chauncey from whom the town takes its name. This group bought up a great deal of land and launched headlong into salt manufacturing on a larger scale than had previously been attempted. Thus, the community grew around the needs of the workers and the industry created there. Later, Chauncey became a part of the burgeoning coal-mining industry and gained national attention with the mine strikes of 1932. Pictured are workers on the Daniel T. Johnson farm across from the Athens County Home, which served the homeless, paupers, single women with children (destitute), and so on, near Chauncey.

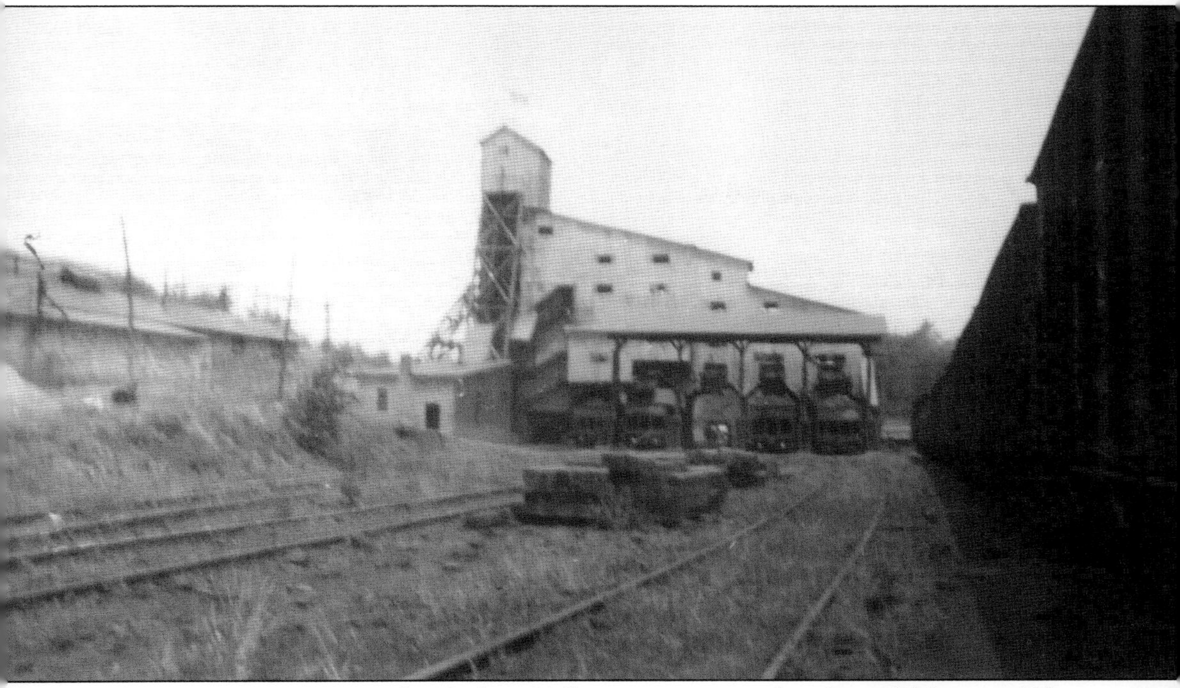

On February 1, 1932, miners in the Hocking Valley went out on strike when told they would be getting a 25-percent wage cut. As was typical of mine operators throughout the second half of the 19th century and well into the first half of the 20th century, the reasons the miners were expected to take losses included a belief on the part of the owners that workers should help them compete with other coal fields (that paid their miners less) and help keep the stockholders' profits up. Typical of miners, they felt oppressed and resented taking losses as rich people got richer; they turned to their unions for relief. Typical of mine owners and capitalists in general, the bosses refused to recognize the union as the voice of the workers. Typical of both mine workers and operators of the era, the situation led to open conflict that resorted to violence. This picture is of the Chauncey coal tipple. (Courtesy of the Anastas Collection.)

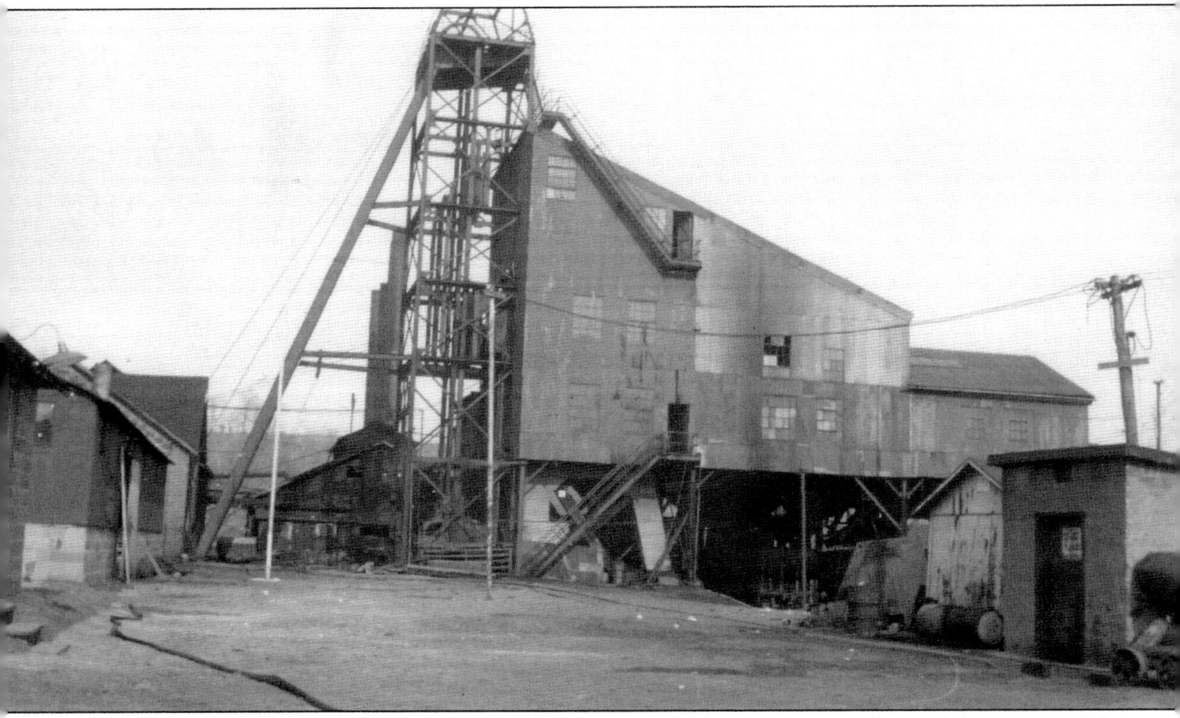

By March 1932, hundreds of Hocking Valley strikers took up arms to withstand the power of the mine owners and to counter the threat of state militia troops being sent in to calm the strikers' "lawlessness." Against advice of union leaders and union sympathizers, strikers stoned a vehicle containing National Guardsmen, Capt. Norman Whiting, and Capt. Harley Johnson. They were also accused of dynamiting a railroad trestle. The state began planning emergency responses of machine-gun squads and other military troops. Meanwhile, operators continued to bring in scabs (also known as "blacklegs") to do the work of the striking miners; owners and operators also threatened total shutdown of operations in the Hocking Valley if miners continued the strike. Threats and violence continued throughout the summer and into the fall of 1932. This picture is of the Chauncey coal shaft in 1941. (Courtesy of the Anastas Collection.)

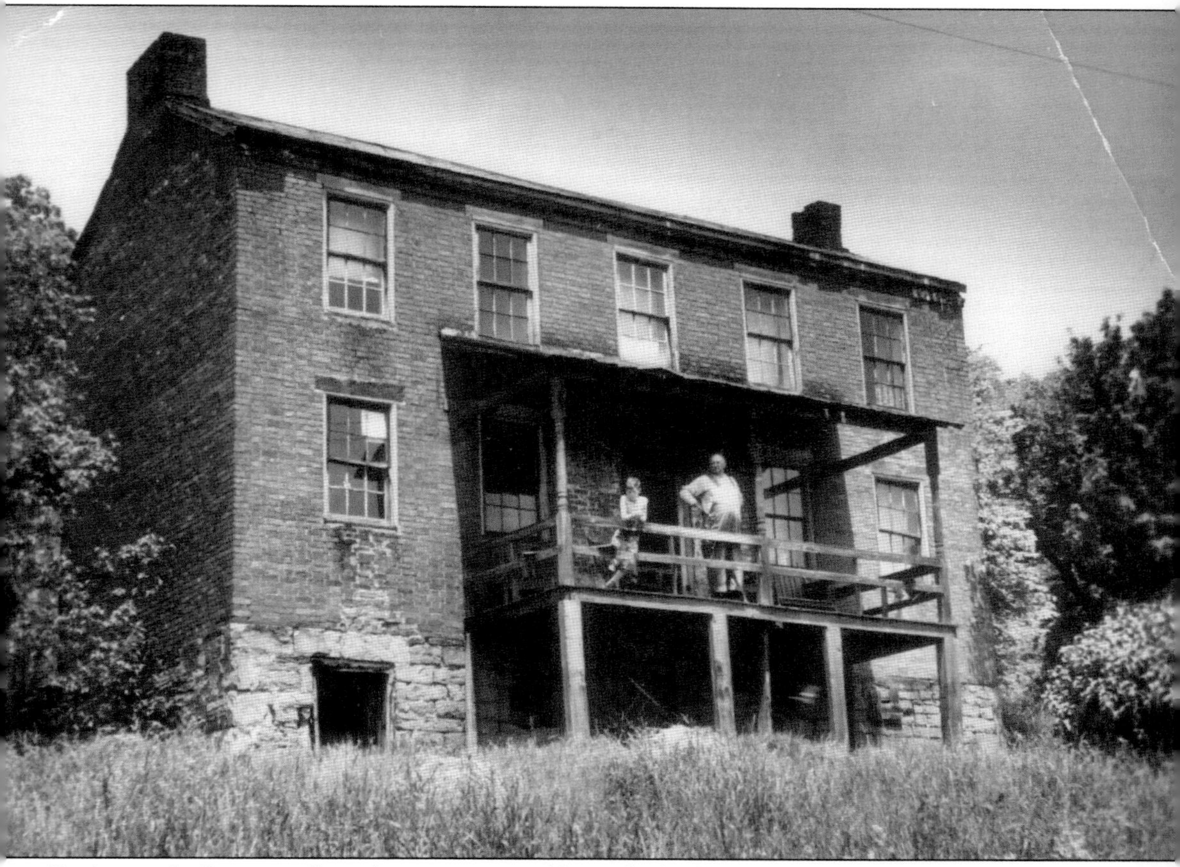

By August, bullets were flying between state soldiers who had been called in and striking miners and sympathizers. Buildings were destroyed by fire. Snipers hid out on hilltops and fired across and down through Chauncey as they and the military attempted to dominate one another. Machine guns fired into the hills to attempt to control snipers. A dynamite blast was set off in Nelsonville (fortunately, hurting no one). Miners demonstrating in the streets were tear-gassed. A secret "Hocking Valley Vigilance Committee" was rumored to be responsible for a fiery cross set up near Nelsonville. A Chauncey feed store owned by the father of a working miner (scab) was attacked and damaged. Shots were fired into homes, windows were broken, and threats made against people associated with operators. Mining superintendent John Schoonover's home was set afire. The tipple of the Essex Mine No. 2 was burned. Many people were wounded, and some were killed. This house was located near Mine No. 25.

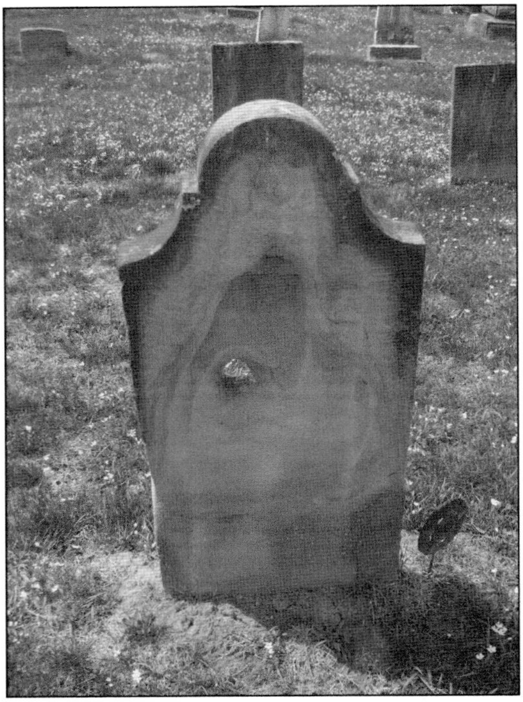

Among those killed was Ray Freeman, an 18-old-miner from Buchtel, who was found lying in the Nye Cemetery at the time of his death. This picture is of the gravestone—with a bullet hole—that young Freeman attempted to hide behind. (Author's collection.)

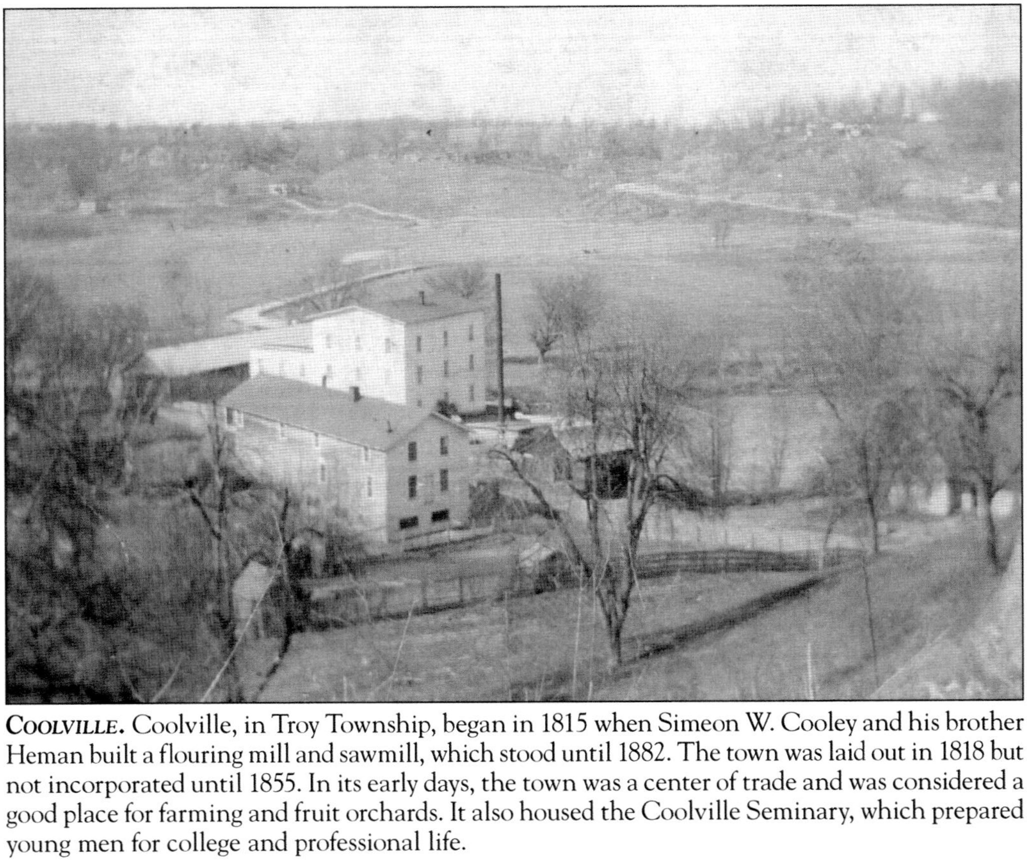

COOLVILLE. Coolville, in Troy Township, began in 1815 when Simeon W. Cooley and his brother Heman built a flouring mill and sawmill, which stood until 1882. The town was laid out in 1818 but not incorporated until 1855. In its early days, the town was a center of trade and was considered a good place for farming and fruit orchards. It also housed the Coolville Seminary, which prepared young men for college and professional life.

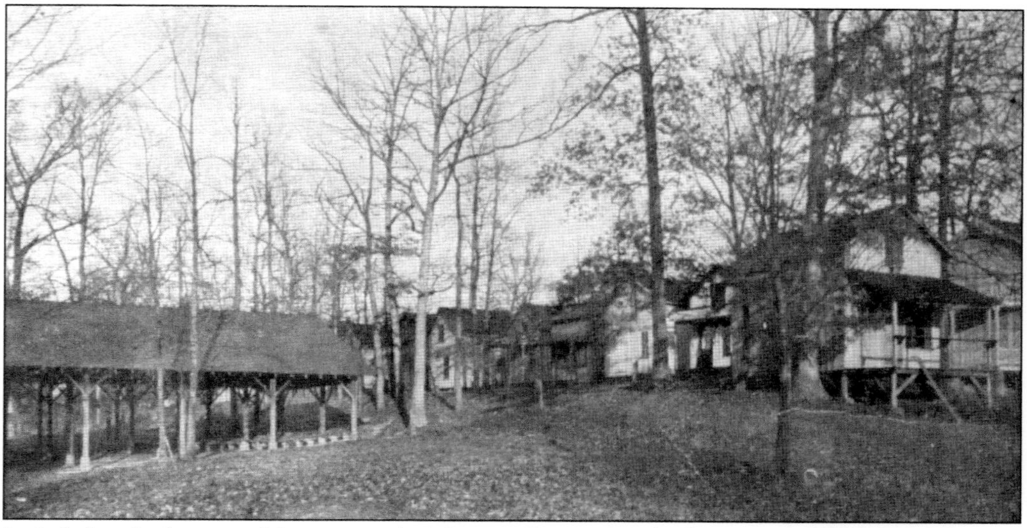

Included in the history of the town is the Marietta District Methodist Episcopal Church camp near Coolville (pictured). According to the *History of Hocking Valley, Ohio*, the camp contained at one time "an auditorium, boarding-house, preacher's tent, and a number of private cottages." The Camp-Meeting Association was organized in 1880 and chose Coolville for its "beauty and convenience of location, a good supply of pure water, and the favorable condition of surrounding society."

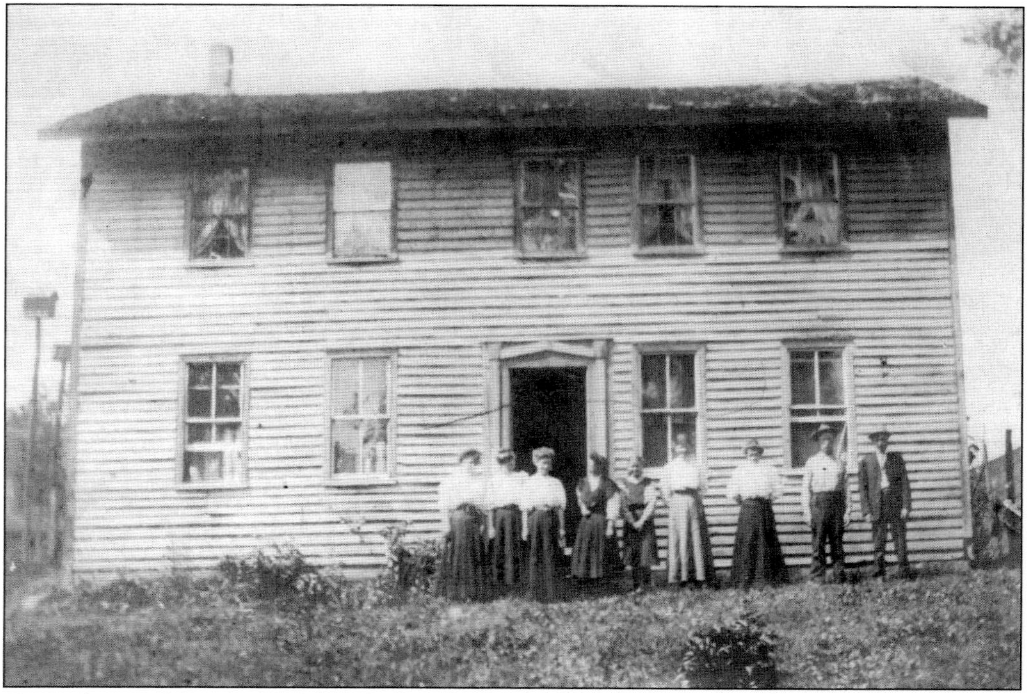

Shown here is the Ira Kincade residence in Coolville in May 1908. The plain style of the structure is typical of many turn-of-the-century homes in Athens County's more rural areas. The vast openness around the home suggests that this was probably in the farming area common not far from the town itself.

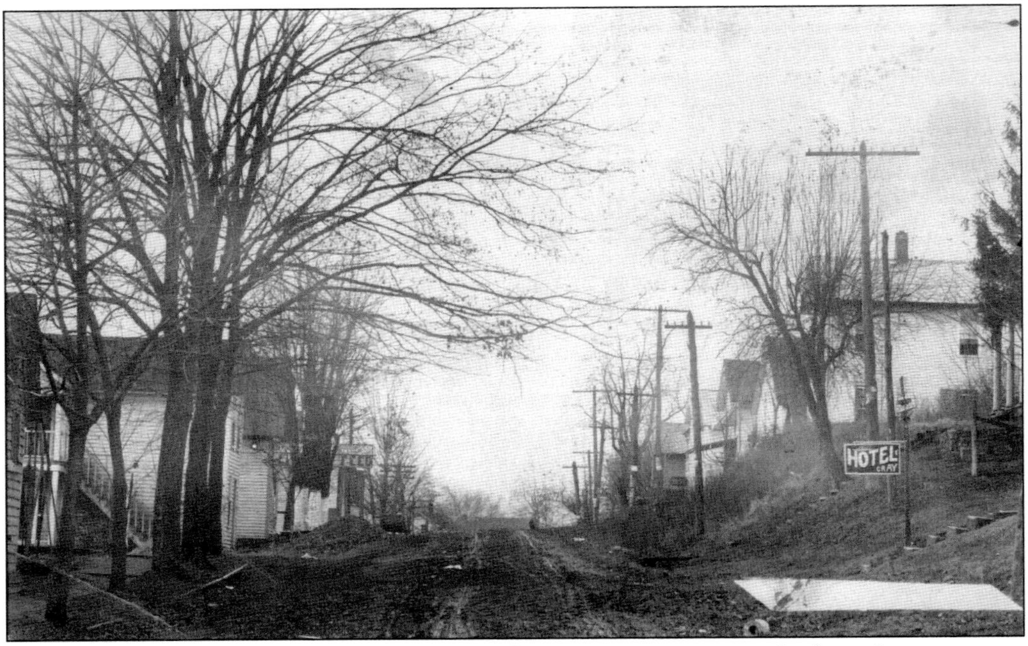

Pictured here is a Coolville Street scene around 1913. At one time, not far from this view, were several general stores, a furniture store, drugstores, grocery stores, millinery shops, shoe stores, a hotel, wagon shops, a tannery, and a saddler and harness shop. The post office had been in place as early as 1822.

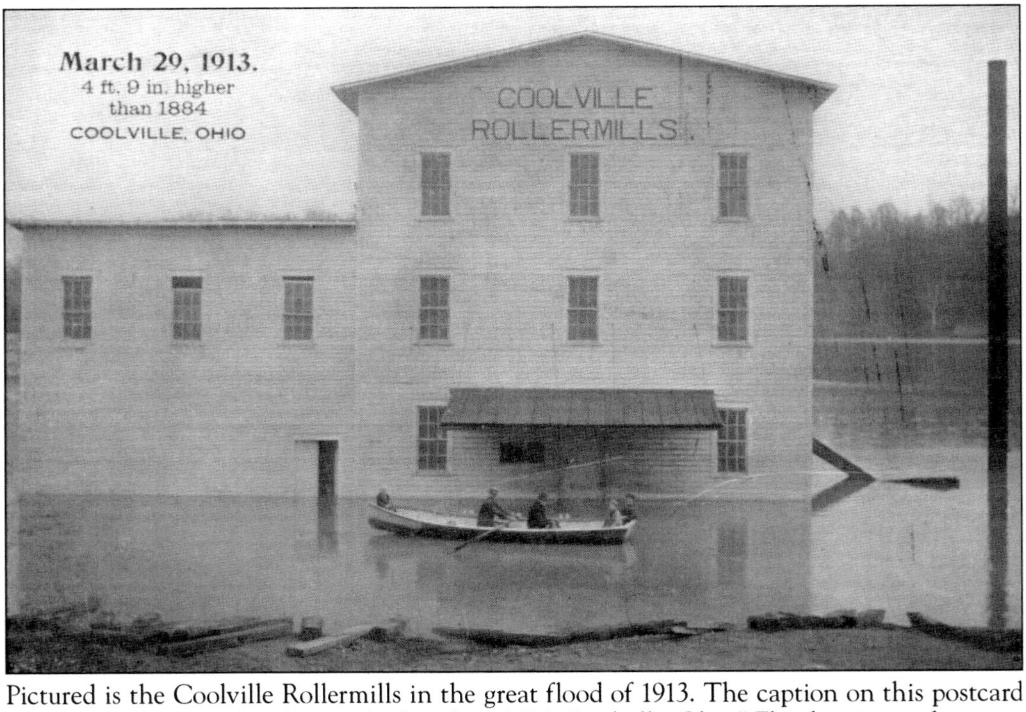

Pictured is the Coolville Rollermills in the great flood of 1913. The caption on this postcard reads, "March 29, 1913. 4 ft. 9 in. higher than 1884. Coolville, Ohio." Flooding in southeastern Ohio has long been a problem. Historians Beatty and Stone date the present mill to about 1927 and state that it was water powered until 1945.

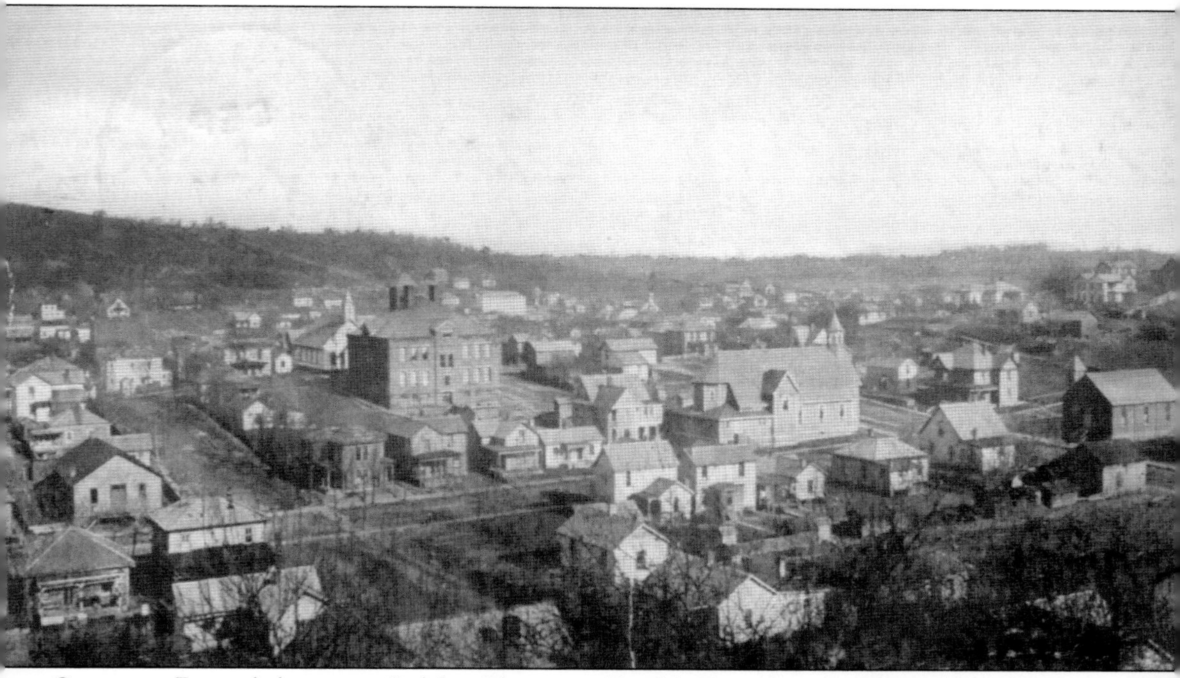

Glouster. Formerly known as Sedalia, Glouster in Trimble Township started out, like all early settlements in the county, with a handful of residents. The *History of Hocking Valley, Ohio*, states, "In 1822 a school was taught, near the forks of the creek . . . by Nancy Bagley, of Vermont." Early on, much of Trimble Township (including the area that would become Glouster) was dominated by farming. However, the town of Glouster only came into being and truly flourished during the great coal mining push of the late 19th and early 20th centuries. According to historians Beatty and Stone, the town was name Glouster by an Englishman from Gloucestershire who bought up much of the land for coal mining; it was incorporated in 1888. The Palmer Mine, in particular, once sat at the edges of the town itself, and its many catacombed, mined-out rooms still lie under the area where stores and homes sit today. Shown here is an early bird's-eye view of Glouster from Gobler's Knob.

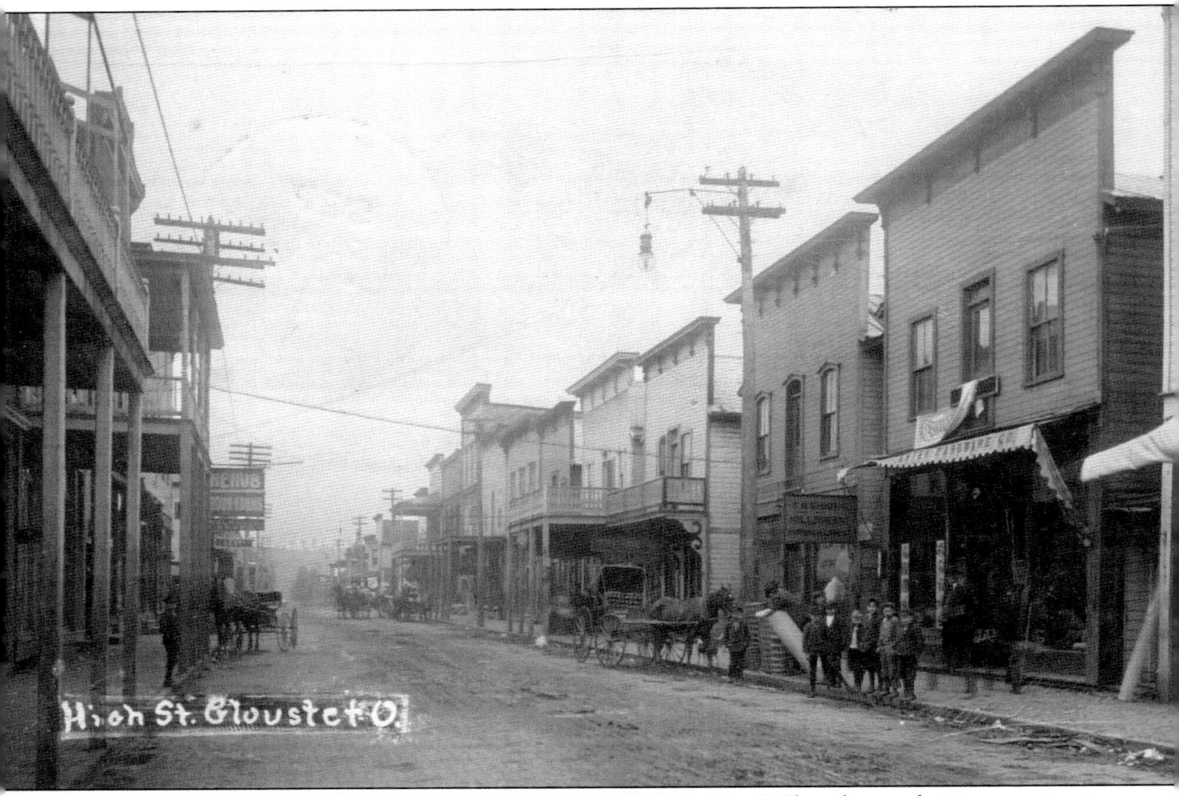

Glouster grew so fast that it was referred to as the "Magic City." Churches and civic organizations abounded. Schools were built, and local government made policies and sought to deal with the social issues that come with a town changing rapidly to accommodate an influx of people and new ideas. Because of the mining that took place in and around Glouster, many people of Italian, Polish, Hungarian, Slovak, and African American descent (and others) moved into the area, dramatically affecting the culture and making Glouster a diverse community. Its neighbors, though, such as Trimble, largely remained white, Anglo-Saxon, protestant, and agrarian in nature and were less affected by the issues inherent in mixing people of race, ethnicity, and culture. Because of its rich amalgamation of people, Glouster produced numerous interesting stories of life in a mining town. This is a pre-1909 picture of High Street in Glouster.

On September 27, 1894, the *Athens Messenger* published an article about Emancipation Day in Glouster, which stated that the town at the end of the 19th century was a progressive community built on the mining industry. Part of the article was focused on the joy of the people of color there on Emancipation Day; it states, "Glouster has many large stores, some fine business blocks, good churches and a beautiful school building, which is an ornament to the Magic City." These 2011 images of two banks in Athens show the commitment of some businesses in the community to maintain their historic appearances. Unfortunately, too many other buildings in the community have not been preserved as well as these. (Both, courtesy of Cyrus Moore.)

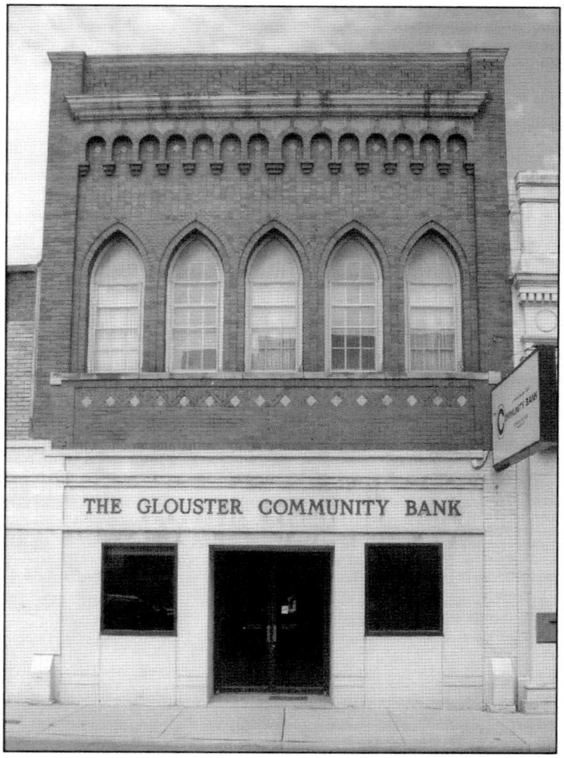

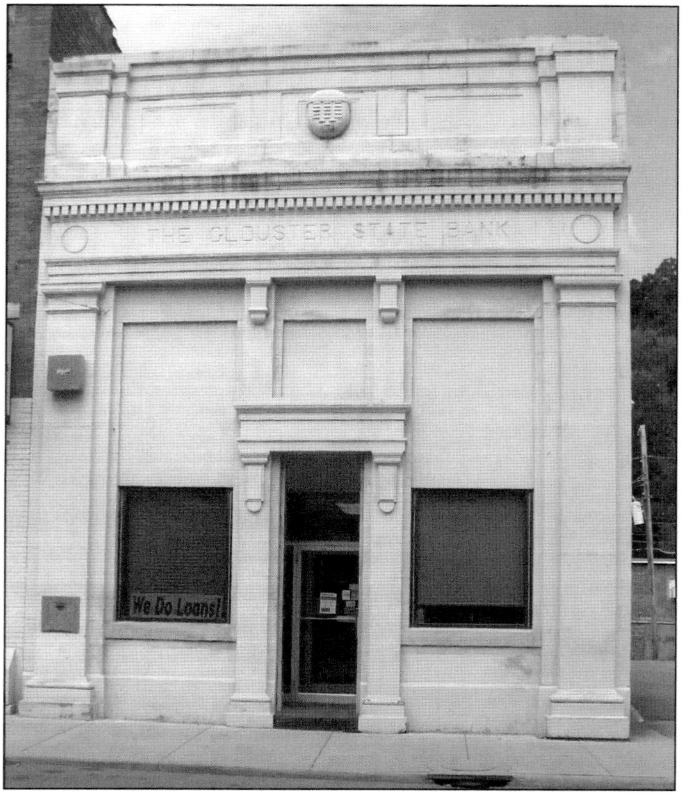

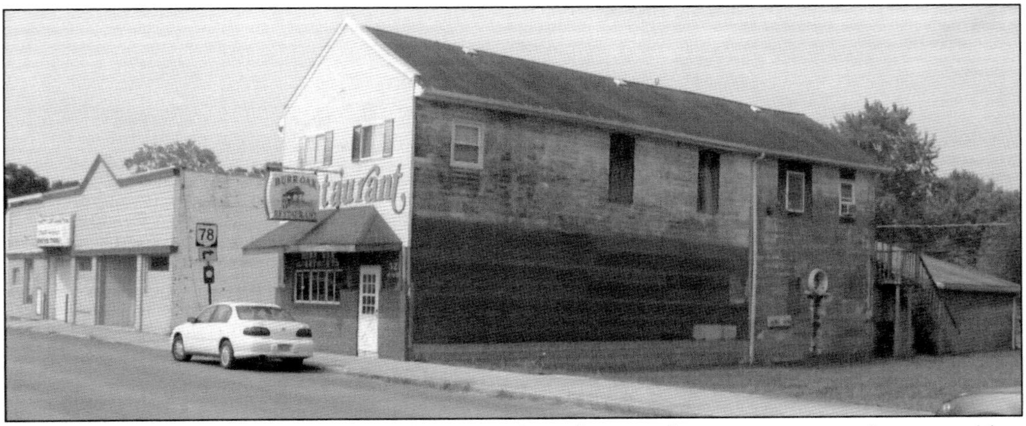

Glouster, home to numerous mine laborers and profligate saloons, was not without troubles. For example, a 1904 report on Fourth of July activities states that a man had his throat cut by a another man in a barroom fight; others were injured by carelessly fired explosives. (Courtesy of Cyrus Moore.)

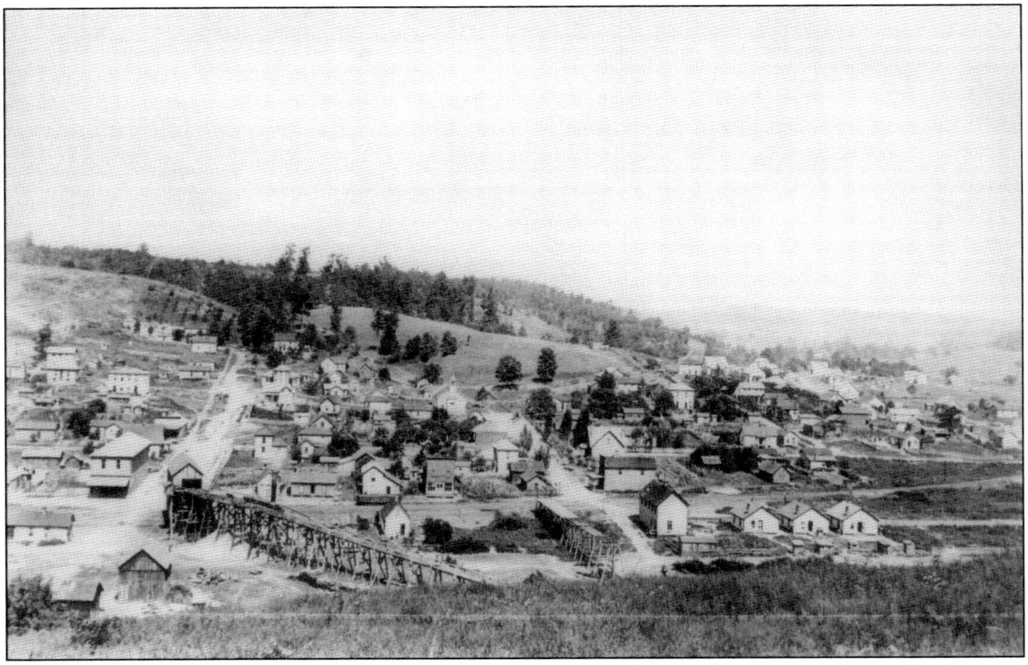

In August 1925, about 1,500 Glouster mine workers returned to work after a walkout. The United Mine Workers of America and local workers were resisting the efforts of mine owners refusing employment to workers at a Sugar Creek mine near Athens. Shown is the Palmer Mine in Glouster, where many men worked for many years.

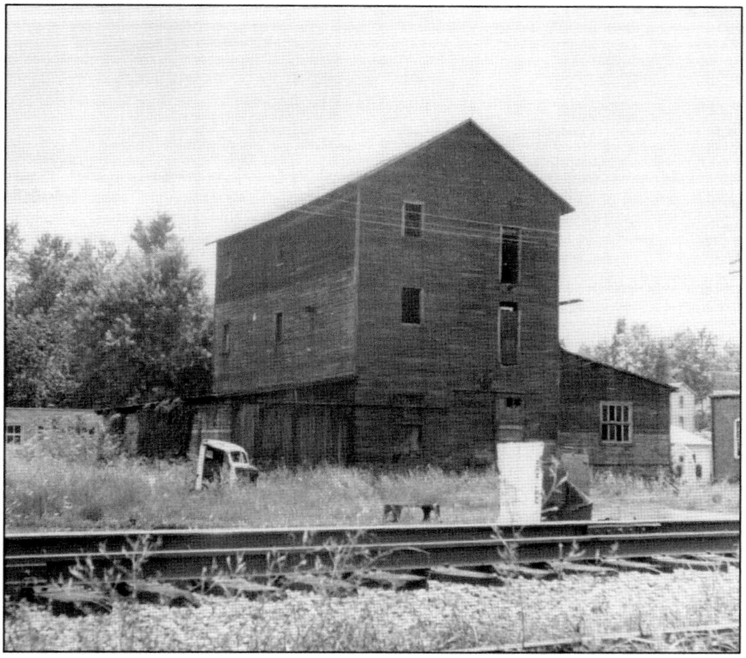

The former Glouster Mill is pictured here. This flour mill sat alongside the Palmer Mine. Directly behind it is Sunday Creek. On the left is the old school bus garage, and on the right is Campbell's car repair shop. Sometime in the late 1950s or early 1960s, Gilbert Bingman turned the building into a greenhouse and mushroom-growing operation. The building has since been razed. (Courtesy of the Anastas Collection.)

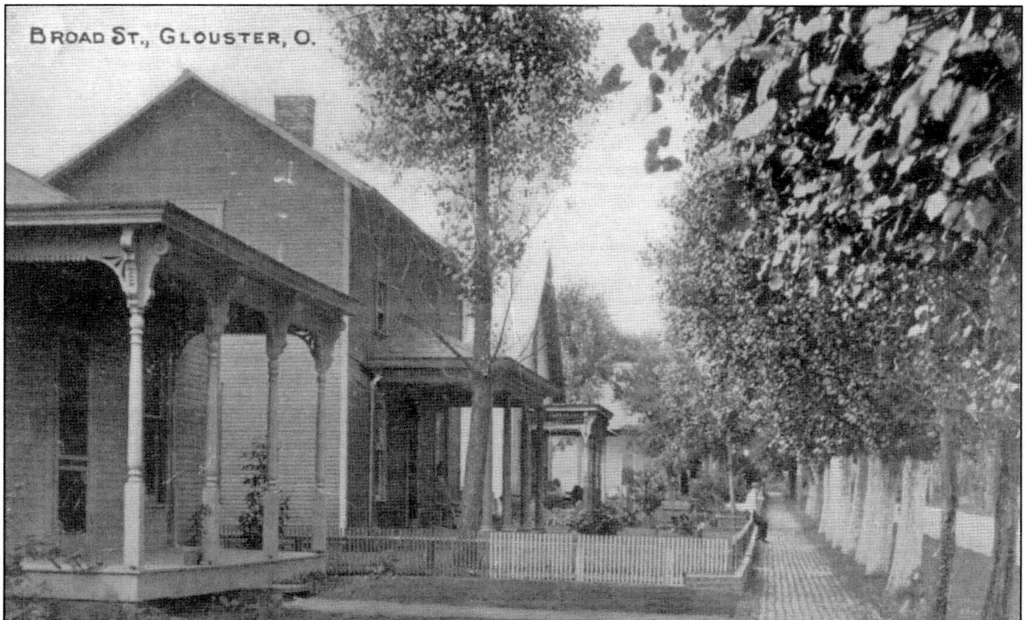

Glouster's streets were once lined with homes meticulously cared for, brick sidewalks, and stately trees. This picture is of Broad Street around 1910. People of Glouster from the beginnings of the town through the 1930s took great pride in the place, engaged in civic affairs, and promoted a vision of a town that would be the pride of Athens County.

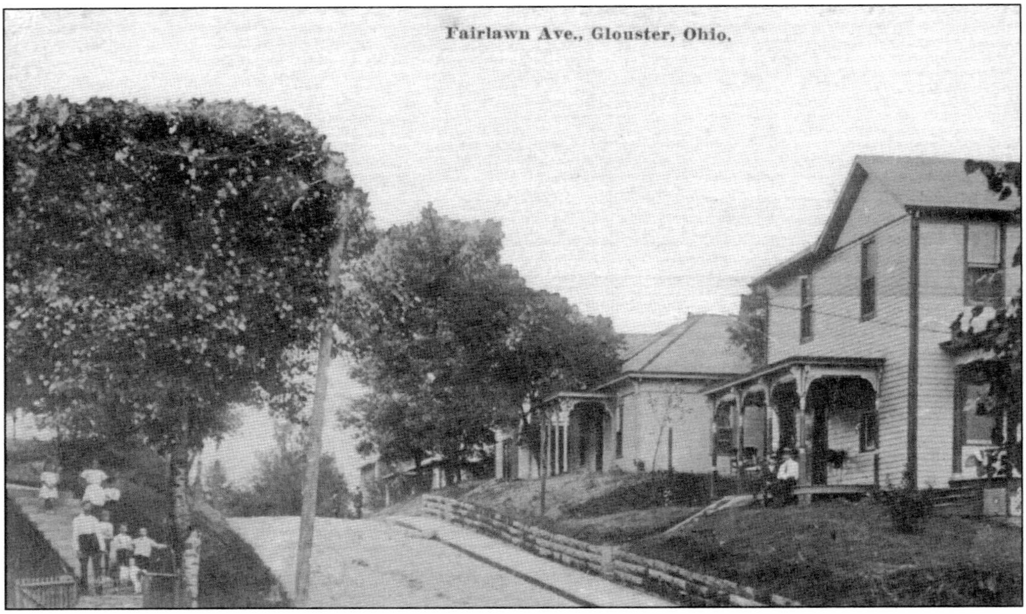

The image above is of Fairlawn Avenue, and the one below is of Republic Street. In Blower's history of Trimble Township, he presents an overview of the commitment early dwellers had for making Glouster a genteel place. In his discussion of Ella Crawford, he states, "She was a born leader in the social and civic affairs of Glouster her whole life through, an active member of the Rothwell Club and a real guide in its work in the civic affairs of the town. She was both gracious and lovely, this combined with her wonderful personality and friendship and her devotion to all things worth while [*sic*] in building a better community for all of us."

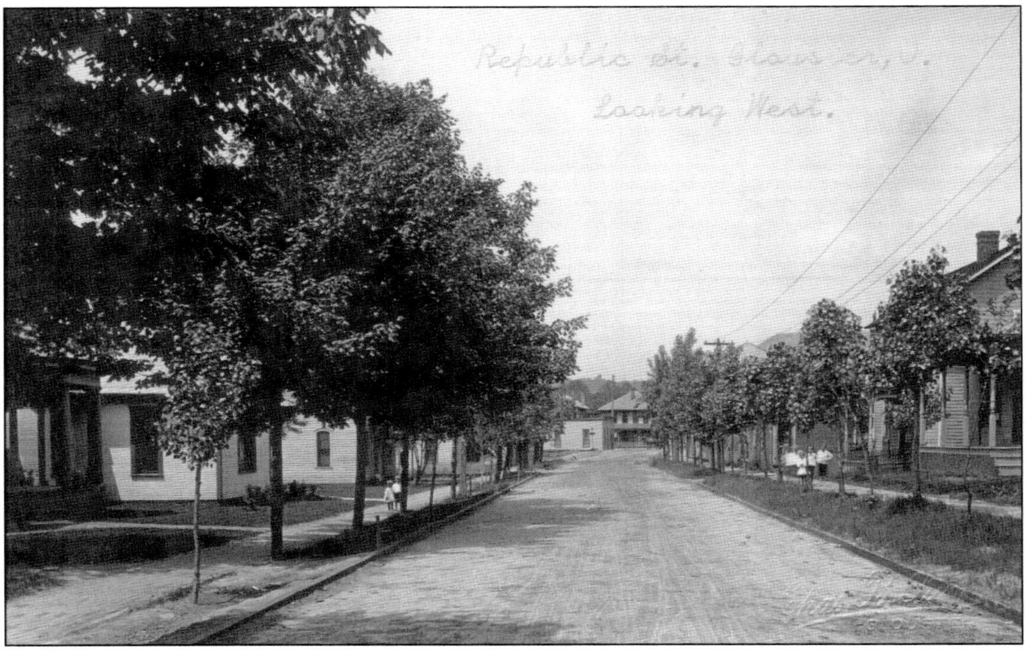

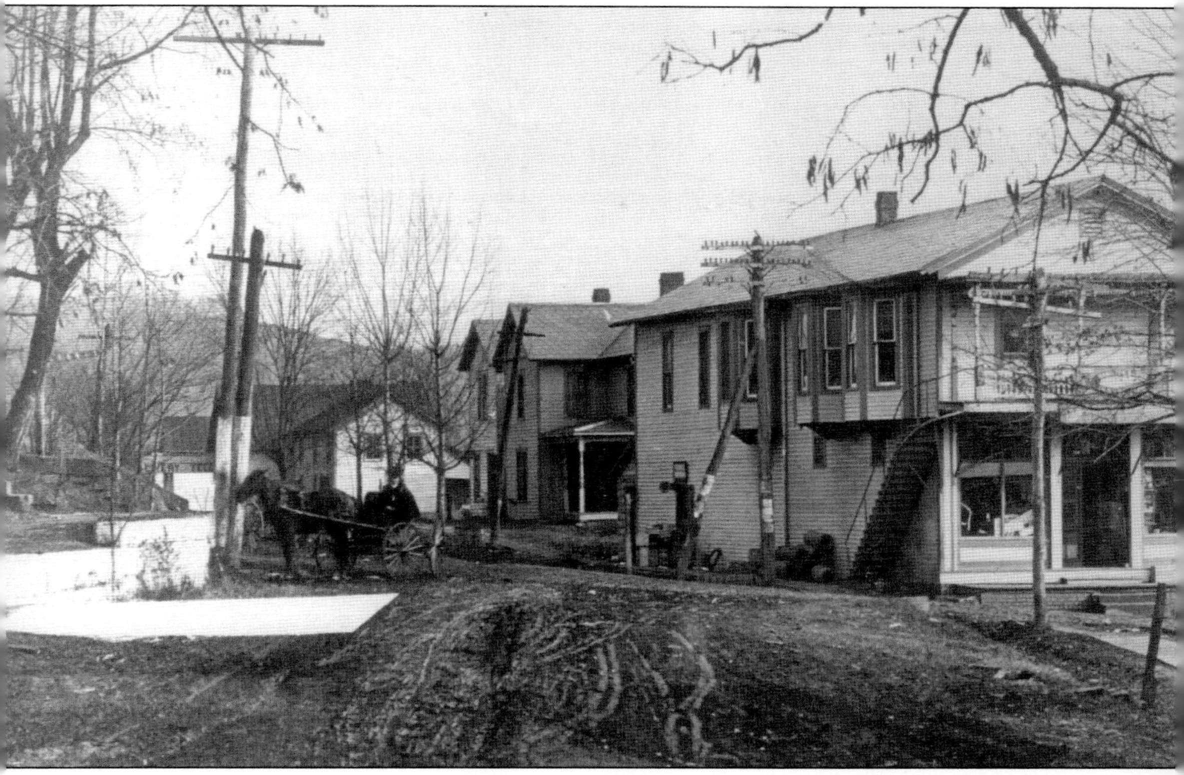

GUYSVILLE. Guysville is located in Rome Township, which was largely agrarian in nature early in its history. According to the *History of Hocking Valley, Ohio*, brothers Charles and Ezra Stewart built the Savannah Mill in what was called Savannah, which would eventually become Guysville. In 1834, Alexander Stewart and George Warren also built a mill nearby, but it was consumed by a fire. Daniel B. Stewart built a three-story grist and sawmill on the site and then added a woolen factory. The village was laid out in 1836 by Chauncey Carpenter. The name Guysville comes from Guy Barrows's efforts to establish a post office there. (Locals still referred to the town as Savannah for many years.) According to historian Nancy Aiken in an interview with Roy Cross for the *Athens Messenger* on September 17, 1997, the Guysville Post Office was established February 24, 1838, and could have had the name Savannah had the community demanded it. However, the name Savannah was appropriated a year later when the town of Clear Creek in Richland County chose, thus Guysville stuck as the official name for this Athens County town. This picture is of Guysville about 1900. (Courtesy of the Anastas Collection.)

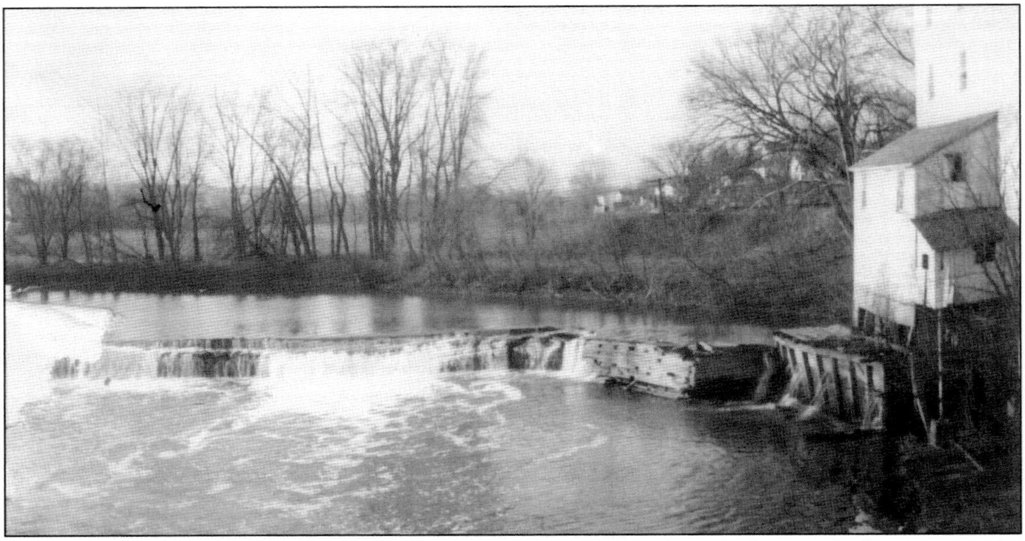

Briefly, Guysville and its bridge across the Hocking River made it the livestock-shipping site for the county. Shipping was further enhanced when the M&C Railroad built its short-line branch to Belpre, linking Guysville with the entire country. Over time, the town attracted professionals and built hotels, stores, and other businesses, most of which are now long gone. This picture is of the Guysville mill and dam in 1935. (Courtesy of the Anastas Collection.)

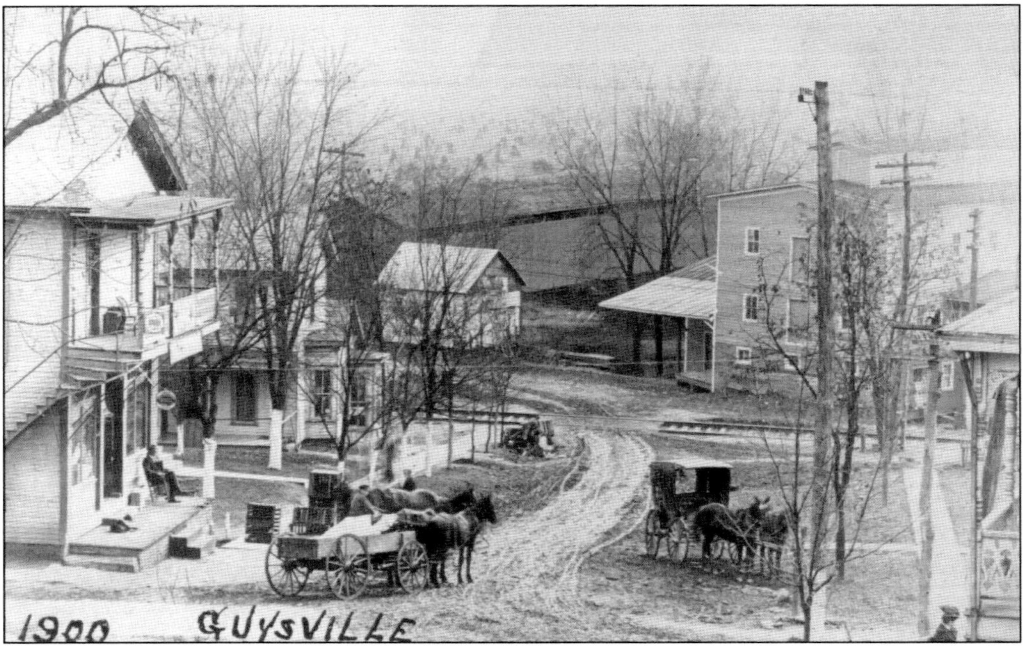

In the late 1920s and 1930s, Guysville's roads were still dirt. According to the December 4, 1995, *Athens News*, a Mrs. Montle told the story of the bridge washing out in a flood when she was a child. The bus driver, who lived on the same side of the river as she, rowed the children across each morning to the bus to get them to school. This picture is of Guysville in 1900. (Courtesy of the Anastas Collection.)

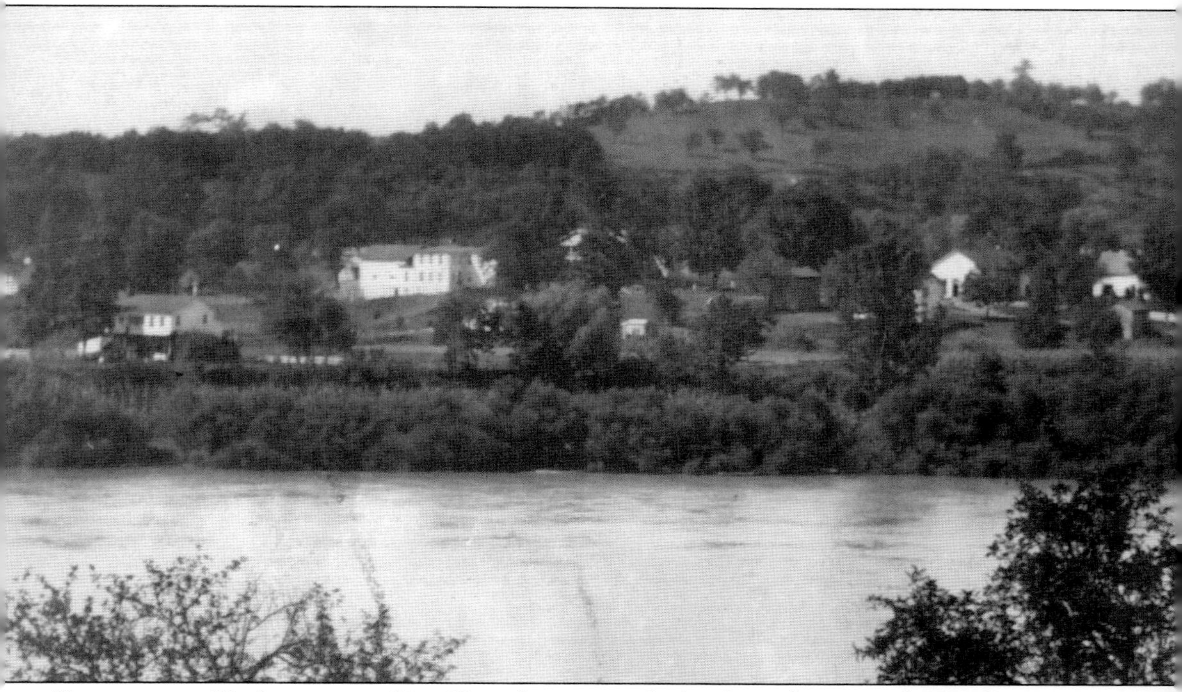

HOCKINGPORT. Hockingport, in Troy Township, sits on the border with present-day Washington County and is one of the oldest settlements in the county. Kingman Dutton and his family had settled at the mouth of the Hocking River as early as 1806. Dutton kept a number of canoes and developed a business of carrying people and goods up the Hocking to other parts of Athens County. The town, once known as Big Hocking (1836–1839), was officially established in 1839. Its service as a port community between the Hocking and Ohio Rivers provided significant promise for business as a shipping port; however, the arrival of railroads and easier and faster shipping neutralized the port's advantages. Among Hockingport's first settlers were Charles Devol, E.H. Williams, Samuel Dutton, Sylvester A. Gibbs, Benjamin Huntington, Benjamin Brookhart, David Davis, George Williams, and Alonzo Williams. In line with what has been seen in other communities in Athens County, education was an important factor. The Southern Ohio Normal School, formerly known as the Hockingport Seminary, existed here. Its purpose was to prepare students for college studies and also provide instrumental and vocal instruction. Shown here is a bird's-eye view of Hockingport in 1907.

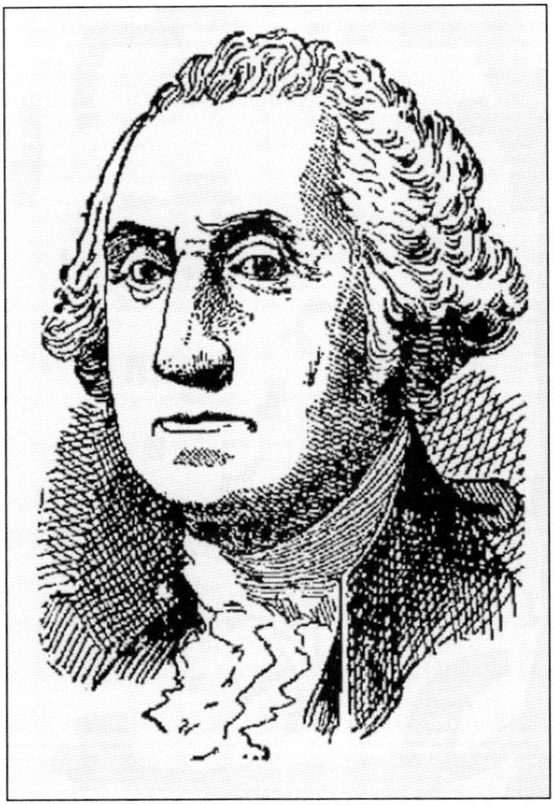

In 1770, George Washington and his party camped at the mouth of the Great Hockhocking River. He had been inspecting "land he owned on the Great Kanawha, near Point Pleasant" on what is now the West Virginia side of the Ohio River, according to Peters's *Athens County, Ohio.* In 1774, Lord Dunmore and troops came to the territory to fight Native Americans. Shortly after arrival, Dunmore signed a treaty and ended hostilities. While at Fort Gower near Hockingport, officers received notice that the First Continental Congress had declared rights for all colonists. The officers declared they would stand with the colonies if the colonies went to war with England. Their resolution was, according to Beatty and Stone, "the first declaration of independence from the Crown in deference to American rights." In 1923, the DAR set a marker, shown below, to commemorate the historic location. The picture of Washington is from an 1800s newspaper.

The resolution at Fort Gower from November 5, 1774, states, in part: "That we will bear the most faithful allegiance to His Majesty, King George the Third, whilst His Majesty delights to reign over a brave and free people; that we will, at the expense of life and everything dear and valuable, exert ourselves in support of his crown, and the dignity of the British Empire. But as lovers of liberty, an attachment to the real interests and just rights of America outweigh every other consideration, we resolve that we will exert every power within us for the defense of American liberty, and for the support of her just rights and privileges; not in any precipitate, riotous or tumultuous manner, but when regularly called forth by the unanimous voice of our countrymen."

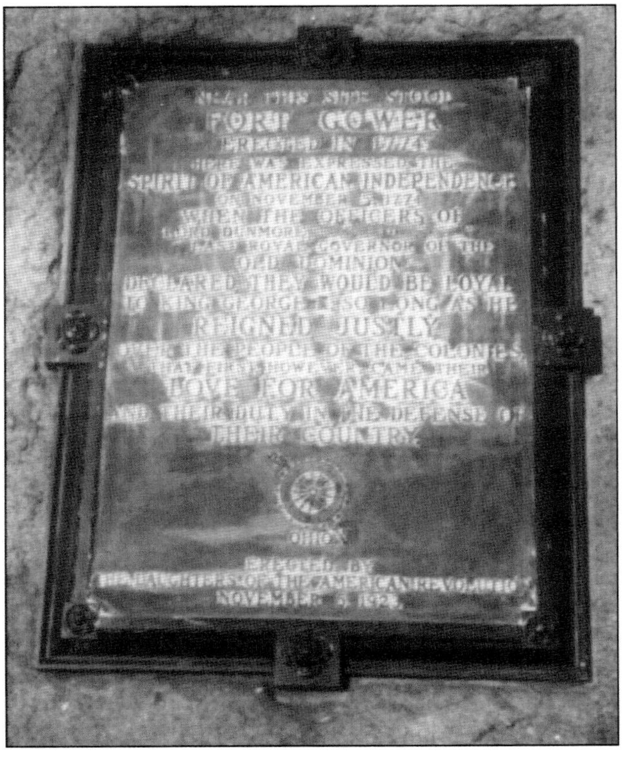

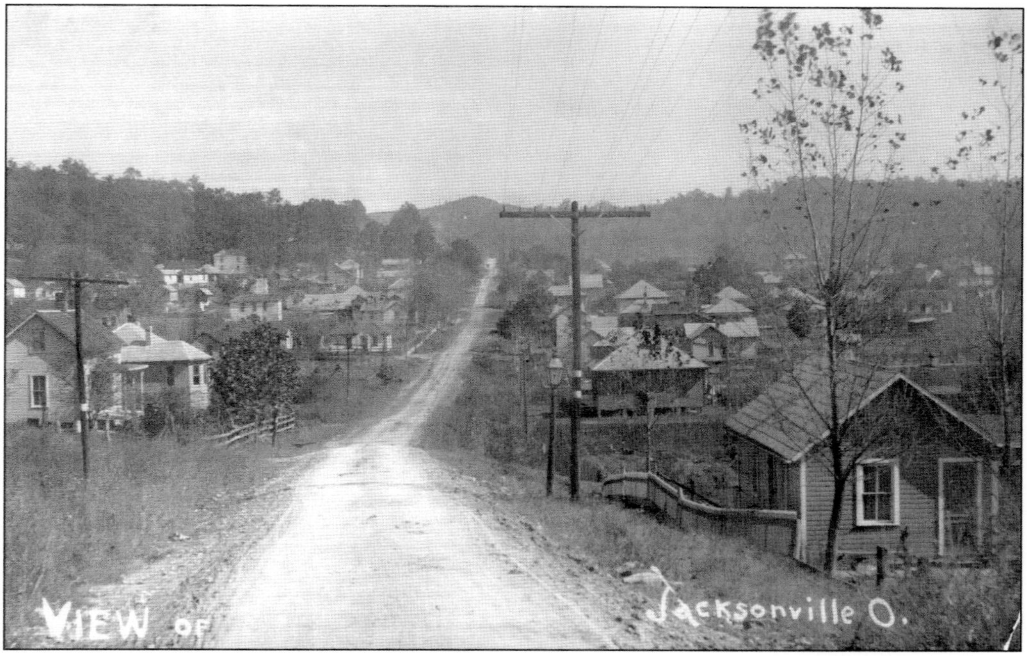

JACKSONVILLE. Jacksonville, in Trimble Township, was named for mine owner Oliver D. Jackson, who bought and leased thousands of acres of land in 1879–1880 for mining. The railroad came through in 1881, thus creating a means for hauling coal out of the region. This picture of Jacksonville was taken sometime prior to 1910.

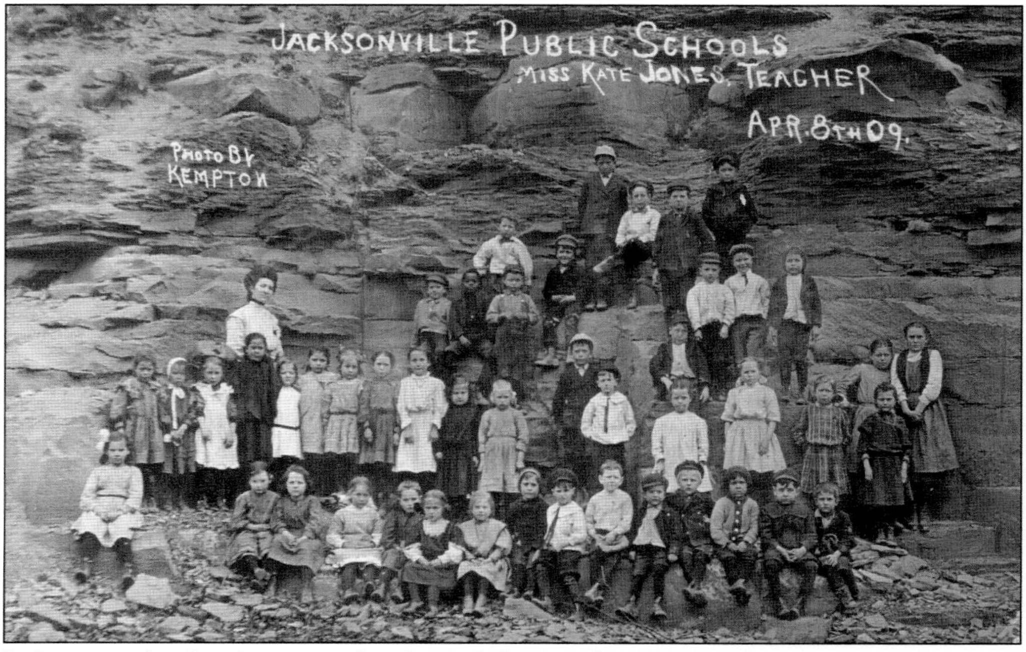

Jackson struck a five-foot vein of coal, which he leased to W.P. Rend, and many workers were needed. As a result, the town grew rapidly and had confectioneries, a theater, grocery, a school, and so on at one time. This picture is of schoolchildren in Jacksonville on April 8, 1909.

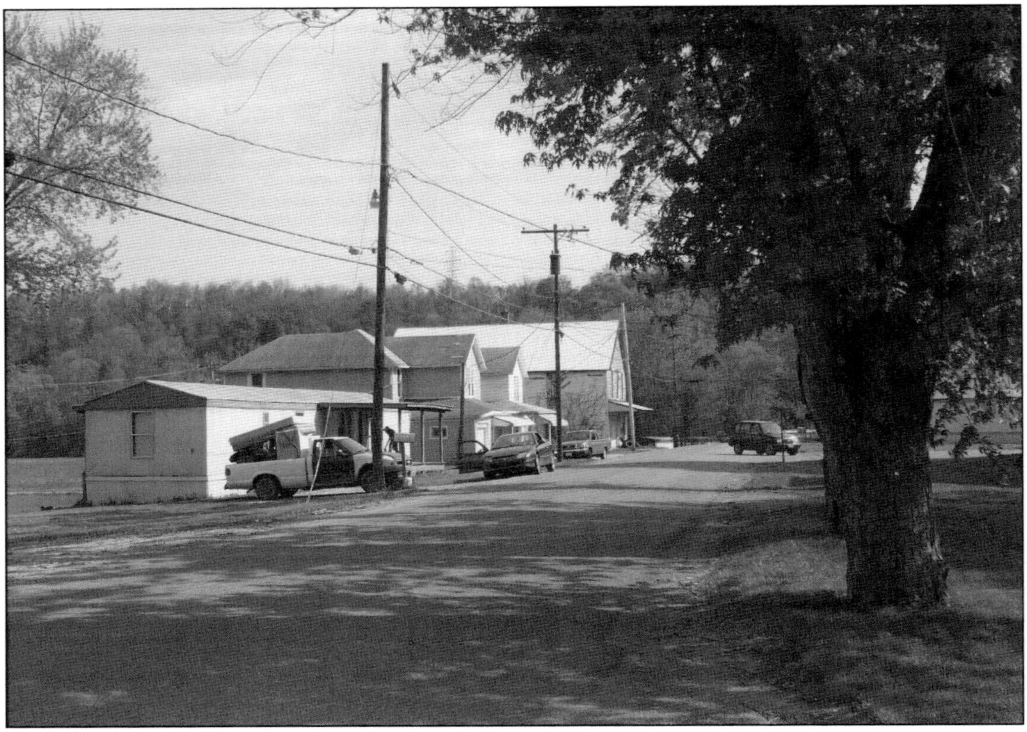

MILLFIELD. W.E. Peters states that Millfield was laid out by John Pugsley in 1826 and was named "for a mill that had been built there in 1802 by John Sweat." The town was formally established in 1834. Sometime prior to 1883, the Ohio Central Railroad had a station in Millfield, but it would not be until the arrival of the coal operators that Millfield would begin to thrive. By 1930, the Sunday Creek Coal Company had bought the mine that would place Millfield on the map of human disasters. (Author's collection.)

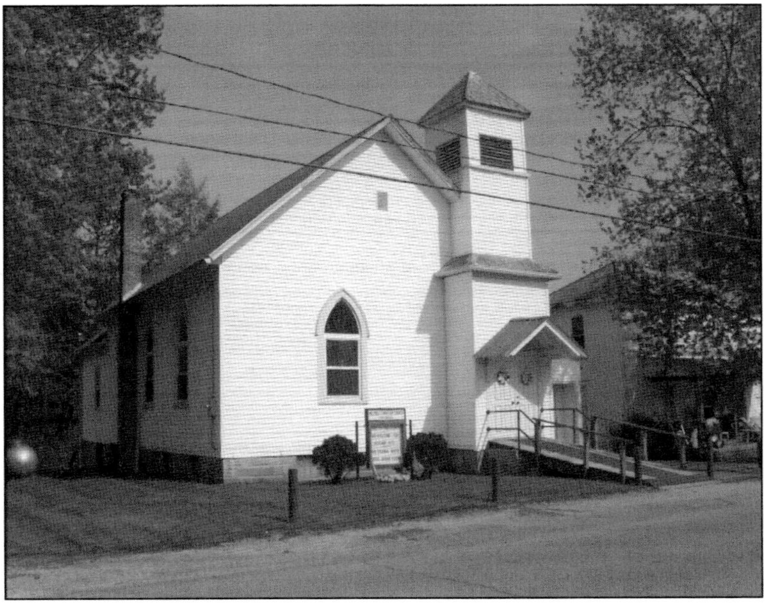

Shown here is the Millfield Christian Church just down the street from the company store. Across the street are the ruins of the old motion picture theater and some small stores. (Author's collection.)

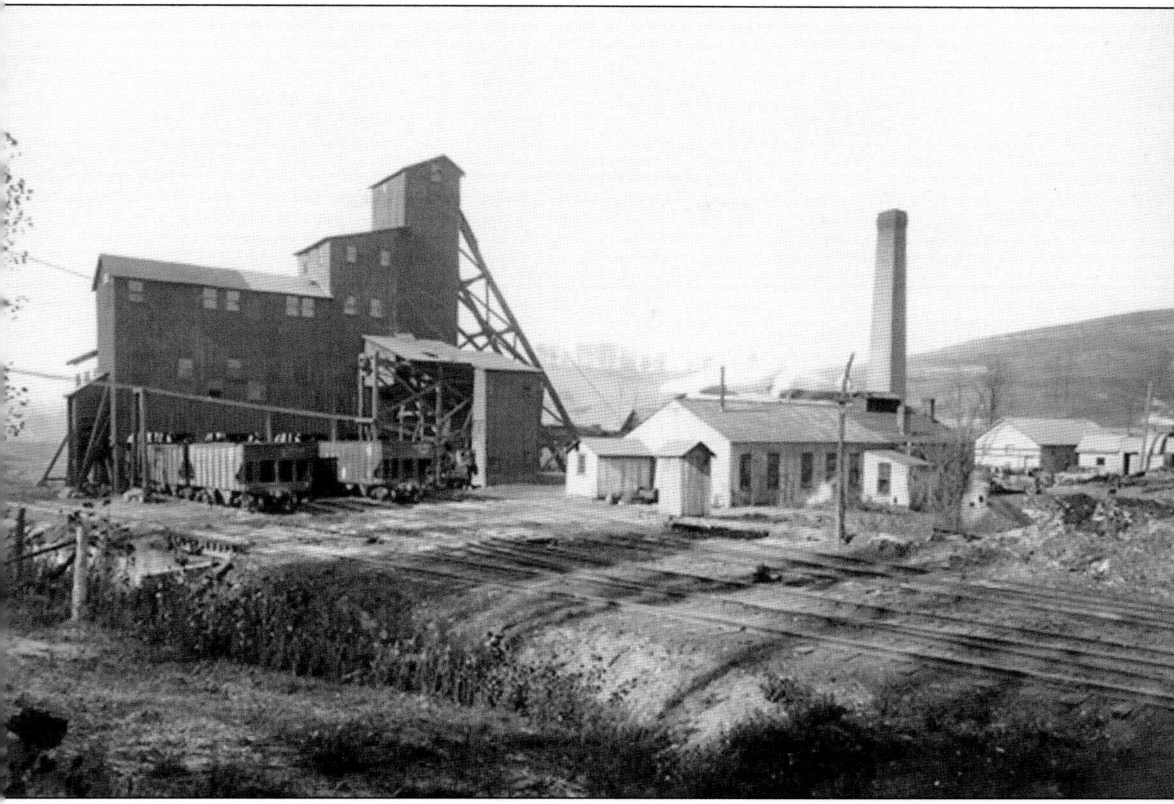

On the morning of November 5, 1930, William E. Tytus, the president of the Sunday Creek Coal Company, and a number of guests—including company officials and business associates—arrived at Mine No. 6 east of Millfield to inspect a new air shaft that had been installed. As workers went about their tasks of mining, the guests made their way deep underground to the air shaft. At approximately 11:45 a.m., an explosion occurred, and a fire engulfed the human beings in the mine. Many miners some distance from the explosion site made their escapes, with some being saved only in their last moments of hope as "bad air" filled every part of the mine. Nineteen men were later found barely alive behind a barricade they had built to protect themselves from the poisonous gases that had killed many of their friends, family members, and coworkers. A total of 82 men lost their lives that day—including Tytus and his entourage. Most died from the lack of oxygen occurring after the explosion and the infiltration of poisonous gases or "afterdamp."

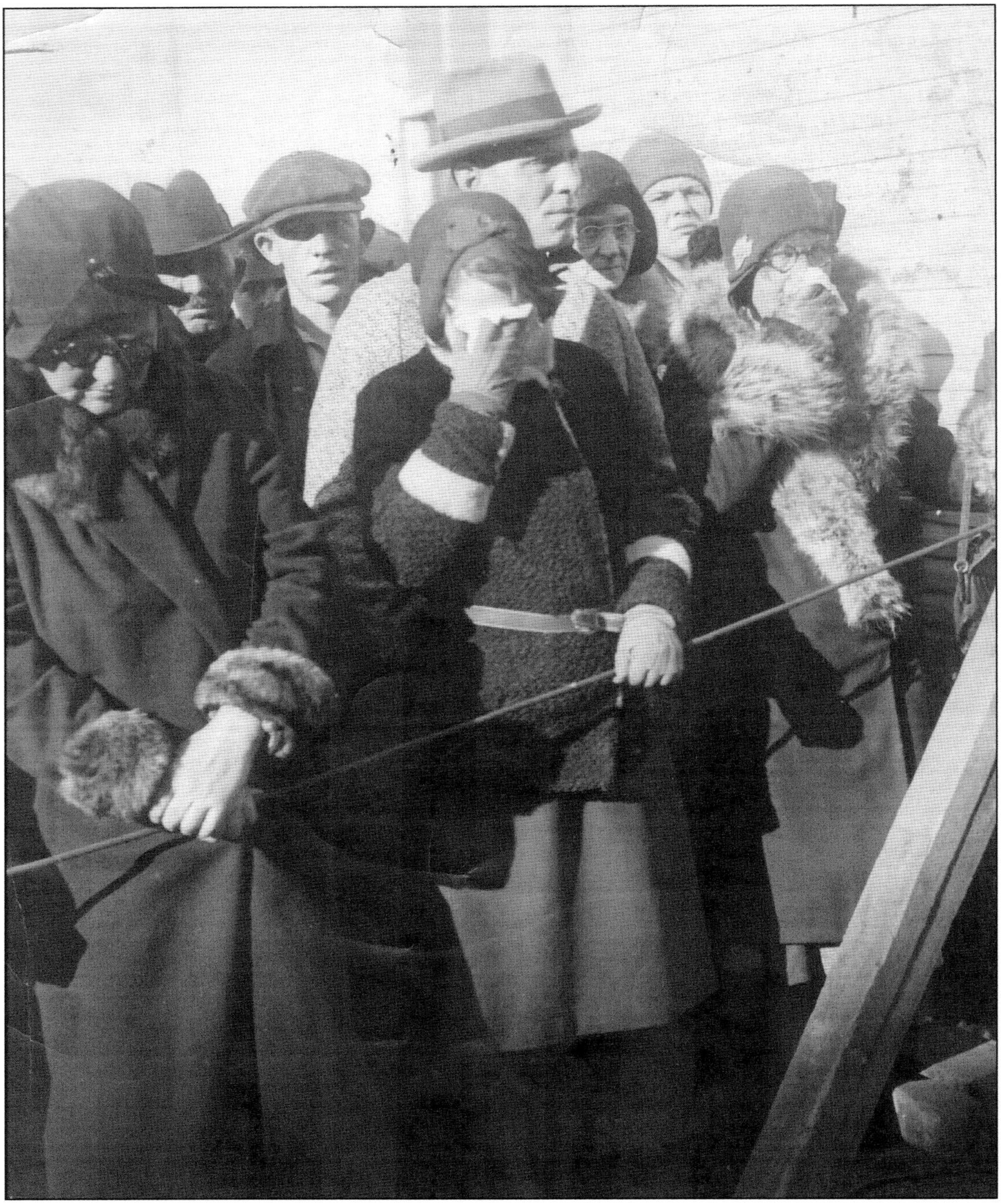

Immediately after the explosion, people from miles around who heard it rushed to find out what happened and learn the fate of their loved ones. When the news of the catastrophe spread, ambulances and emergency equipment had difficulty getting to the site because of the numerous cars blocking the road. Unfortunately, many of those hindering rescue efforts were merely sightseers or "gawkers" drawn by the desire to witness devastation; others were people who wanted to help. The National Guard had to be called in to handle the crowds and to make way for the rescuers to do their jobs. Most people who got to the grounds did what good people do in times of crisis: they offered support and provided meals for the rescuers and the waiting families of miners not yet found, while some prayed or just stood around dazed by the horror. Many of the miners who survived the blast and fire, or who had not been working on the shift when the mine exploded, came to the mine in hopes of going in after their coworkers.

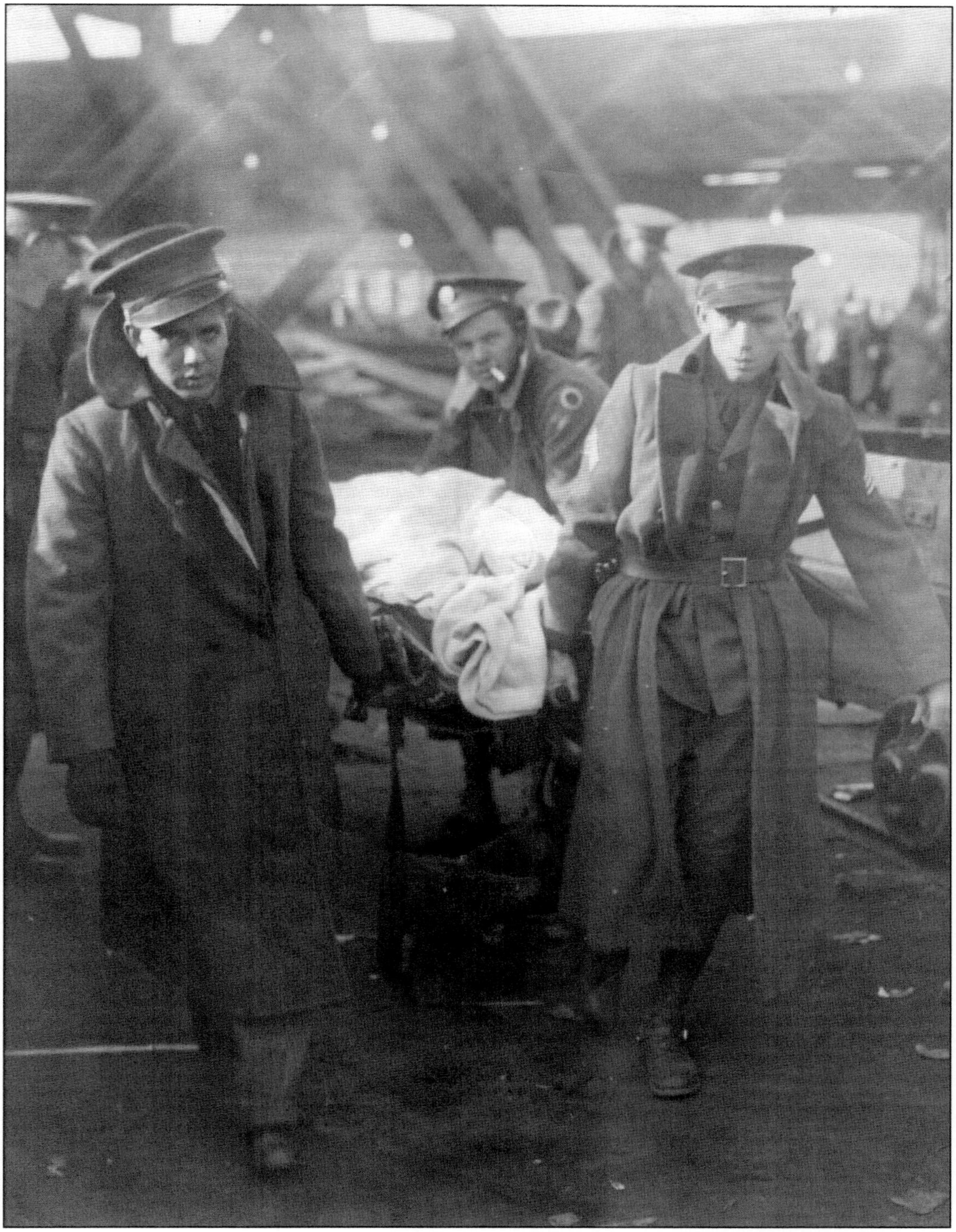

Unfortunately, until the poisonous gases could be cleared from the mine shafts and tunnels and more gas masks could be shipped in from Columbus and elsewhere, it was almost impossible for more than a handful of people to go in quickly. It took almost 10 hours to get to the 19 survivors who were hidden behind a makeshift barricade referred to as a brattice. When they were found, most were within minutes of dying from the gases that had seeped through and the lack of breathable air. It would be another full day before most of the bodies were found. This picture is of stretcher-bearers at the disaster site in November 1930. (Courtesy of Melody Bragg of Technical Information Center & Library, National Mine Health and Safety Academy.)

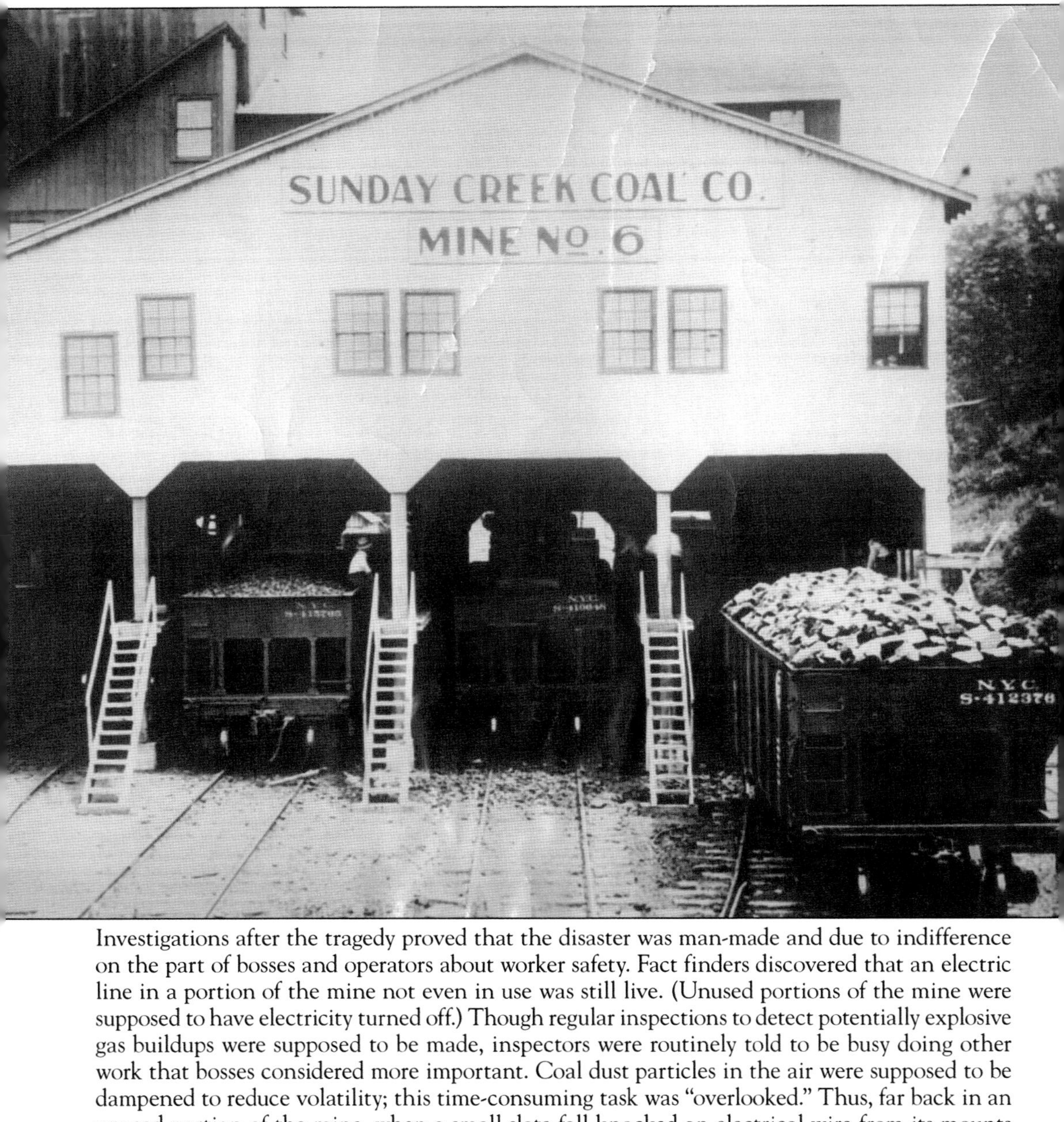

Investigations after the tragedy proved that the disaster was man-made and due to indifference on the part of bosses and operators about worker safety. Fact finders discovered that an electric line in a portion of the mine not even in use was still live. (Unused portions of the mine were supposed to have electricity turned off.) Though regular inspections to detect potentially explosive gas buildups were supposed to be made, inspectors were routinely told to be busy doing other work that bosses considered more important. Coal dust particles in the air were supposed to be dampened to reduce volatility; this time-consuming task was "overlooked." Thus, far back in an unused portion of the mine, when a small slate-fall knocked an electrical wire from its mounts on the ceiling, the live wire fell across a steel rail. The arc caused by the touching of the wires to the rail ignited the gas and coal dust and set off the worst mine explosion in Ohio's history. No one was formally held accountable, fined, or jailed. Early on, only a secret report meant for the owners acknowledged the owners' fault for the tragedy that occurred and the lives lost.

Shown here is the Millfield Mine Company Store. During the chaos of the explosion and extrication of the dead miners, this building was used as one of several temporary morgues. Undertakers from throughout the southeastern Ohio area were called to deal with the unprecedented number of bodies, all needing care at the same time. (Author's collection.)

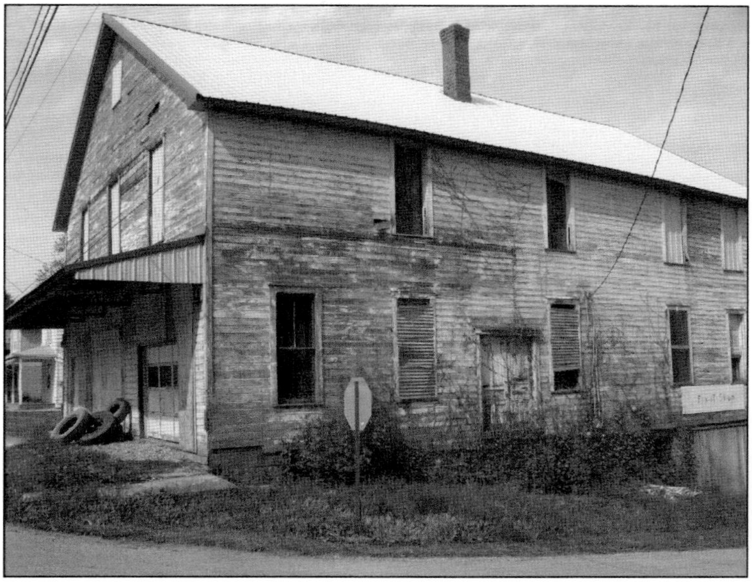

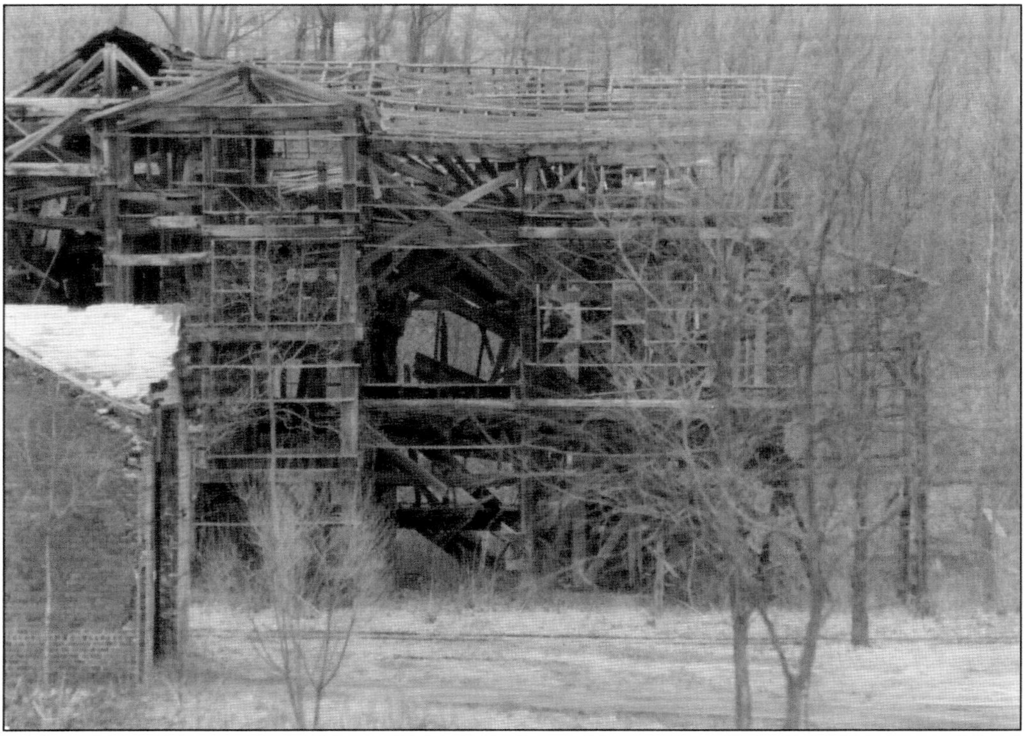

Standing like a ghost in this picture are the remains of the Millfield Sunday Creek Mine No. 6 in 1984. The structure was finally razed shortly thereafter. All that remains of the disaster site now are a single crumbling tower and small portions of some buildings. In the town of Millfield is a stone monument to those who died needlessly so long ago.

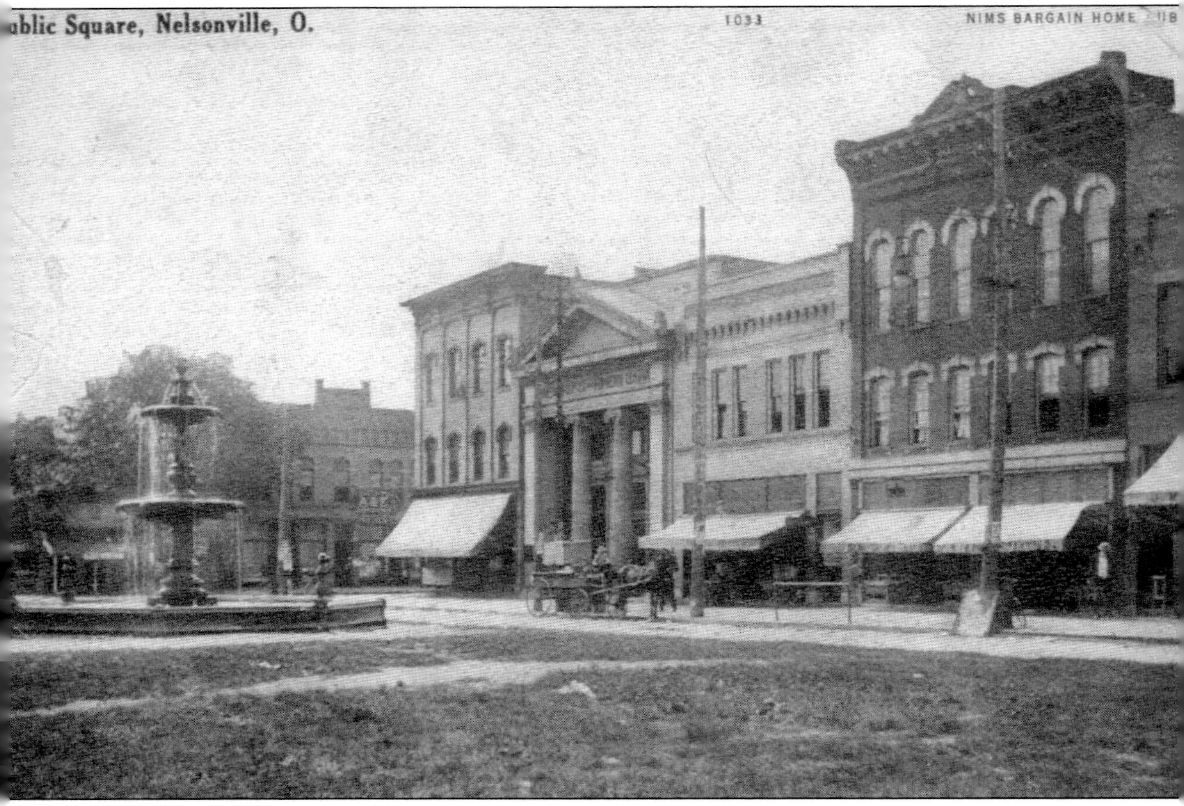

NELSONVILLE. Nelsonville was laid out in June 1818 by Daniel Nelson of Shrewsbury, Massachusetts, and incorporated in 1838. Nelson (for whom the town was named) had purchased the land that became Nelsonville directly from the Ohio Company in 1814. Prior to Nelson's arrival, two families had settled near what would become the town. According to the *History of Hocking Valley, Ohio,* they were the Johnsons and Hurlberts, and they were all that stood for civilization between Athens and a budding community at what is now Logan in Hocking County. Nelson's original plat for the town comprised 57 lots. In 1823, Nelson gave the community lot No. 48 for a school and a place of worship. Simultaneously, he donated the land known as "the public square" to the community and stated in the deed that it is "to be forever kept open to the use of the said town of Nelsonville." This picture is of Nelsonville's Public Square in 1908.

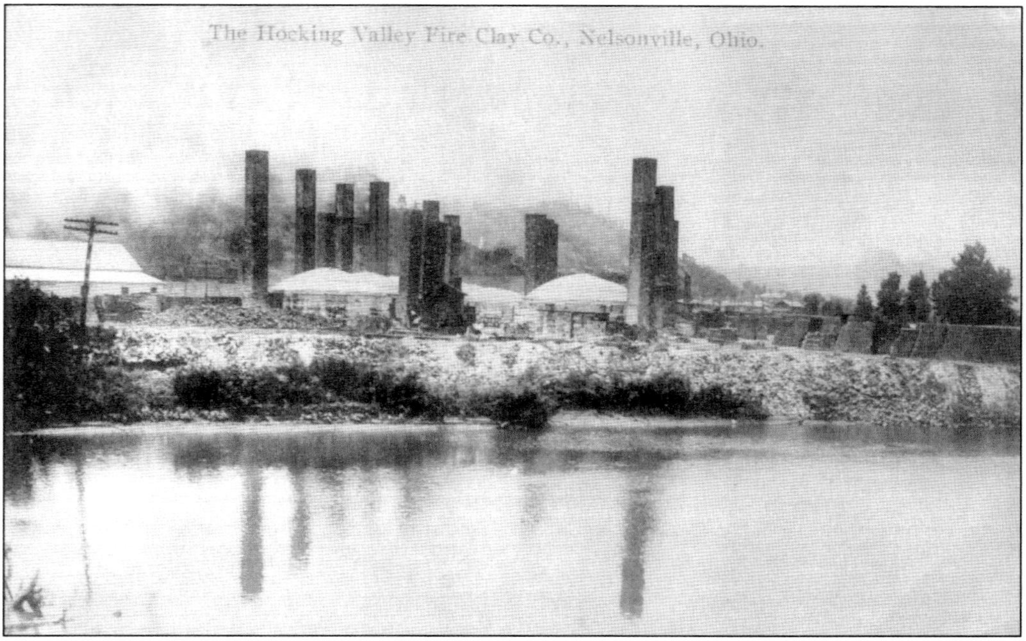

At one time, Nelsonville was noted for its mills, brick manufacturing, coal mining, shipping on the canal, railroad accessibility, and prosperity. At the time of the writing of the *History of Hocking Valley, Ohio*, published in 1883, it was referred to as being "destined to retain the prestige she now holds of being the largest and most important city in the rich and beautiful valley of the Hocking River." Today, the community struggles to find ways to reclaim its former glory. Though its mineral resources have been consumed, active community groups continue to try to lure businesses and customers to the city and are working to maintain its rich history. Both pictures are of the Hocking Valley Fireclay Company.

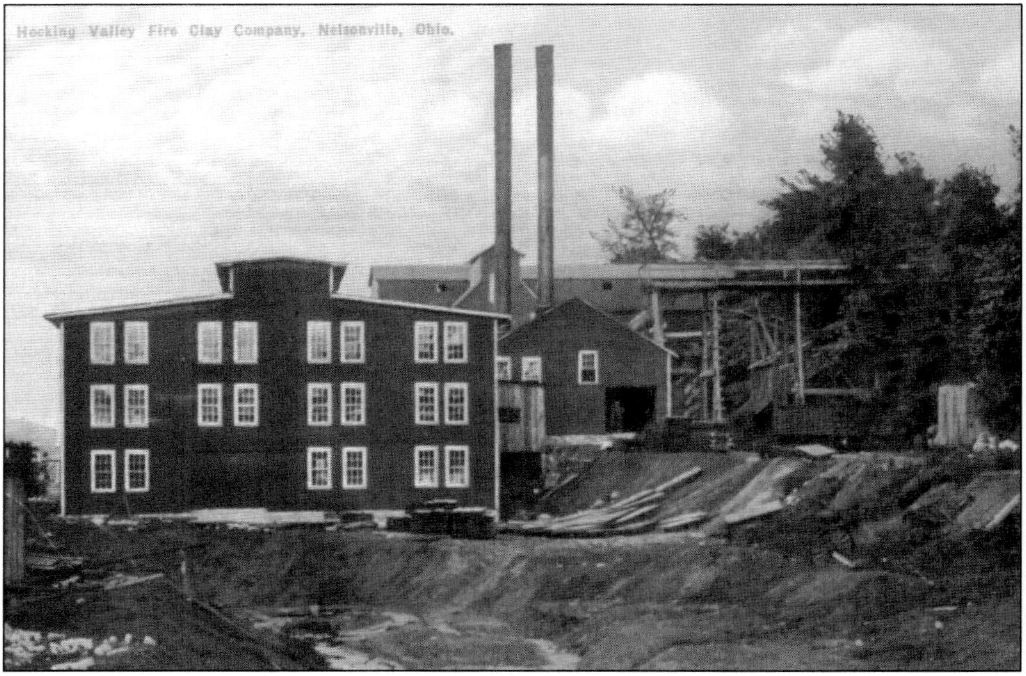

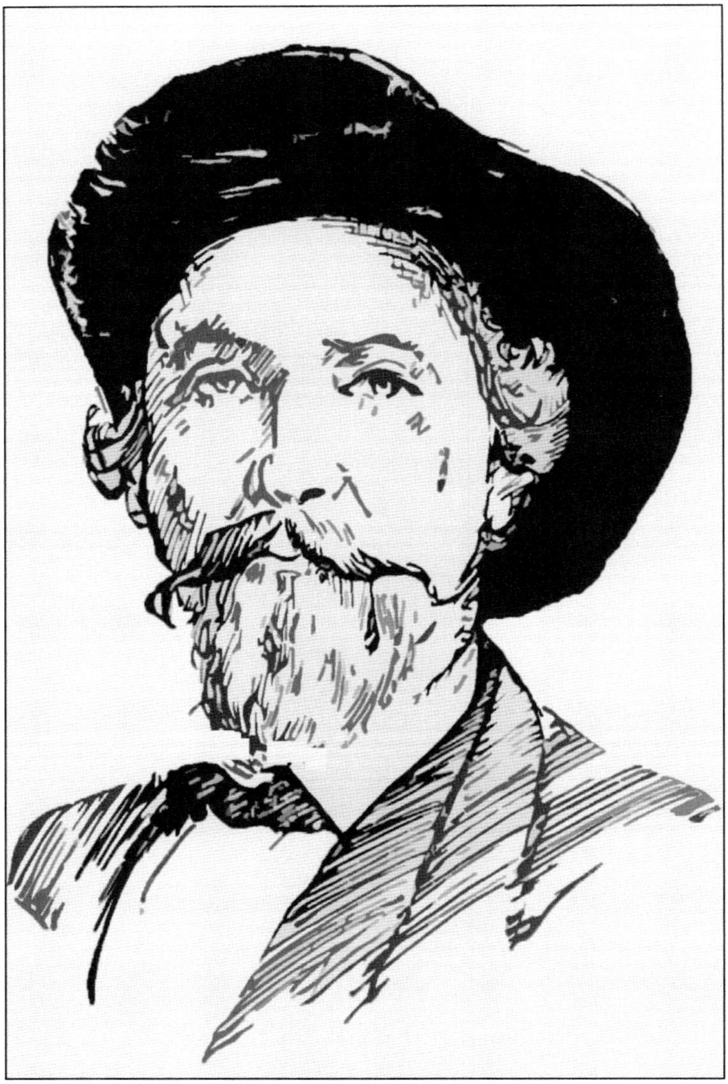

Among Nelsonville's many claims to fame is one of its most famous unwanted and uninvited guests—rebel general John Hunt Morgan—who arrived unannounced on July 22, 1863, at approximately 9:00 a.m. Pursued by Federal cavalry and still reeling from defeat at the Battle of Buffington Island, Morgan entered Nelsonville looking to rest and feed his weary men and horses. The raiders entered from the west, coming down the East Clayton Road (Route 278) from Starr in Hocking County. Believing Morgan's men were farther south, local militia had been sent there and left Nelsonville unguarded. During Morgan's brief stay, which lasted no more than three hours, the raiders burned 10 canal boats, a bridge over the Hocking Canal, and L.D. Poston's coal mine. Morgan spared the Steenrod flour mill after the tearful pleas of a Mrs. Steenrod affected him and spared a canal boat owned by Charles Stuart who convinced Morgan that it was his family's houseboat rather than a coal boat. Morgan's men helped themselves to local provisions, taking large amounts of food from the townspeople and raiding four stores where they acquired whiskey, cigars, and candy. After taking 36 horses from the town, Morgan and his men left Nelsonville around noon, following the Old Marietta Road up Snow Fork of Monday Creek through present-day Buchtel and Murray City toward Perry County. Four days later, Morgan was captured in a small battle with Federal forces in Columbiana County, Ohio.

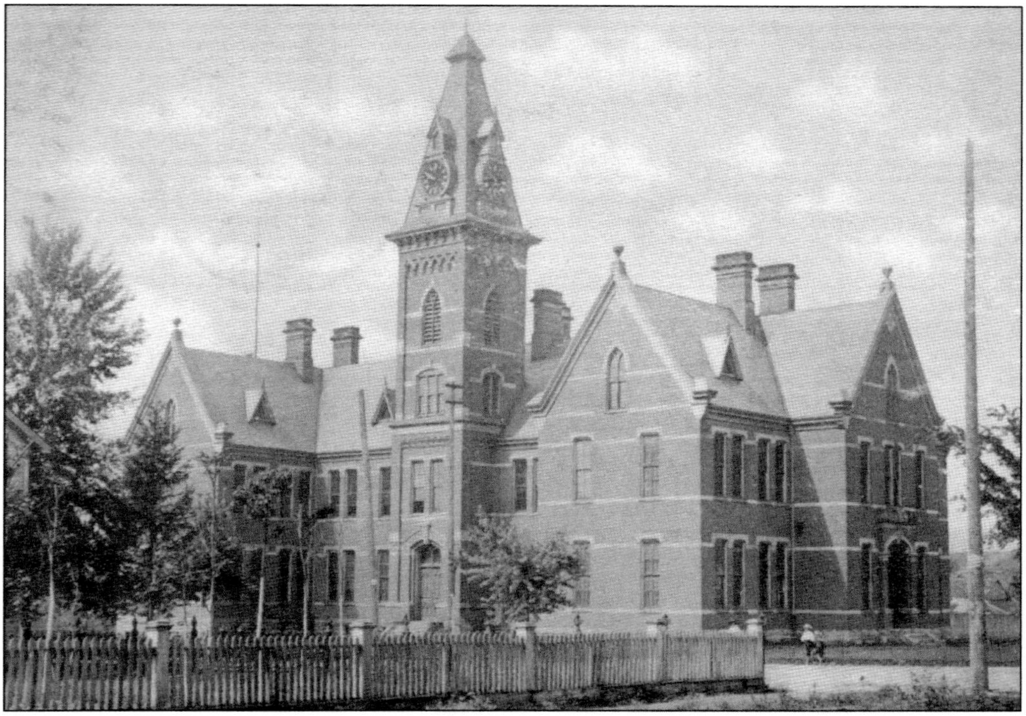

The old Nelsonville Central School in 1907 is shown here. This magnificent building once sat at the north end of the public square. The Victorian Gothic building opened in 1885. Unfortunately, the building was razed long ago, and the lot was used for various purposes. Today, a pharmacy and parking area are located here.

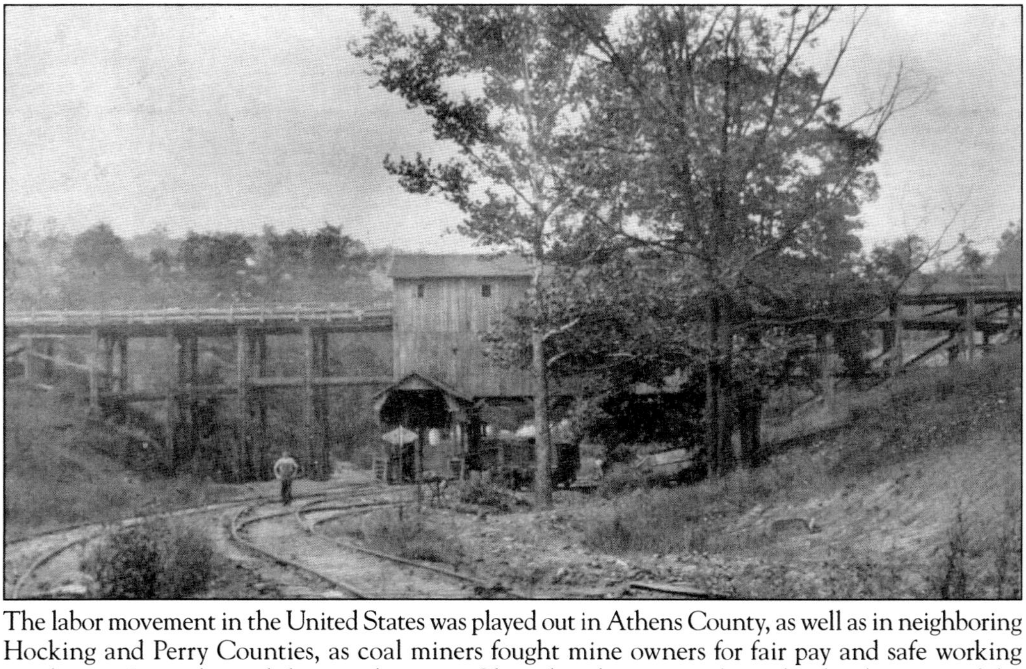

The labor movement in the United States was played out in Athens County, as well as in neighboring Hocking and Perry Counties, as coal miners fought mine owners for fair pay and safe working conditions. It can be said that southeastern Ohio played a major role in the development of the United Mine Workers of America. This picture is of the Baird Brothers Mine at Nelsonville.

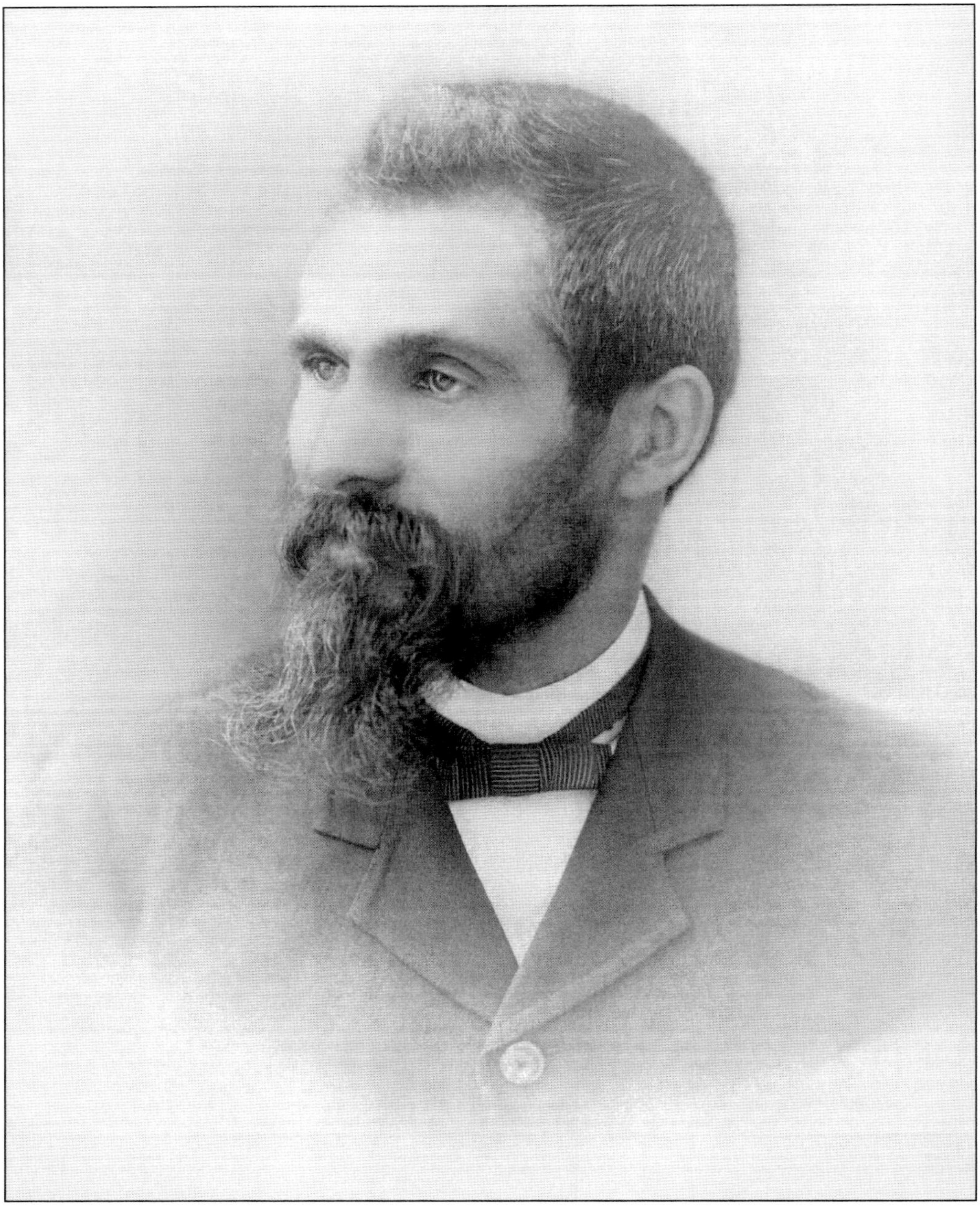

Labor struggles in this country have bred many noteworthy leaders. Chris Evans, one of the great leaders of his era, spent many years of his life calling Nelsonville home. Evans was born in Upper Gornal, South Staffordshire, England, on March 8, 1841. In 1869, he came to the United States with his wife, Caroline, and daughter, Rachel. He had been a miner in England and probably brought a rich understanding of mining and unionization with him to Pennsylvania, where he first lived. In 1875, he was sent by his local union to the Hocking Valley Coal Fields to seek funding for striking miners in Pennsylvania. Evidently, Evans was impressed by the spirit of miners in southeastern Ohio and decided to relocate. He and his family first moved to New Straitsville (Perry County) in 1877. He was a leader of the 1884–1885 Hocking Valley Strike—a devastating battle of wills between miners and owners and a focus of attention across the nation.

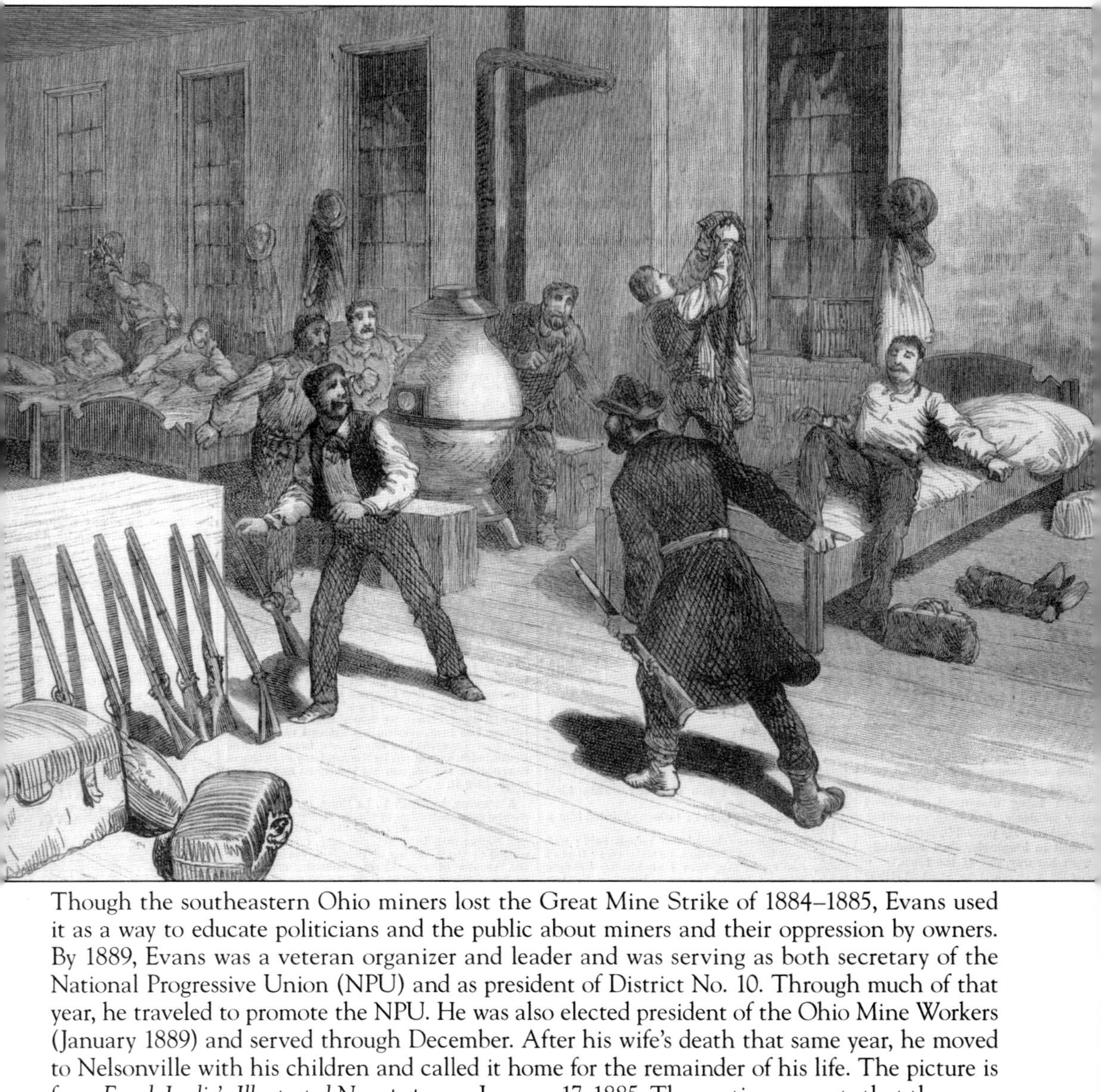

Though the southeastern Ohio miners lost the Great Mine Strike of 1884–1885, Evans used it as a way to educate politicians and the public about miners and their oppression by owners. By 1889, Evans was a veteran organizer and leader and was serving as both secretary of the National Progressive Union (NPU) and as president of District No. 10. Through much of that year, he traveled to promote the NPU. He was also elected president of the Ohio Mine Workers (January 1889) and served through December. After his wife's death that same year, he moved to Nelsonville with his children and called it home for the remainder of his life. The picture is from *Frank Leslie's Illustrated Newspaper* on January 17, 1885. The caption suggests that these are miners getting ready for the coming battle with the Pinkerton detectives and other hired guns of the mine owners.

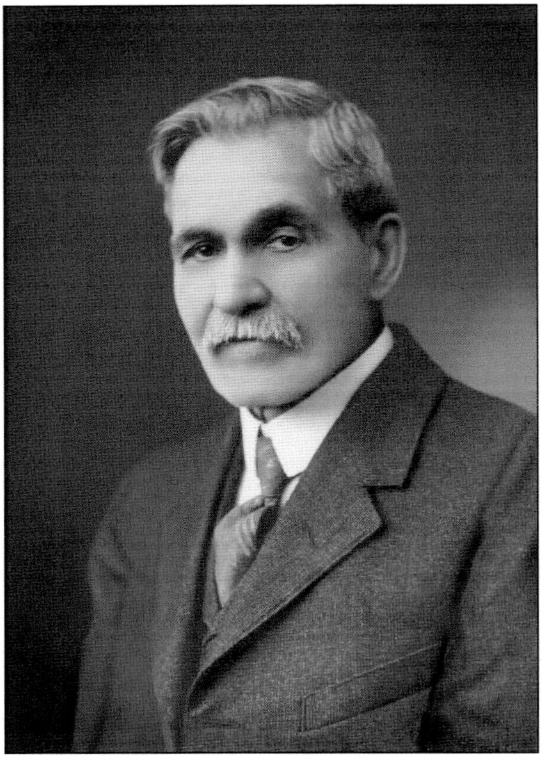

Evans retired in 1908 to Nelsonville, wrote a history of the United Mine Workers of America (UMWA), and died October 2, 1924. The *Athens Messenger* aptly gave Evans's obituary bolder type than those around him and read as follows: "DEATH CALL IS ANSWERED BY A FAMOUS MAN: Chris Evans, 83, Passes Away at Home in Nelsonville; NATIONALLY KNOWN; For Half Century Devoted Efforts to Labor's Cause."

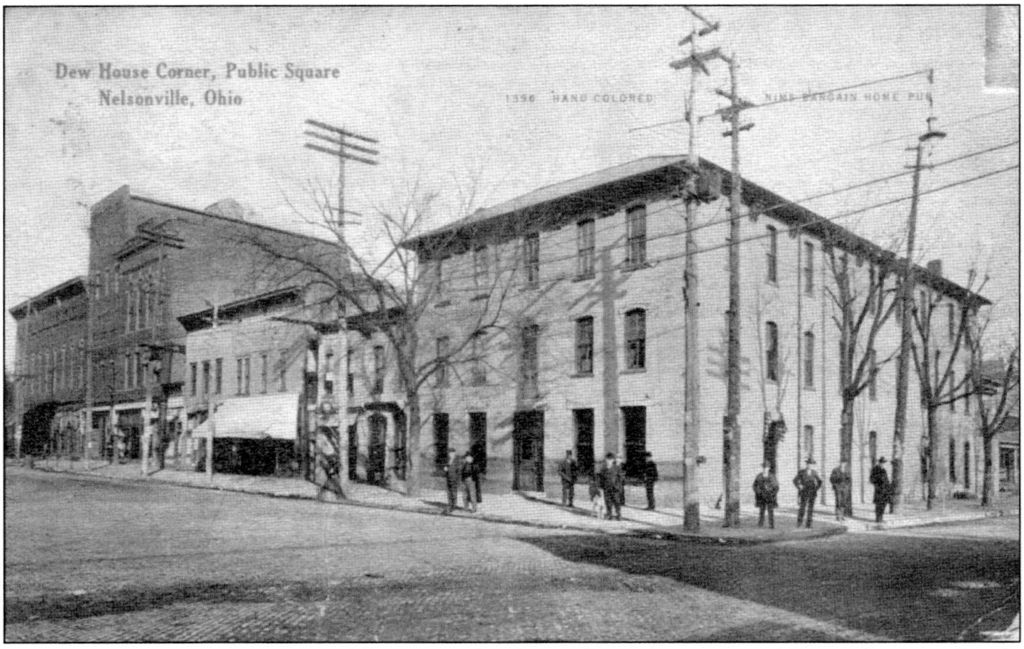

One of the more tragic stories of the town of Nelsonville is about Samuel Dew. The Dew family was prominent in the community from the late 1830s and members were builders of the famous Dew House, a hotel. Samuel was what one might call a "black sheep" of his family. His parents died when he was very young, and he became a ward of relative Sen. James Dew and later of W.W. Poston. This picture is of the Dew House in 1914.

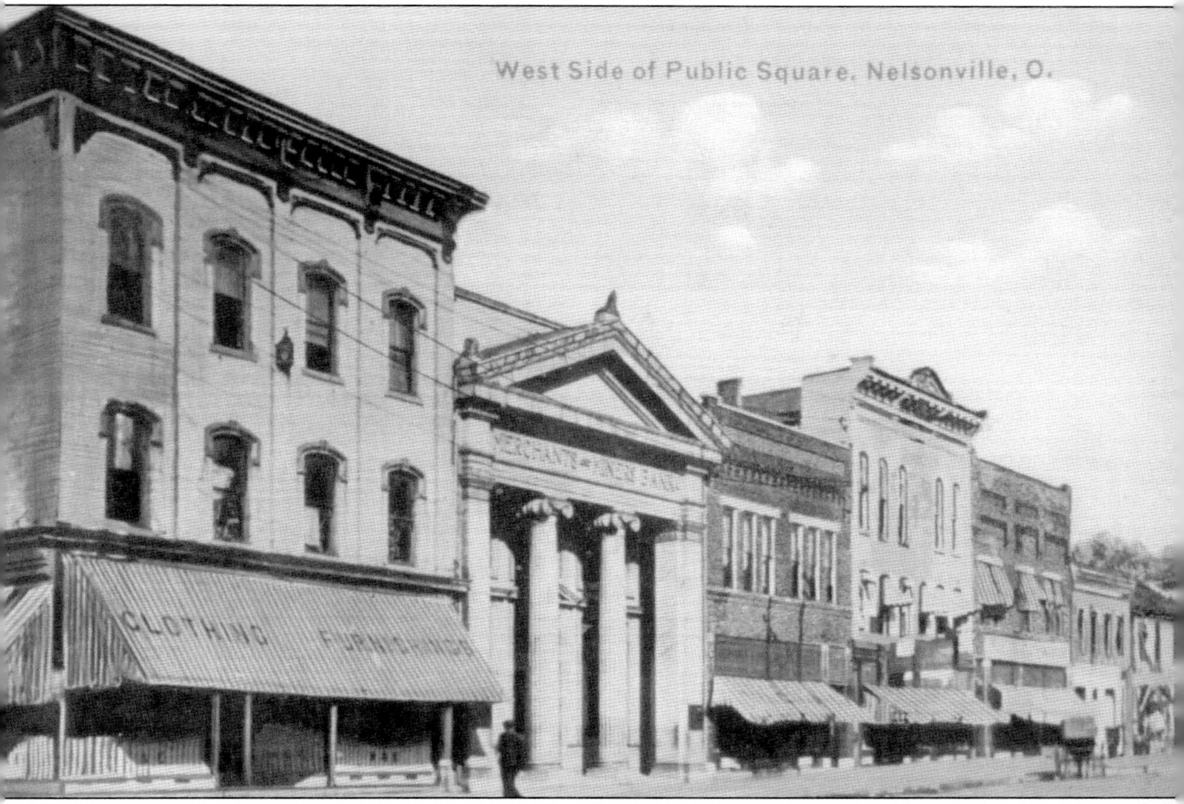

Young Dew was known for being "on the wild side." Though he was married to Mary Winifred Rosser and had a child, Mary, by the time he was 20 he was also a drinker and had run-ins with the law. Apparently, Dew believed he was being persecuted by young assistant marshal Edward H. Davis, particularly after Davis stopped Dew from racing too fast around the square. Sometime shortly after the reprimand, Dew found Davis standing on the Public Square in front of the Dew House. Davis seemingly had no reason to fear for his own safety and was not prepared to defend himself. Dew simply walked up to Davis, pulled out a gun, and fatally shot the sheriff. He then ran north down the Public Square and, realizing what he had just done, put the gun to his own head and shot himself in front of Stuart's Opera House. The entire community was shocked and appalled by the activities. The story has become an ongoing part of the city's lore. Pictured is the west side of the Public Square in 1914.

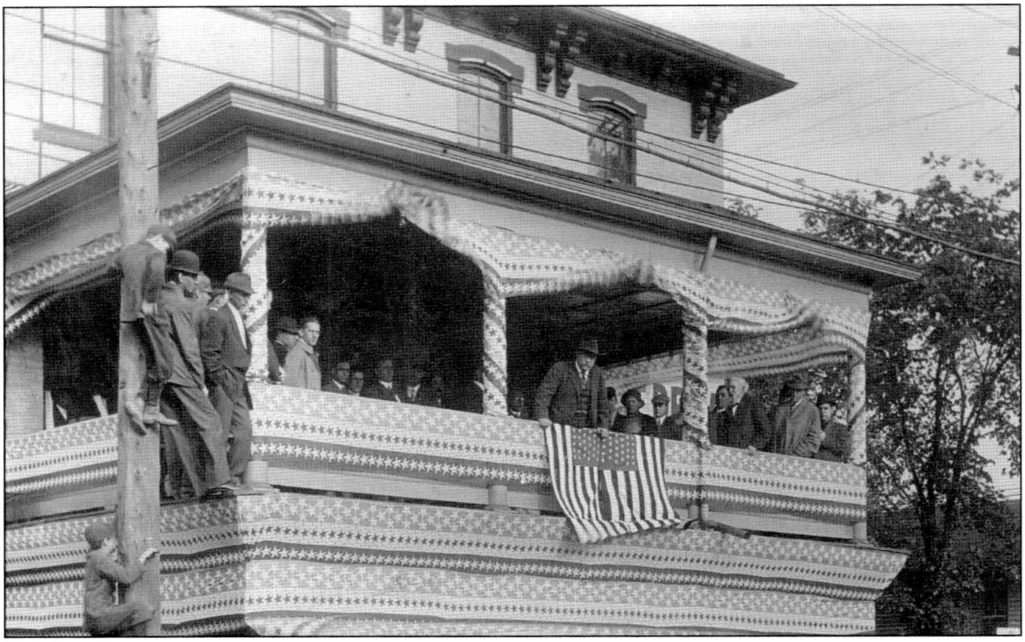

As a thriving town, there were (and still are) many events in Nelsonville worthy of mention in a future history of the community. Many prominent Athens County families have played out their lives there. Pictured here is Teddy Roosevelt giving a speech from the Dew House porch. The Dew House was built in 1839 as a two-story hotel and was renovated in 1878. A third floor was added at that time.

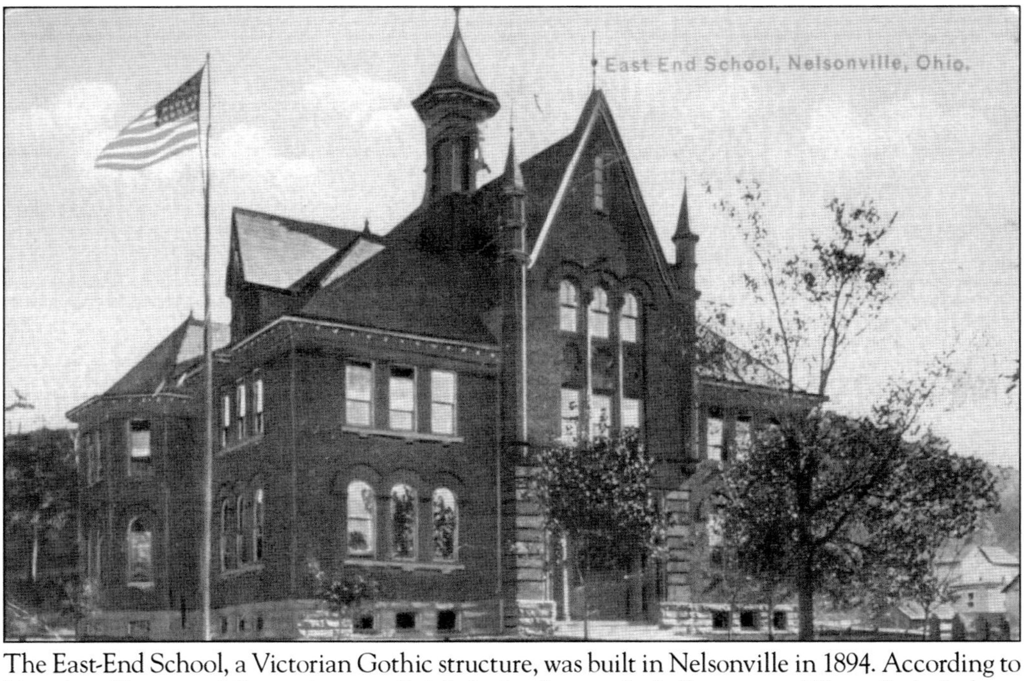

The East-End School, a Victorian Gothic structure, was built in Nelsonville in 1894. According to historians Beatty and Stone, it was redbrick, had a slate roof, a bell tower, and "lots of spirals, bays, and turrets." Beatty and Stone go on to state that it cost $18,000—at that time, a staggering amount of money. One can only chuckle at the kind of building that money would pay for today.

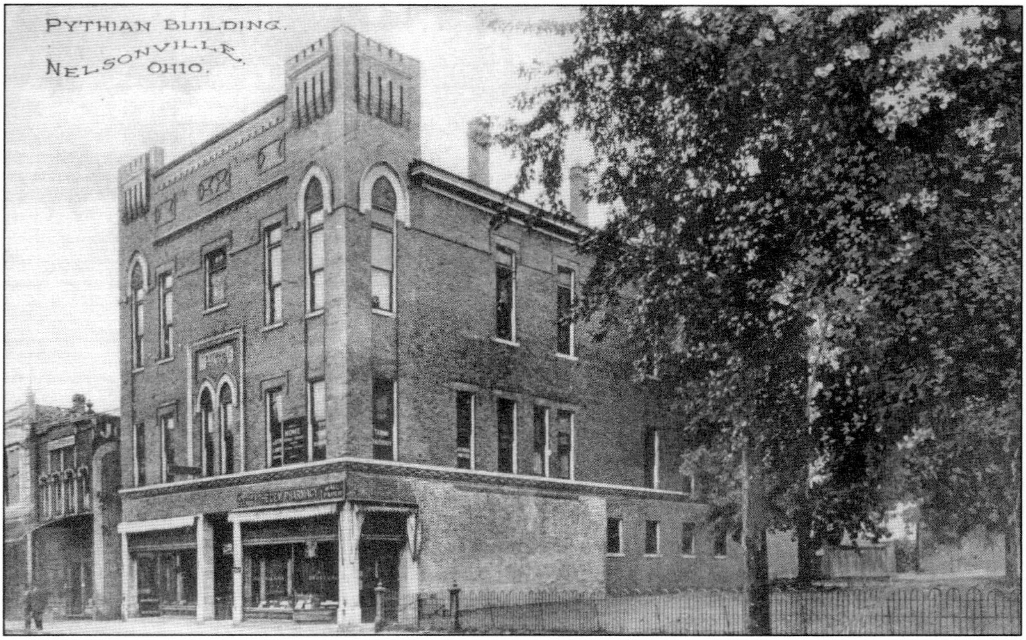

The Knights of Pythias Building, shown above, still stands on Washington Street in Nelsonville next to the lot that once housed the old Central School. The building was first used by the Knights in 1884. Over the years, membership dwindled, care and maintenance costs grew, and the building was finally sold. The Knights still meet but no longer in their own building. The picture below shows Knights of Pythias members dressed in uniforms from the Hocking Valley Lodge No. 75 in Nelsonville. According to their website, "The Order of Knights of Pythias is an international, non-sectarian fraternal order, established in 1864 in Washington, DC, by Justus H. Rathbone and was the first fraternal order to be chartered by an Act of Congress." The order promotes, peace, friendship, and goodwill among its members and the communities they serve.

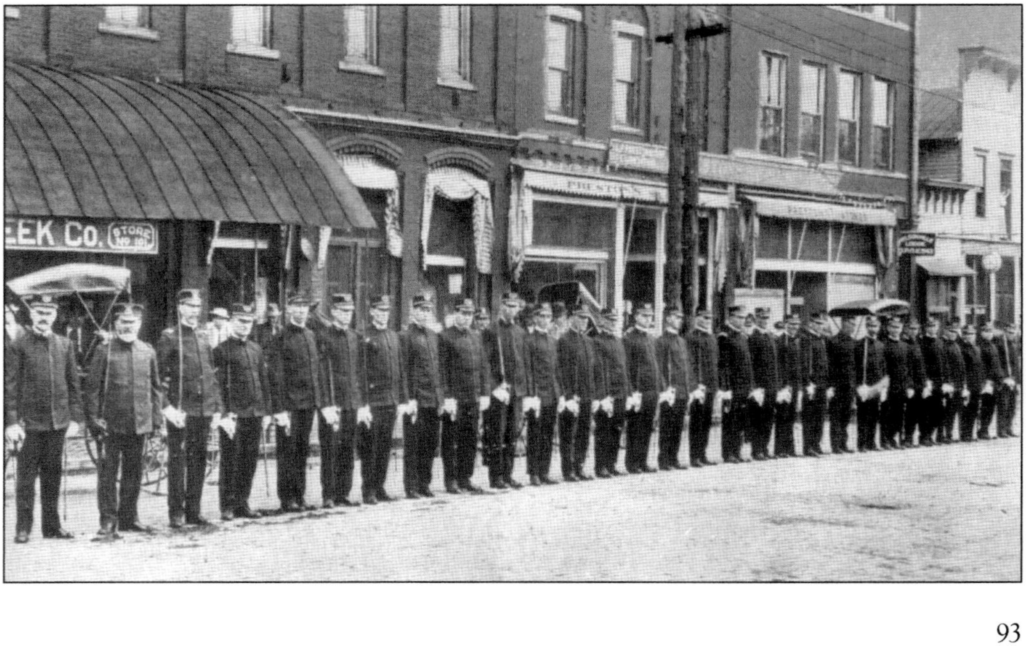

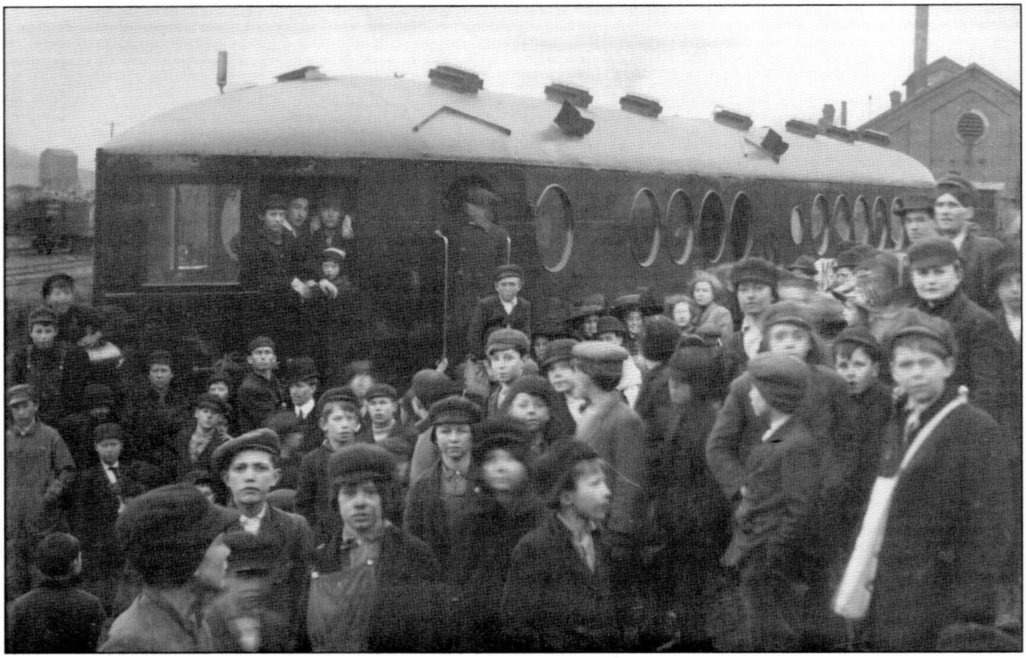

In the image above, young people gather around the traction car in the Nelsonville train yards. A traction line started in Nelsonville in 1909 and reached Chauncey in 1912. It reached Athens in 1915. The image below shows the Nelsonville traction car in 1911. Among those pictured here are Charley Vorhes, Gaston Coe, Marcellus Kreig, Ed Shafer (manufacturer's representative from Omaha, Nebraska), Warren Badger, Colonel Tutt, Ed Young, and "Hud" Price; the operator of the car, Jim Beard, is in the front window. The car is on Columbus Street at the south end of the Public Square. According to Beatty and Stone, the traction line was built by E.B. Young of Athens and C.D. Shafer of Nelsonville.

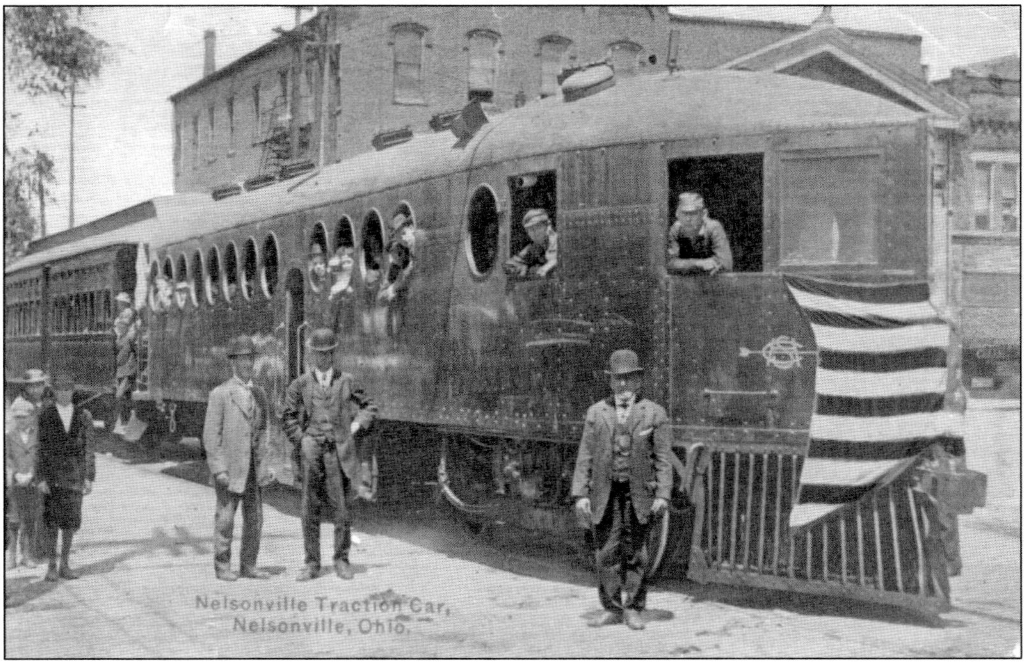

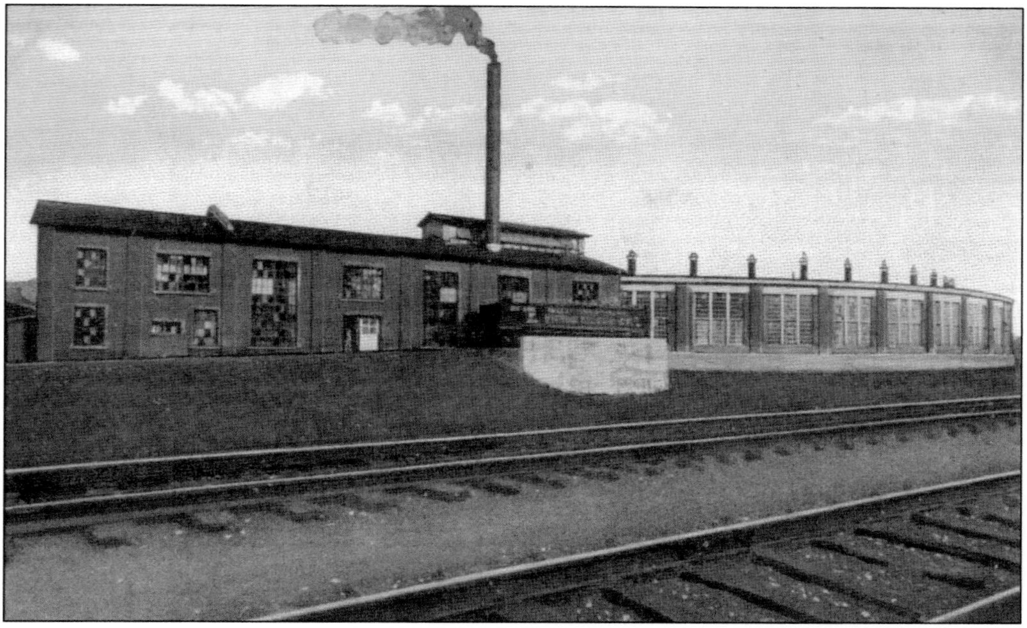

Shown here is the roundhouse in Nelsonville at the train yards. At one time, multiple tracks ran through the community, requiring repair buildings, switching operations, and a host of other facilities to serve both the train companies and the traveling public. The Nelsonville depot still operates today for the Hocking Valley Scenic Railroad.

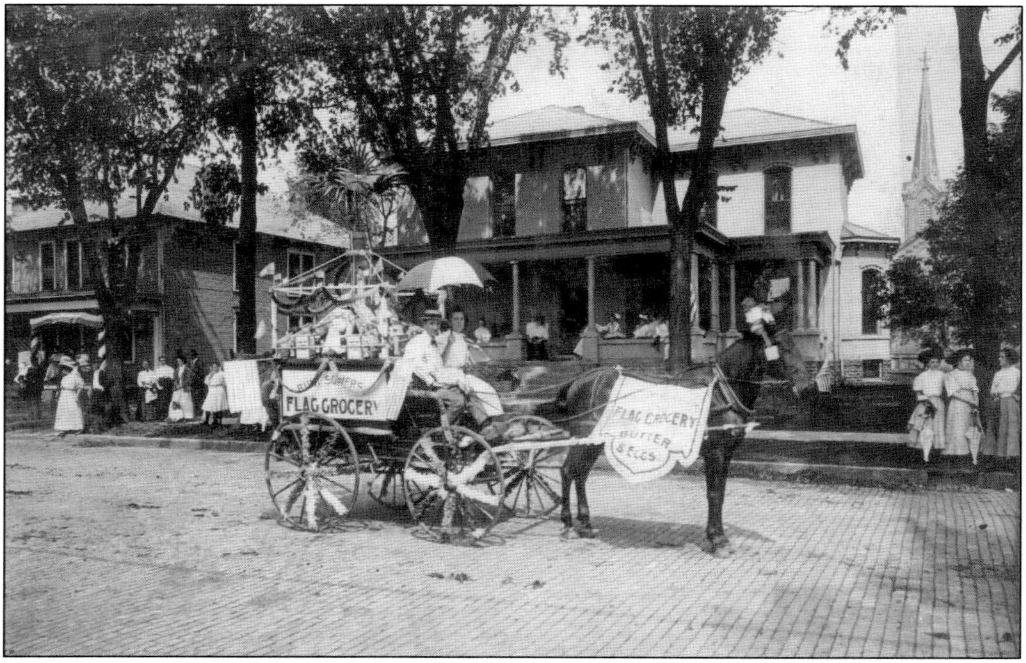

Shown here is the Flag Grocery wagon advertising butter and eggs in a parade that took place in Nelsonville (date unknown). Like today, parades were an opportunity to call people's attention to local business. At the time of this picture, a small neighborhood grocery could sustain its owners by selling local farm products.

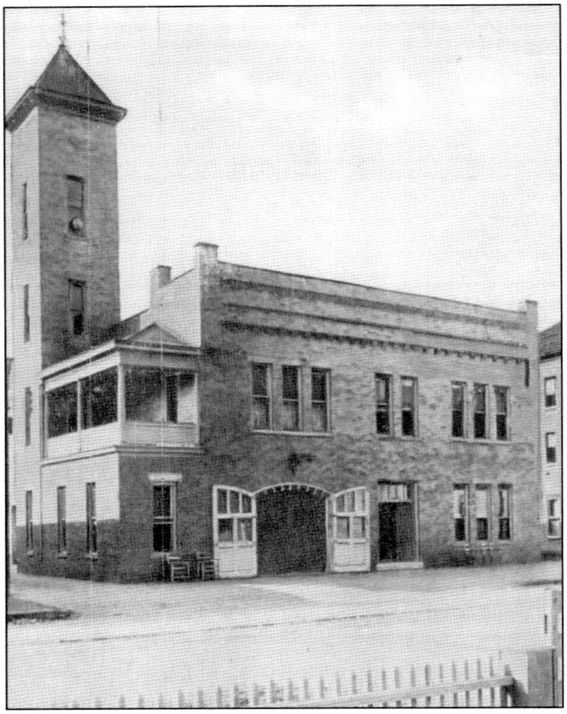

The Nelsonville City Building is shown here in 1920. The building is now owned by Brooks Shoe Company, one of the largest businesses in Nelsonville other than Hocking College, and is used for office and meeting space. The new Nelsonville City Building is now on Route 278 in a much more modern, one-story building.

This is the George Freer and Brothers Planing Mill. The Freers were dealers in wood products for home builders and also did custom sawing, turning, and millwork. The mill was located across the canal (which was filled in and now serves as Canal Street) from the main part of the town. A Methodist church now sits on the land once occupied by the mill.

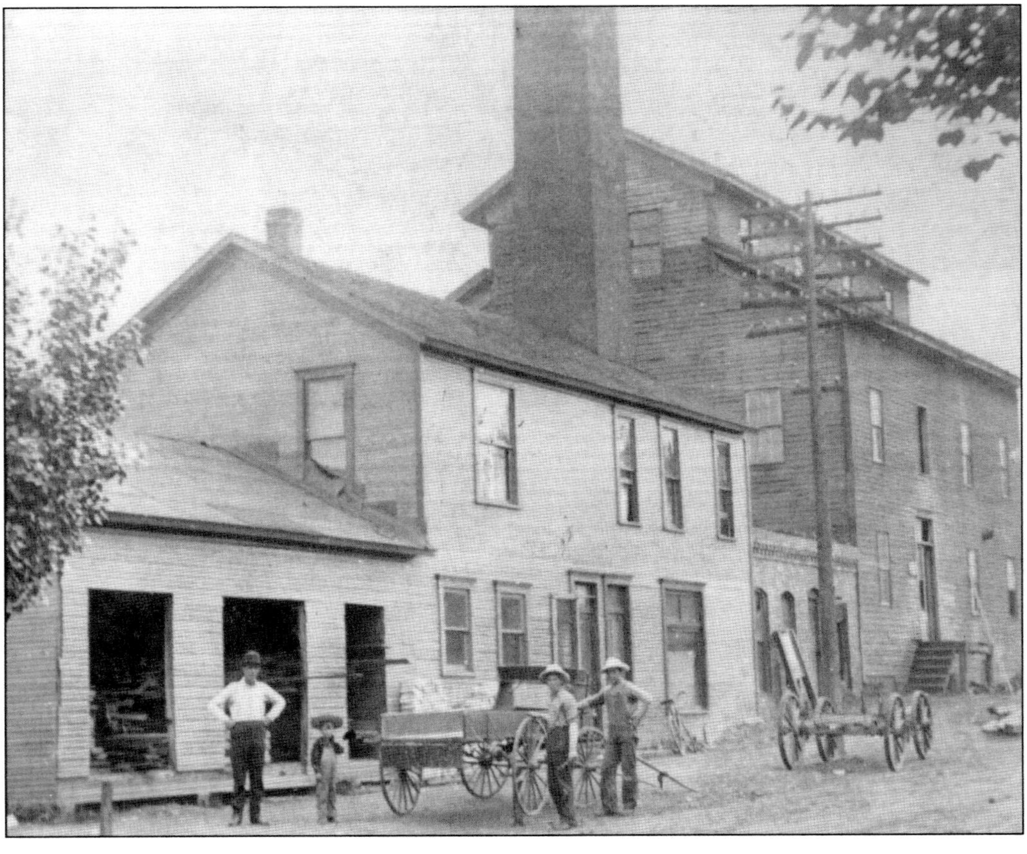

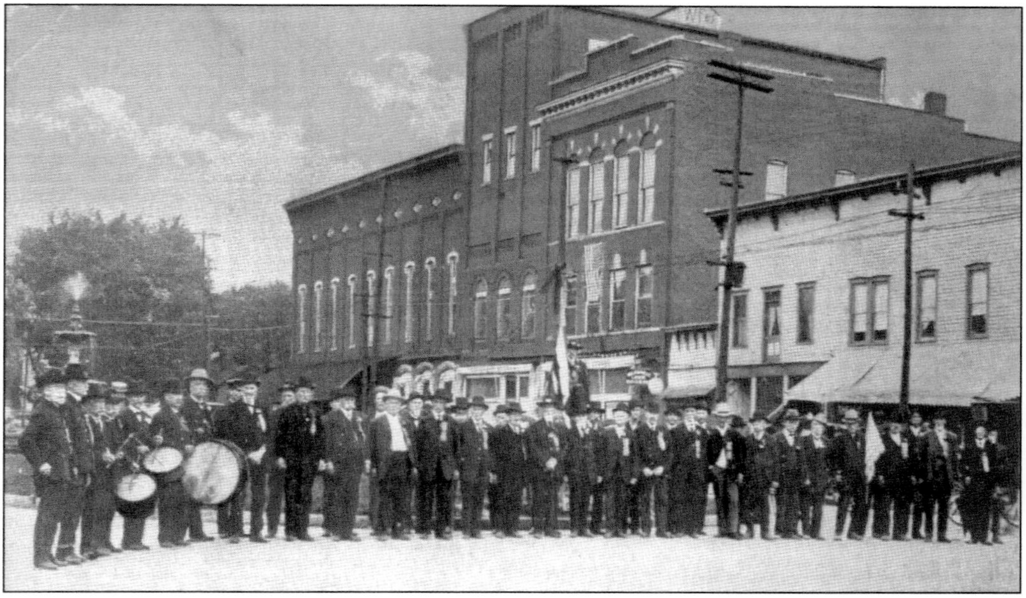

The "Last of Civil War Veterans," GAR No. 38, pose here for a photograph in Nelsonville. It was common practice after the Civil War, or more properly "the War of the Rebellion," for veterans to be honored in formal ceremonies to the ends of their lives. This image was probably taken between 1910 and 1915.

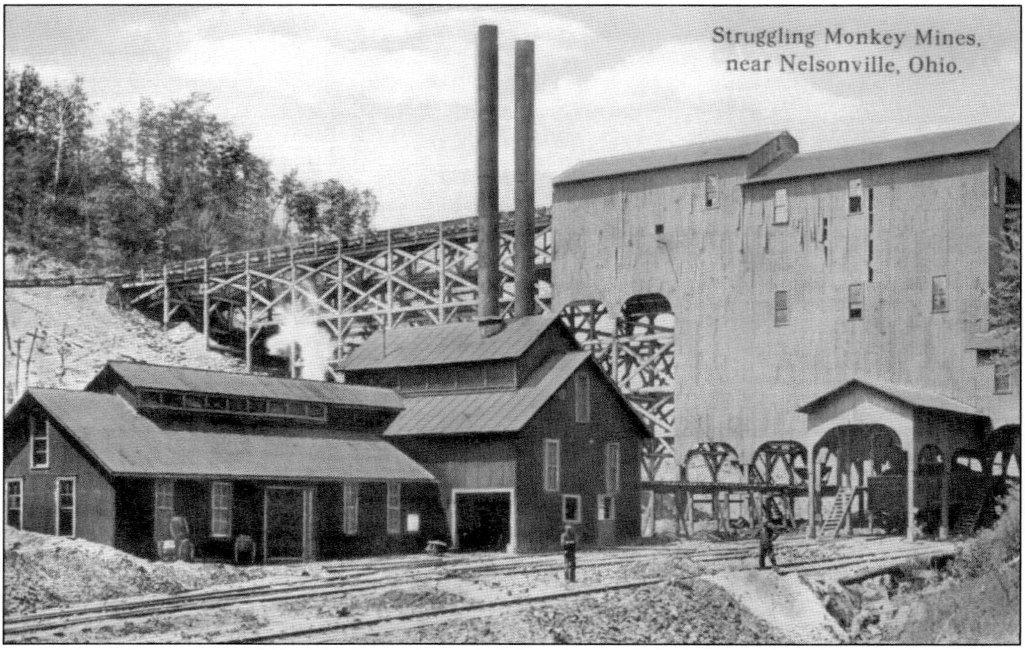

Near Nelsonville was the strangely named Struggling Monkey Mine, shown here, operated by the Vulcan Coal Company. The company also operated the Strong Union Mine. These mines carried coal out on a track of the New York Central Railway to markets well beyond the area and the state. For a while, these mines provided much needed work for their employees.

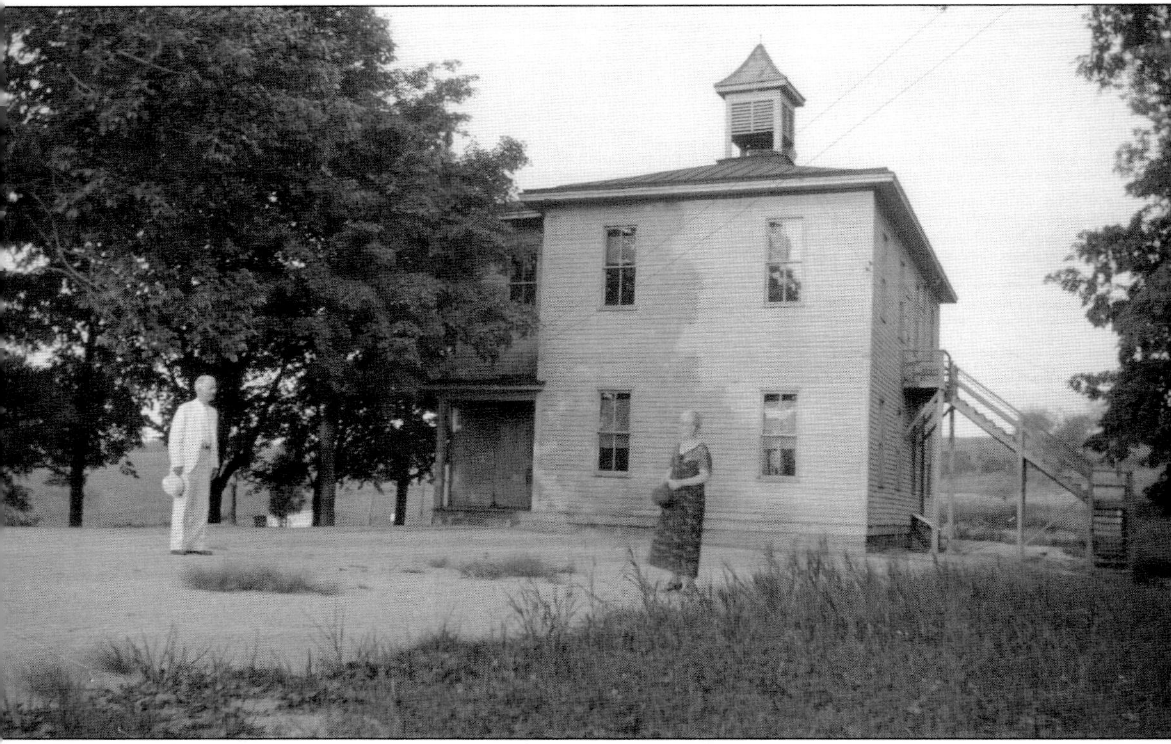

NEW MARSHFIELD. New Marshfield (formerly Marshfield), in Waterloo Township, is situated on land lying between Raccoon and Margaret Creeks. According to W.E. Peters, the town is named for George Marsh, who laid it out in 1854. Its post office was not established until 1859. According to Beatty and Stone, "[New] Marshfield developed as a busy rail community as the result of coal mines opening in the area." It once had stores, barbershops, the Swaim Hotel, and other common railroad town amenities. It sat on what had once been the Cincinnati, Washington & Baltimore Railroad. When the first phone lines were brought into the county in 1899 by the Chillicothe-McArthur Independent Telephone Company, a switchboard was located in New Marshfield, making it a part of a "modern" communication system. The town that was built around the railroad industry began to decline as the railroad industry faced economic problems and new modes of transportation replaced them. This picture is of the New Marshfield School, with Allie Bellows Herron and Frank Lester Bellows, and is dated August 26, 1933.

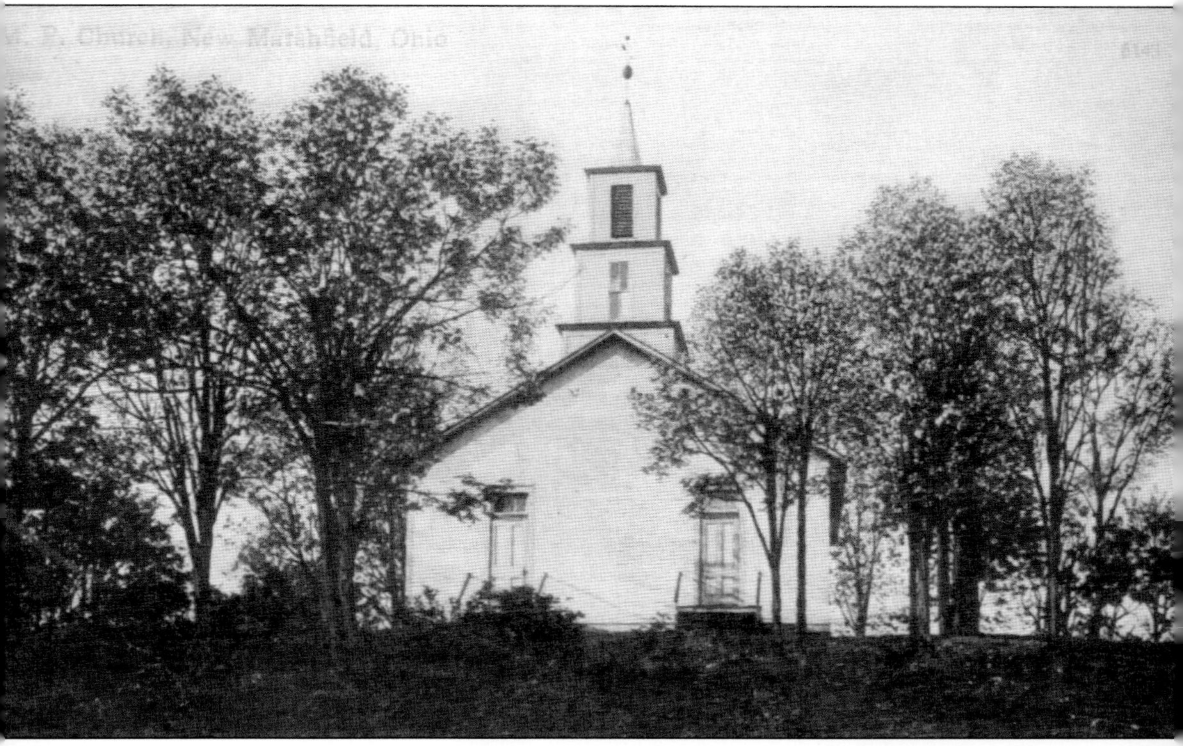

New Marshfield, like most towns in southeastern Ohio, is generally a quiet, peaceful place where people live, work, and enjoy their lives. On the other hand, the town faced all of the problems that go with communities everywhere. For example, fires are not specific to southeastern Ohio towns, but one incident at New Marshfield says a great deal about the community as it existed in 1953. The March 22, 1953 *Athens Messenger* reported that an entire block at New Marshfield had been destroyed. The fire took "two apartments, a house, a three-car garage and barn the previous evening . . . [including] the Hysell General Store, Dickens Garage, and Madge Baughman's house." According to fire chief Charles Dalton of the Athens Fire Department, "The blaze started on a rear porch of the Hysell Store. Linseed oil and feed were stored on the porch." Mrs. Jake Lyons and her husband ran the store and were present when the fire broke out. Mrs. Lyons and an employee noticed the flames at approximately the same time a neighbor did. Jake Lyons was up on the roof painting when the fire started but was able to escape. This image is of the New Marshfield Church in 1918.

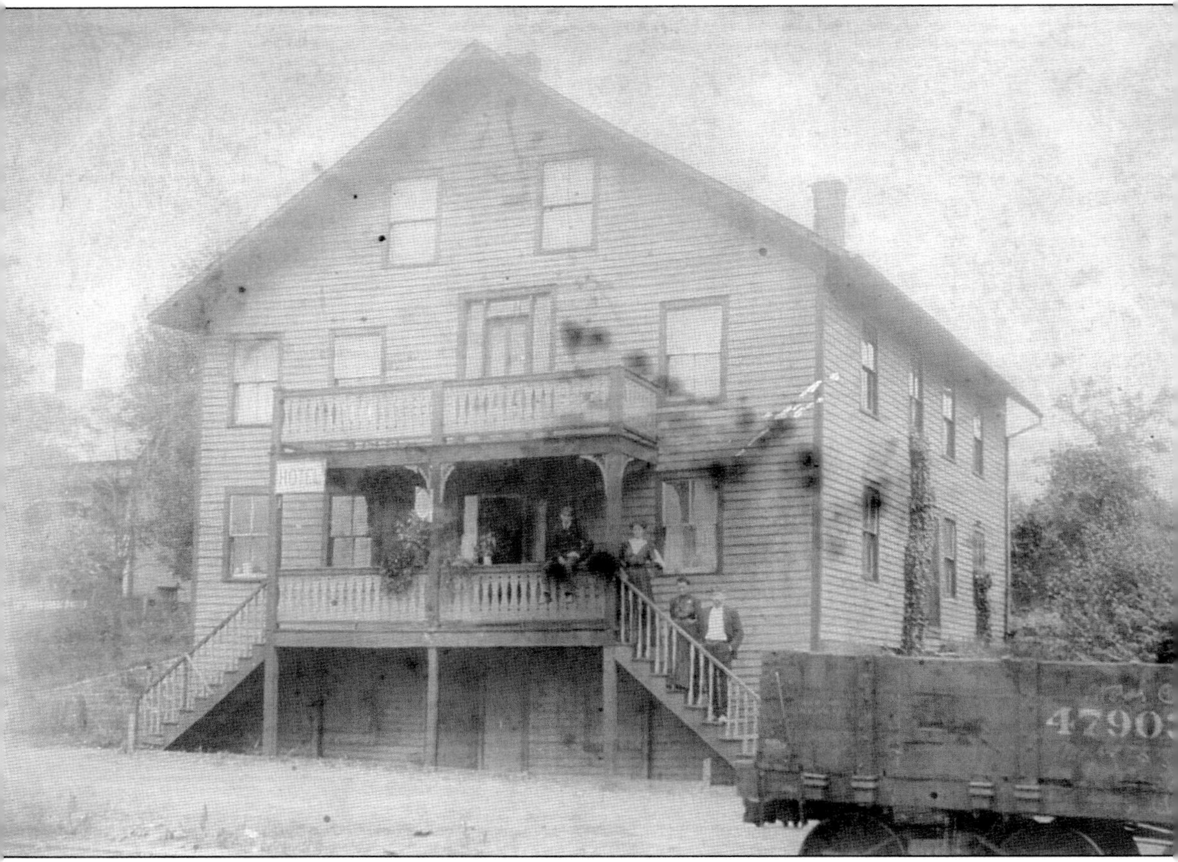

When firefighters arrived to fight the New Marshfield fire, there was not much water readily available, so community members (including numerous women) set up a bucket brigade for transporting water. With the help of the community, access to private cisterns, and a small "booster-type hose," the firefighters and community members were able to keep the fire from spreading into the nearby Steinmeyer farm store and the Gilham-Frank Post VFW Club, an abandoned confectionery, a barbershop, the Hoodlett funeral home, and the village post office. Though much was lost, the willingness of community members to work tirelessly together to overcome the fire and save the town speaks volumes about the good people of New Marshfield at the time. This picture shows the New Marshfield Hotel around 1908.

William E. Peters, one the most noted historians of the area, is the only person known to tell the story of John Lady, whose gravestone (erected by Peters) is pictured here. Where and how Peters learned of the story is unknown, and the Athens County Historical Society and Museum has not yet confirmed it. Given Peters's veracity, it is difficult to discount the story; therefore, local lore embraces it. The story persists because of Peters's placing of the stone seen here at his own personal cost. Where John Lady came from or lived before or during his time in Athens County, whether or not he was truly a traitor to the confederacy, whether or not he was married or had children, and so on, remain for historians to uncover in the future. Perhaps, the entire story will be disproved, leaving a strange curiosity about Peters's determination to place the stone. (Both, courtesy of the Anastas Collection.)

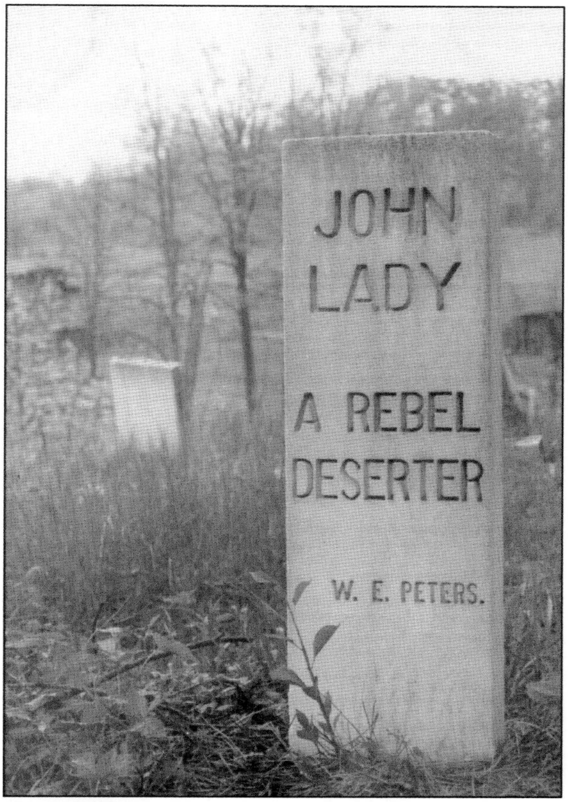

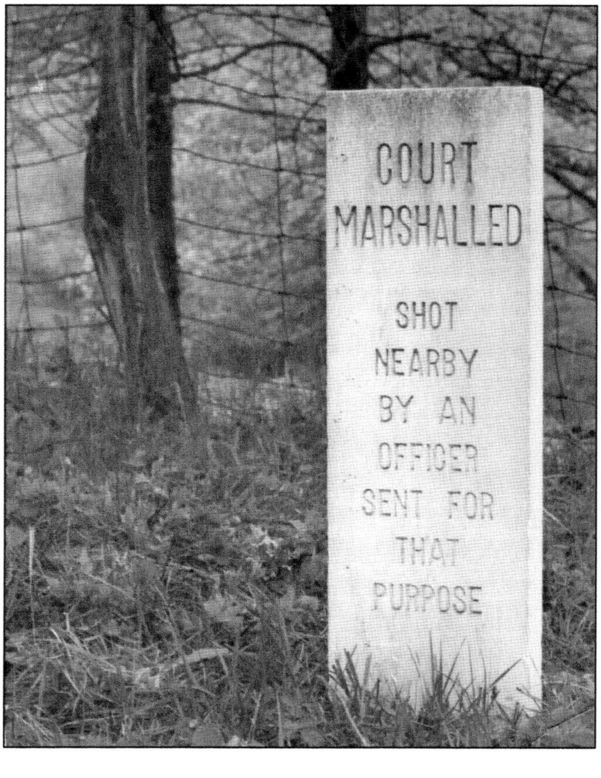

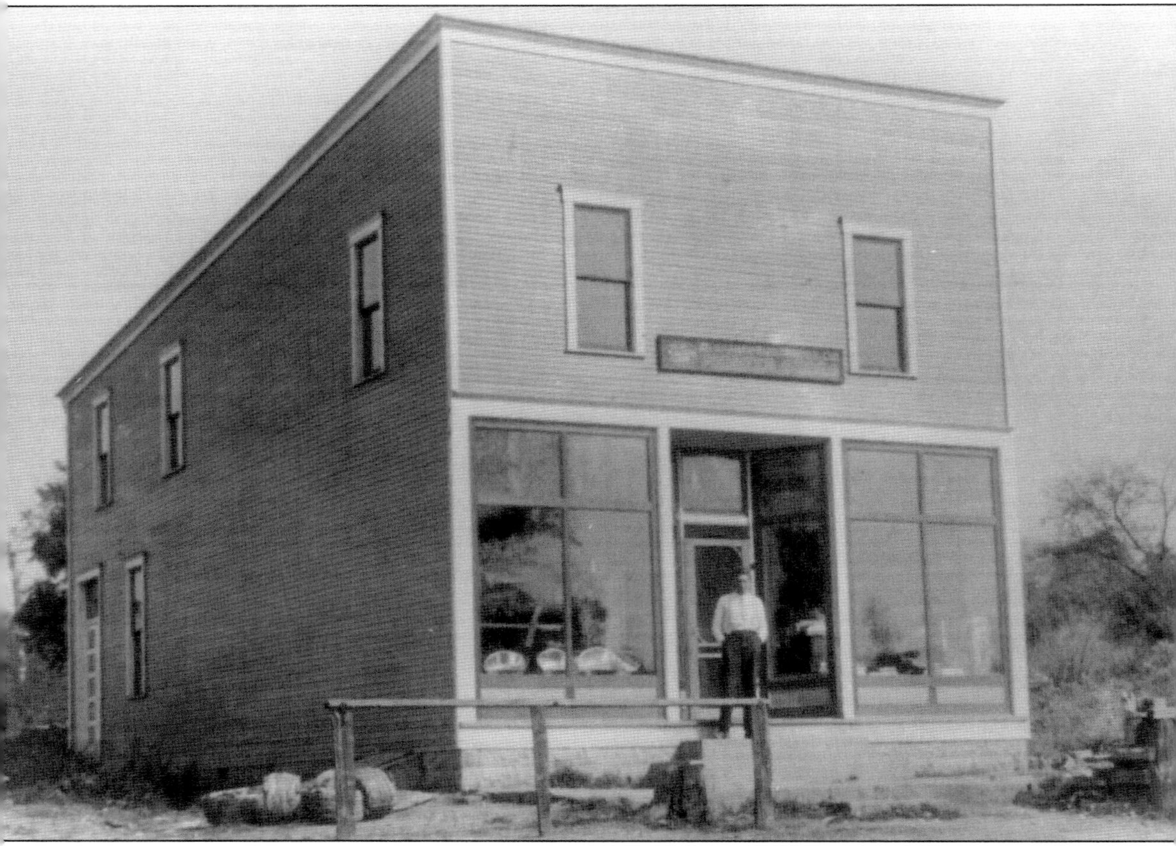

SHADE. According to Walker, a post office was established in Shade in 1839. In the 1883 *History of Hocking Valley, Ohio*, the writer refers to the place as Jerseyville and states that it contained "two stores, one harness shop, one blacksmith shop, one hotel, a postoffice [*sic*], one cabinet shop and two churches—Methodist Episcopal and Christian. Its population is about 175." Beatty and Stone note that the place was first called Pleasant Valley, then Jerseyville, and then Shade once "Route 33 was paved and the highway department erected signs making the name Shade official." This would seem to conflict with Walker's reference to Shade in his 1869 rendition of communities in Lodi Township and the official publications of the US post office declaring that Shade was officially a post office in 1837. After talking with locals, it is clear that the community has been called any and all of the three names at various times and was referred to as all of these names in newspaper accounts over the years; however, it is clear that the official mailing address has long been Shade, Ohio. Pictured here is the Shade General Store. Bill Pruden built the store in 1914.

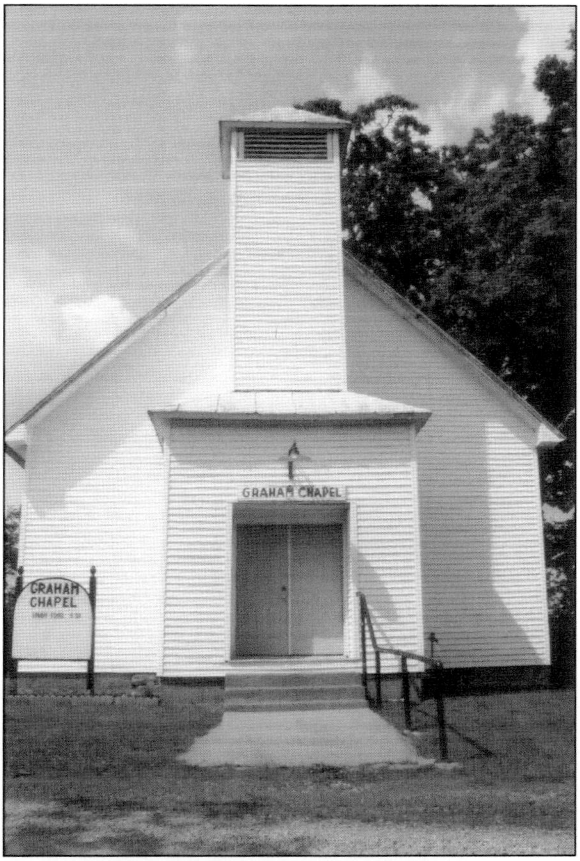

Joseph Thompson was both the first settler in Lodi Township and also its first miller. He built a gristmill near present-day Shade about 1815. In addition to the milling business, the land in much of the Shade area was largely used for agrarian purposes. However, as in the other townships of Athens County, concern about educating people was prevalent. According to Peters, the Pleasant Valley Seminary "was opened to students in December of 1867 when a two-story frame building (30 feet by 40 feet) had been erected at a cost of about $2,000.00, the voluntary contribution of the citizens." The image at right is of the Graham Chapel, and below is the Shade United Methodist Church. (Both, courtesy of Brenda Ruth.)

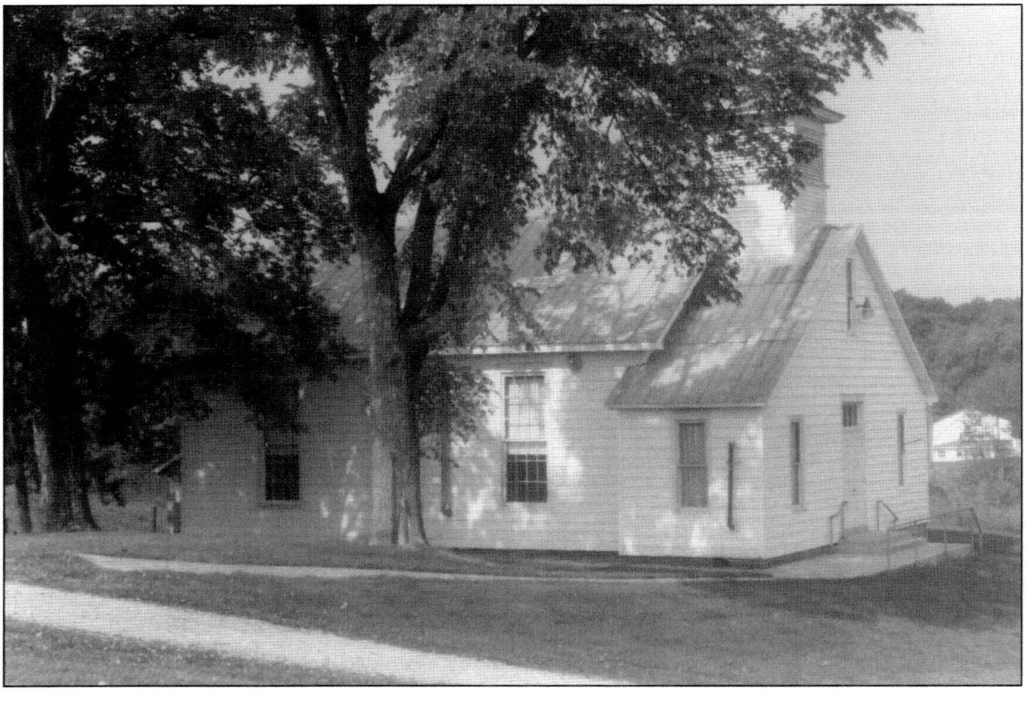

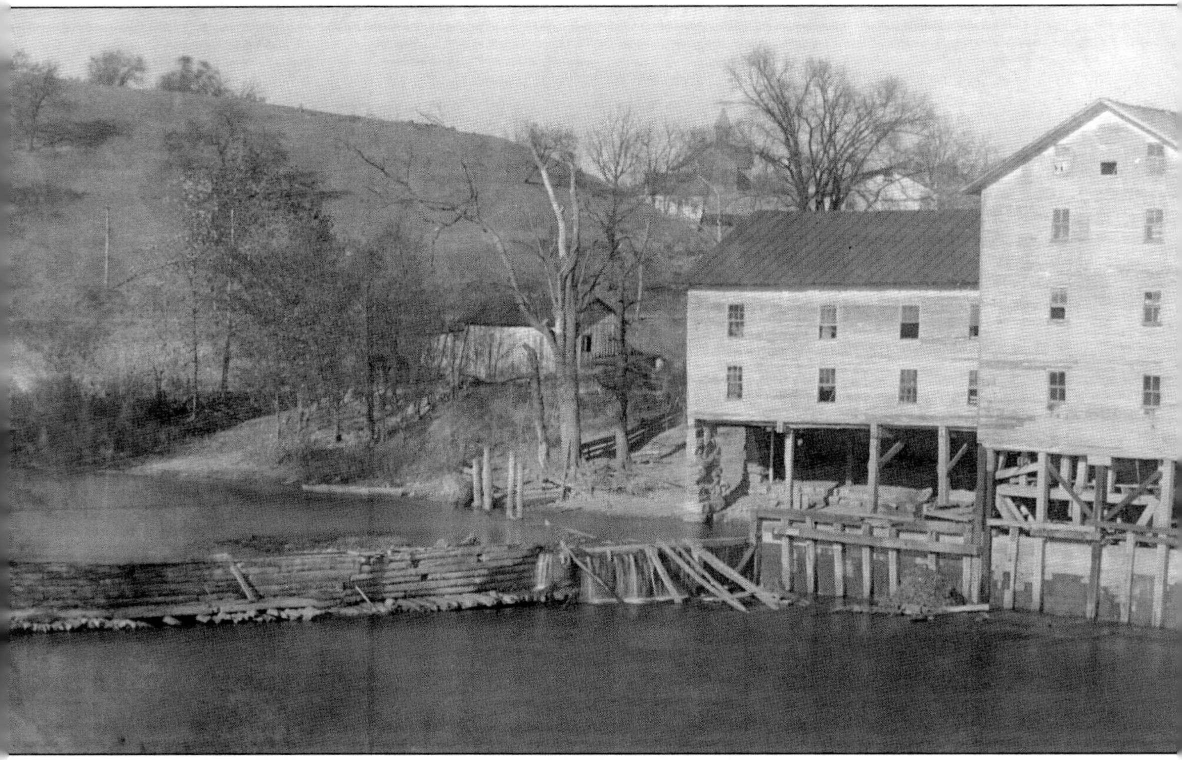

STEWART. Daniel B. Stewart Sr., a former Revolutionary War soldier, arrived in Athens County in 1802. According to the *History of Athens County,* Ohio, by Walker, he had "an orchard of three thousand bearing fruit trees—two thousand peach, and one thousand apple trees—at that time probably the largest orchard in the state," by 1810. Stewart Sr. was considered a publicly spirited man who gave freely of his time and money. "He was one of the first two justices of the peace in the [Rome] township [Elijah Hatch being the other], and acted as such, altogether, more than twenty years." It is for him and his family that the town of Stewart is named. Daniel B. Stewart Jr., born at his father's farm in 1812, was an adept young man with a head for business. He started out working for his father in his mill. Two years later, he bought it, then sold it a short while later and went into the mercantile business in Meigs County and then in Coolville. Pictured is the old Stewart Mill. (Courtesy of the Anastas Collection.)

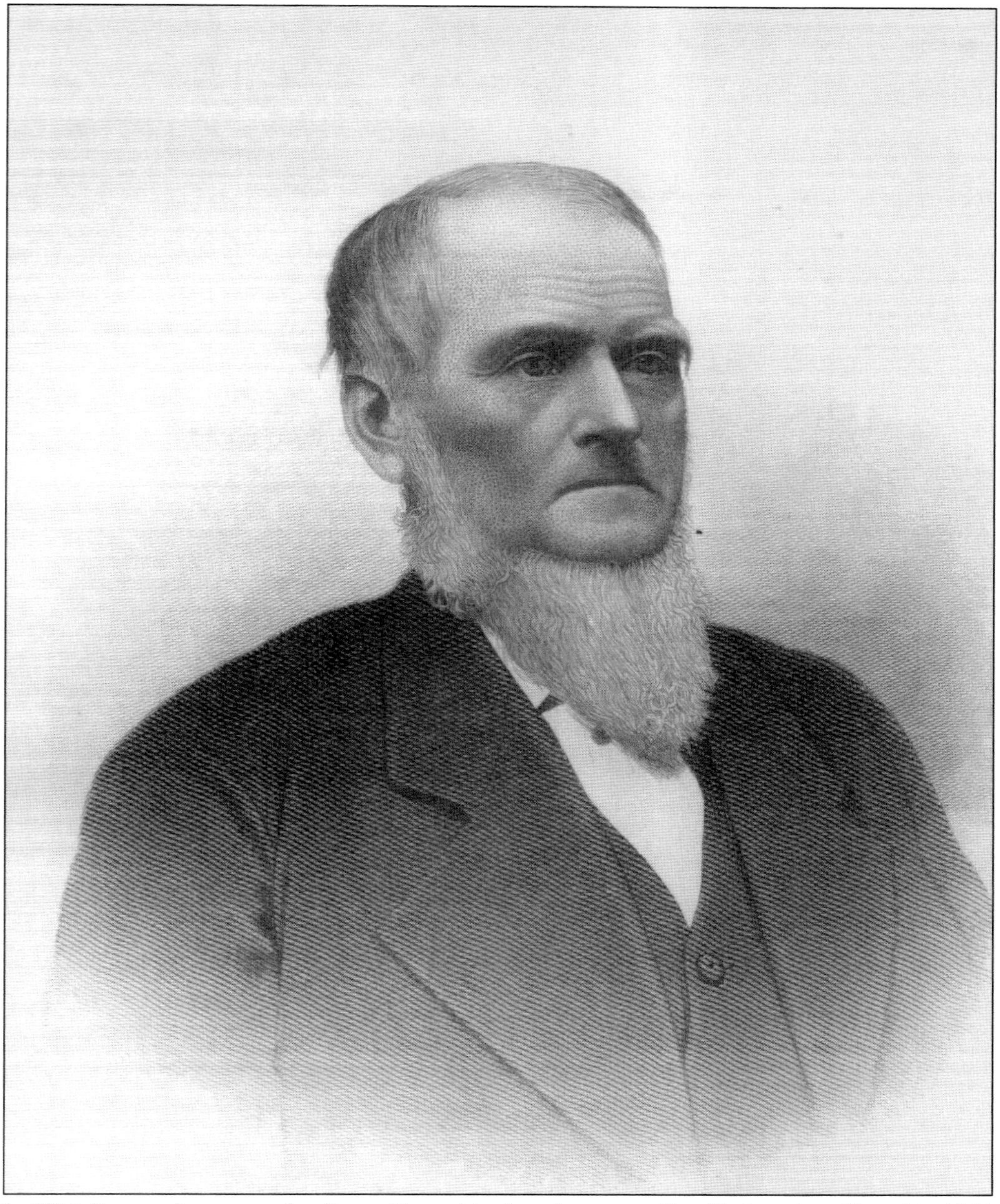

In 1836, Stewart Jr. returned to Rome Township, bought a sawmill, added a gristmill, and in 1844 added a woolen factory. According to Walker, "At one time he was the owner of four mills on the Hockhocking, and part of the time also cultivated five farms in Rome township [*sic*], raising as high as four thousand five hundred bushels of wheat in one year. He served as justice of the peace twenty-one years, and in 1860 was chosen presidential elector for this district." He owned the land that became the town on part of the original Stewart homestead and platted it in 1874 when the railroad came through. According to the *History of Hocking Valley, Ohio*, the post office was called Federalton prior to the establishment of the town of Stewart. This picture of D.B. Stewart is from the *History of Hocking Valley, Ohio*, and appears on a flyleaf between pages 258 and 259.

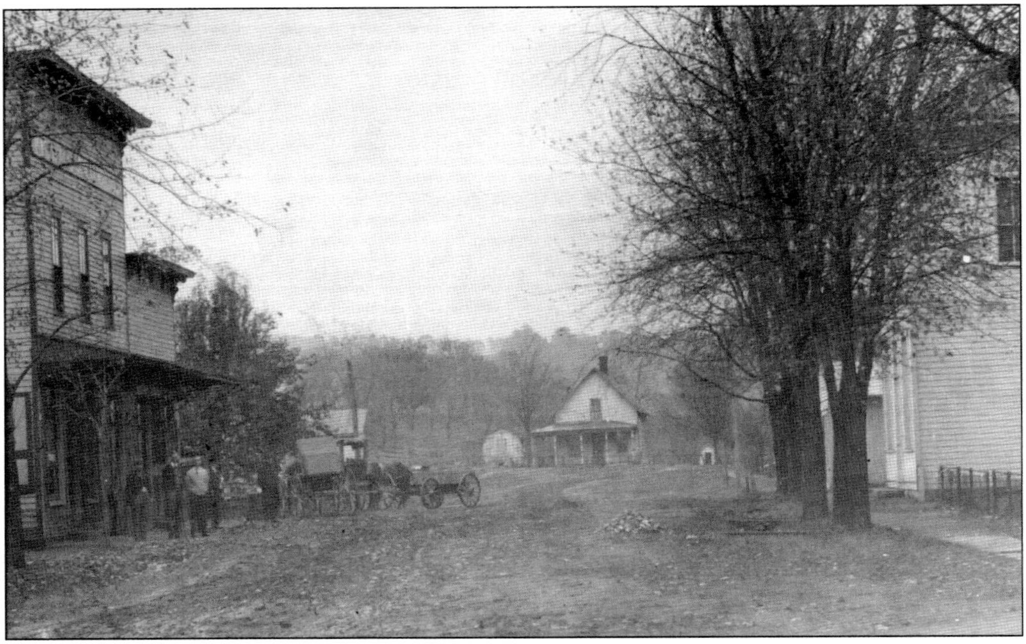

The Harvey Smith Store once stood on Elm Street in Stewart. It is known that by 1883 the town had a church, a flouring mill owned by Mrs. Ruth Byron, a planing mill owned by D.B. Stewart, physician Dr. W.E. Webb, two stores owned by H.G. Smith and S.N. Hobson, and a post office run by S.N. Hobson.

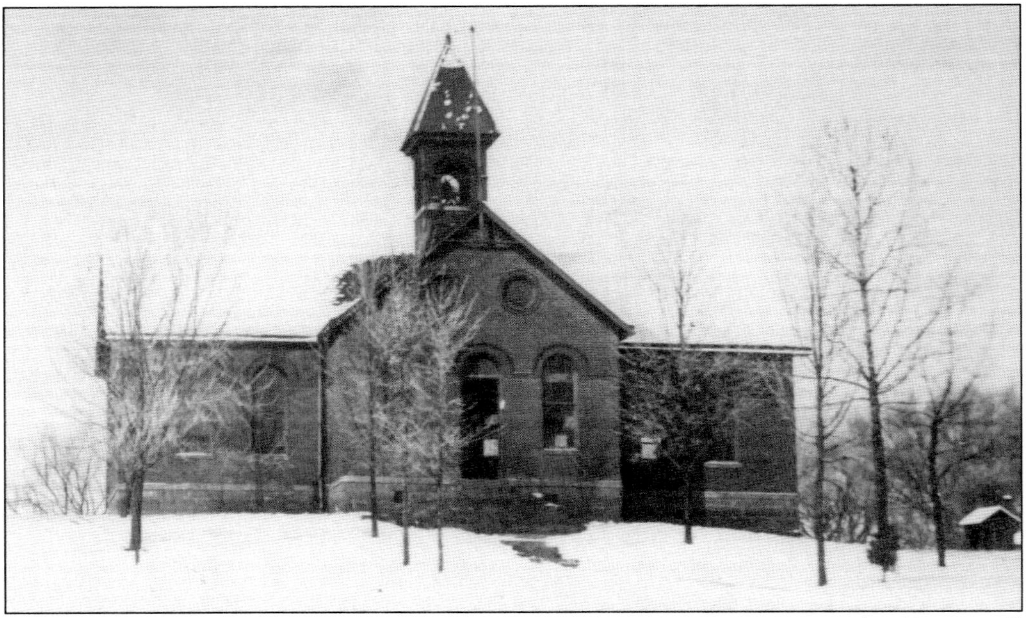

One of the more interesting buildings in the town is the old 1897 two-room schoolhouse still in reasonably good shape and worthy of restoration. This picture, dated 1915, shows its original appearance. Buildings were added to the property in 1922, 1934, and 1938. The 1922 update removed the front portico of the original building but retained the essential schoolhouse, steeple, and bell. The buildings were in full use until 1998 for education and have been used since for other purposes.

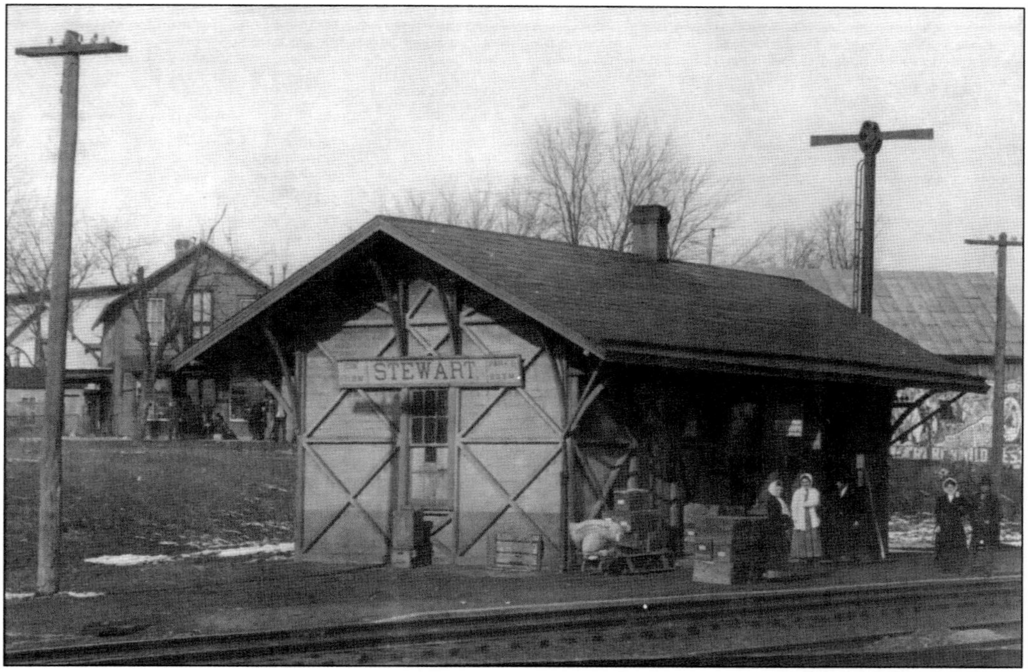

Shown here is the Stewart Railroad Station around 1910. D.B. Stewart Jr. was a shareholder in the M&C Railroad. According to Beatty and Stone, when Stewart learned that the B&O short line would be bringing a track through the Hocking Valley, Stewart made plans to build a railroad through the Federal Creek Valley to join the new line "at the town he would lay out on family land."

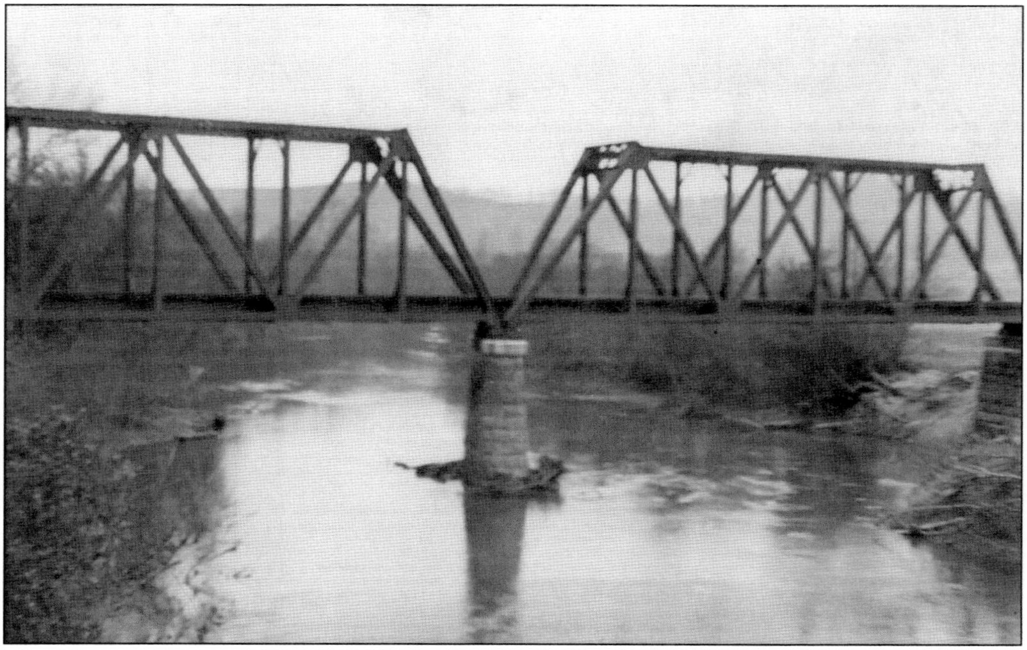

This 1909 picture shows the railroad bridge crossing the Hocking River at Stewart. The railroad that had been built to come down the Federal Creek Valley carried coal out of the Sharpsburg and Lathrop areas and connected with the Marietta & Cincinnati lines through Kilvert and Stewart.

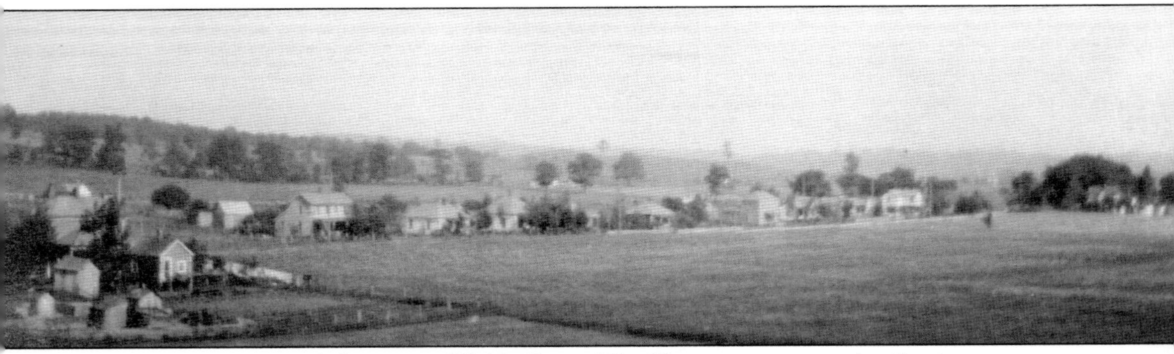

The Plains. Formerly known as Wolf's Plains, The Plains is most noted as "an important center for the American Indian," according to Beatty and Stone. Numerous Indian mounds and ritual circles once dotted the landscape here. Anna C. Rose and others affirm that Christopher Wolf once owned the area, having purchased it "from William and Hannah Martin, and for payment, they received a pony, a pair of buckskin breeches, and two gallons of whiskey." Prior to Wolf's ownership, the area had been referred to as Hickory Glades. Wolf sold all of his property, including his beautiful brick home, and moved to what is now Haydenville in the late 1830s. Wolf's Plains ultimately was shortened to The Plains. According to Rose, a post office was not in place until one was removed from Beaumont and transferred to Wolf's Plains in 1908. This image provides a view of The Plains in 1952 and suggests why it is named as it is.

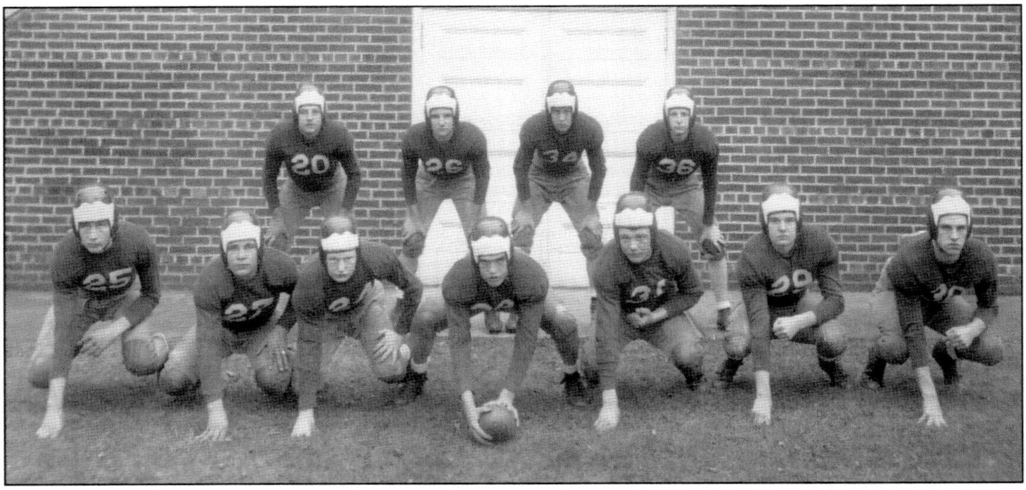

The Plains has become closely associated with the city of Athens because of the close proximity of the two communities. Athens High School is located in The Plains, and its auditorium and sports fields are a major part of the life in Athens, The Plains, and other communities in the county. The Athens Messenger Building is also in The Plains; the *Athens Messenger* newspaper (long housed in the city of Athens) continues to report city and county history.

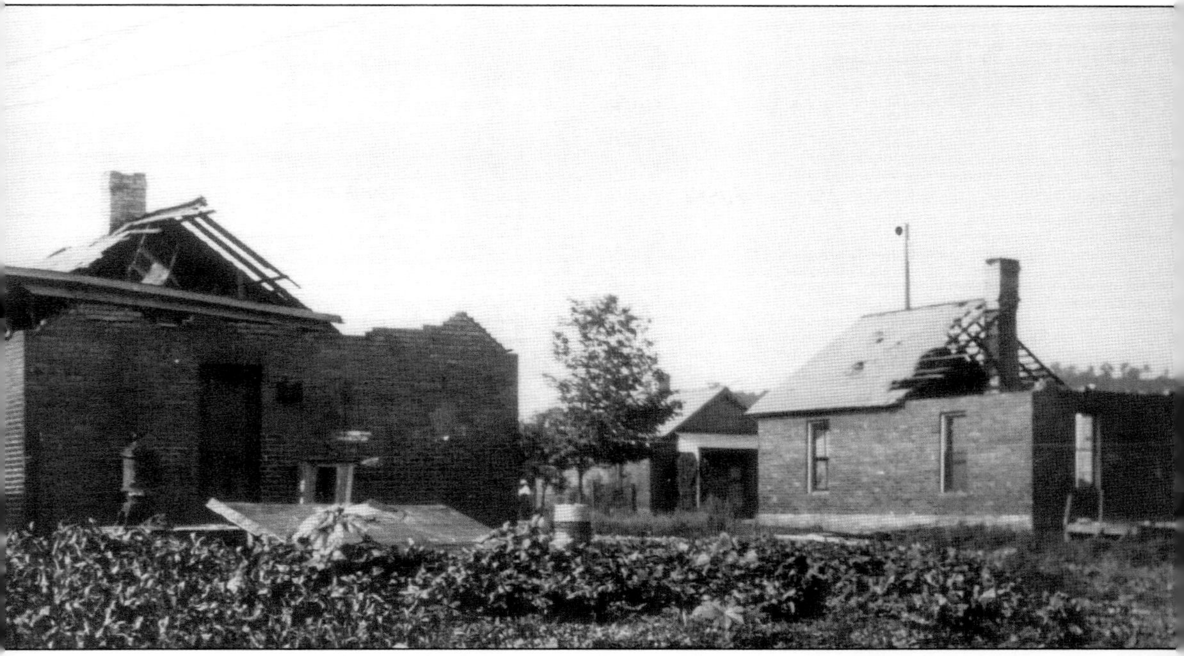

In September 2010, tornados touched down in Athens and in The Plains, causing significant destruction. Basil Rutter Field at the high school was almost completely destroyed, and portions of the Athens Messenger Building's roof were blown away. It has taken a year of focused community effort to restore the damages. The devastation of the 2010 tornado was similar to a tornado that took place in nearby Chauncey many years ago pictured here.

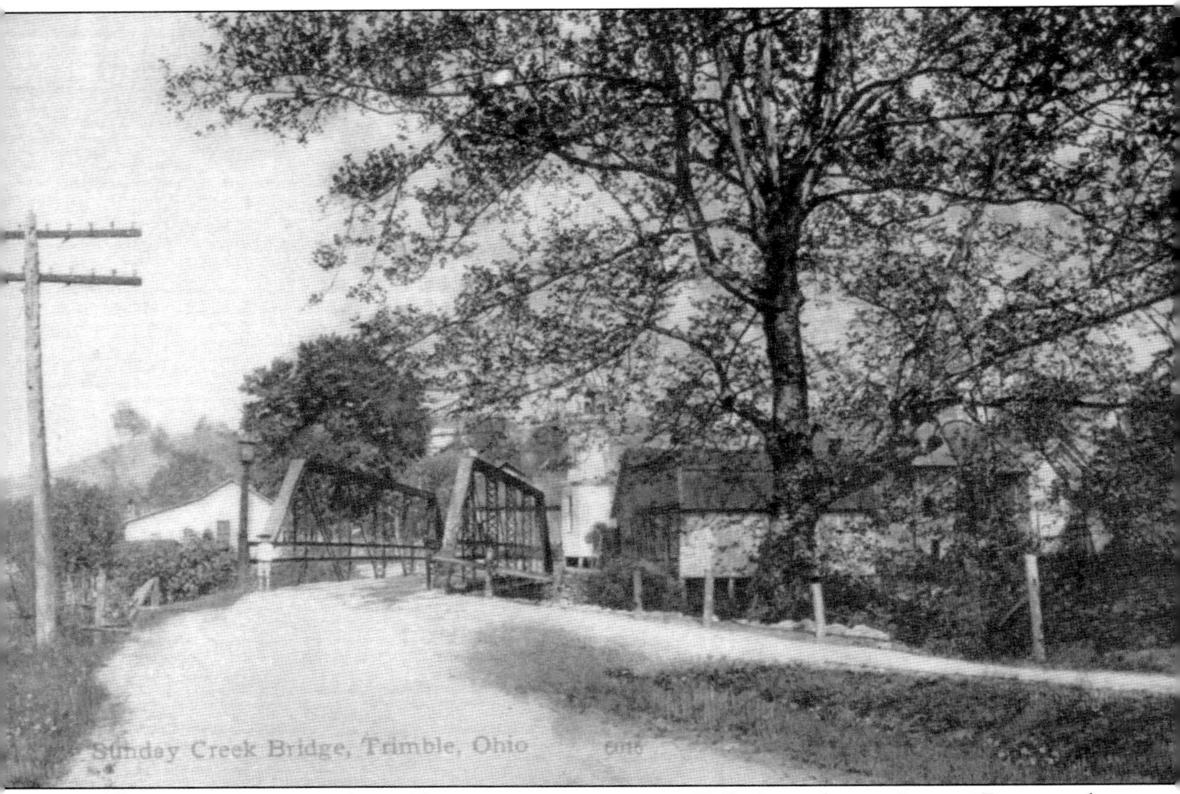

TRIMBLE. The town of Trimble came into existence in 1841. According to Peters, "For a number of years . . . it [current-day Trimble] was known as 'Oxford' from the fact that a man by the name of Watkins, who had stolen an ox near Logan, while on his way to McConnellsville to sell it, was overtaken by a vigilance committee at Trimble where he forced the ox to ford the swollen Sunday Creek." How Peters verified the story is not known, and it raises questions about whether or not the Watkins referred to by Peters was the same Watkins who is known to have built a mill at the site. Walker states, "In 1825 Jonathan Watkins built a mill at the village. . . . It was at first only a saw mill, but, after two or three years, a gristmill was connected with it . . . [and] continued to be the principal one in the township till 1865, when it was destroyed by fire." This picture is of the Sunday Creek Bridge in Trimble.

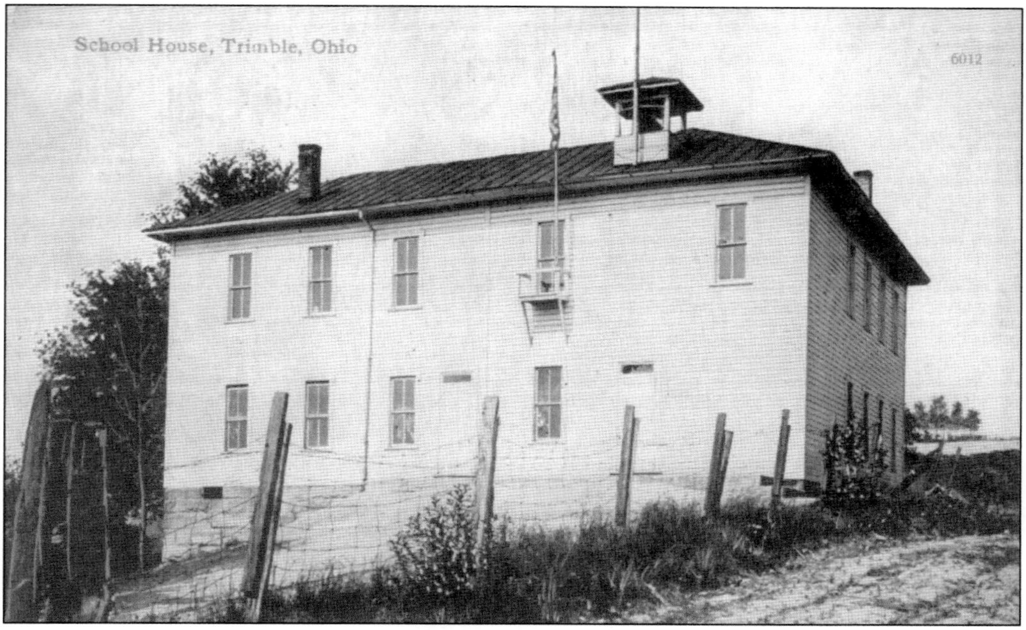

This image is of the old schoolhouse in Trimble. Because of transportation issues, it was common for even small towns like Trimble to have a school to meet the needs of its people for education. When travel improved and busing came into being, consolidation began and many of the small-town schools disappeared. Not much information is readily available about this school. Unfortunately, it was razed long ago.

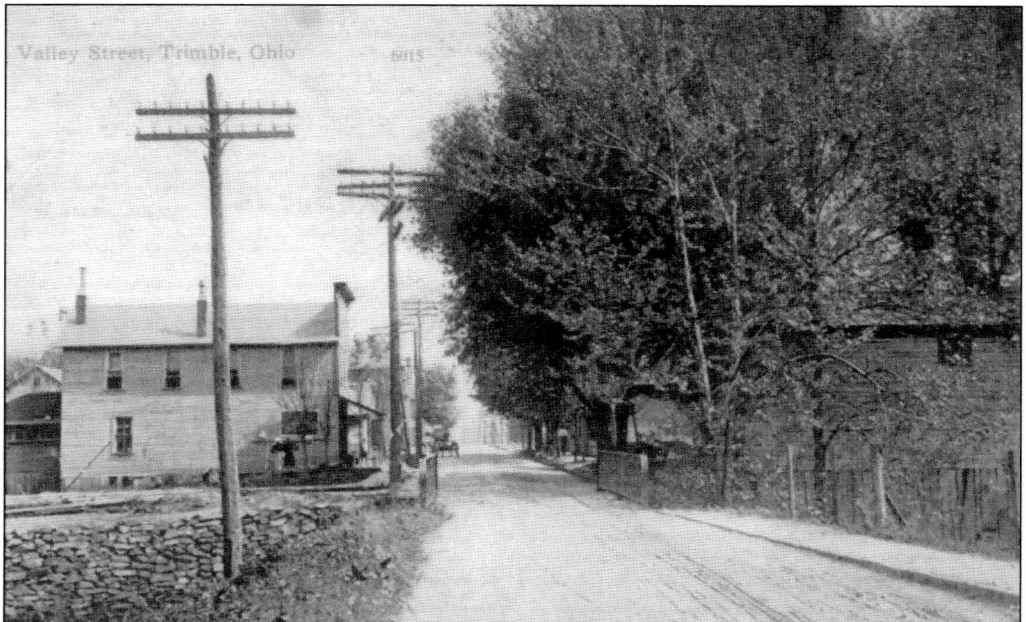

Brick making and coal mining were major factors in the successes of Trimble; however, unlike its neighbors, Trimble remained largely agrarian in nature and remained relatively stable despite the ups and downs of mining and the depletion of shale product for brick making. Pictured is Valley Street in Trimble.

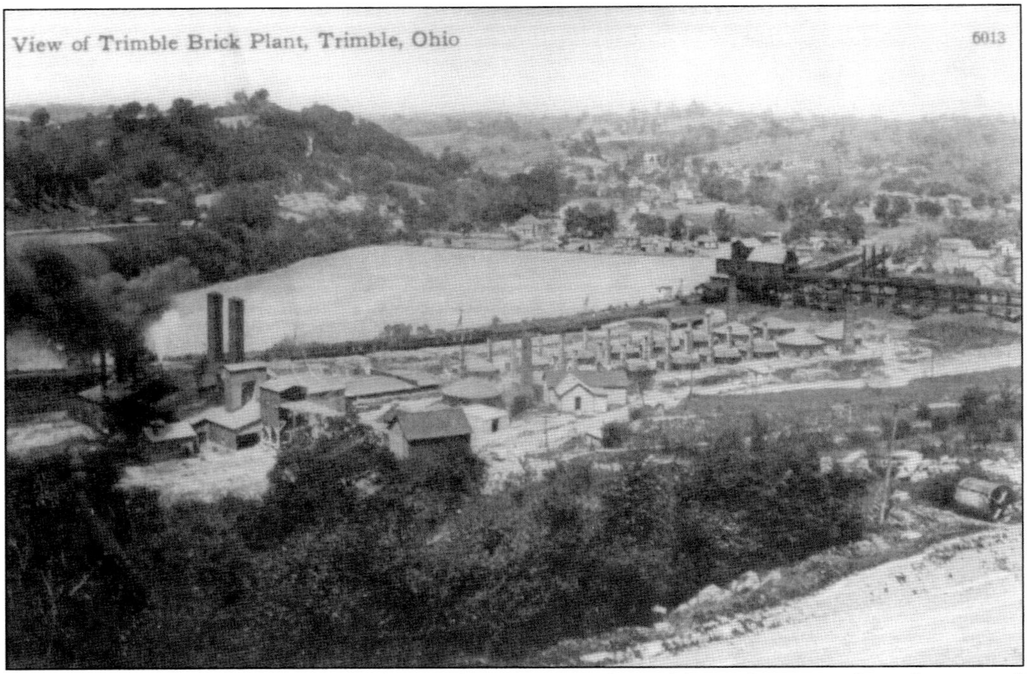

The Trimble Brick Factory is shown here. The area around Trimble was known to have "immense" deposits of fireclay. According to historians Beatty and Stone, the plant shown here was started around 1900 by Thomas Mason, Isaac Lafolet, and William Hyde. The plant operated for approximately 20 to 30 years until the shale (needed for brick production) was depleted from nearby hillsides.

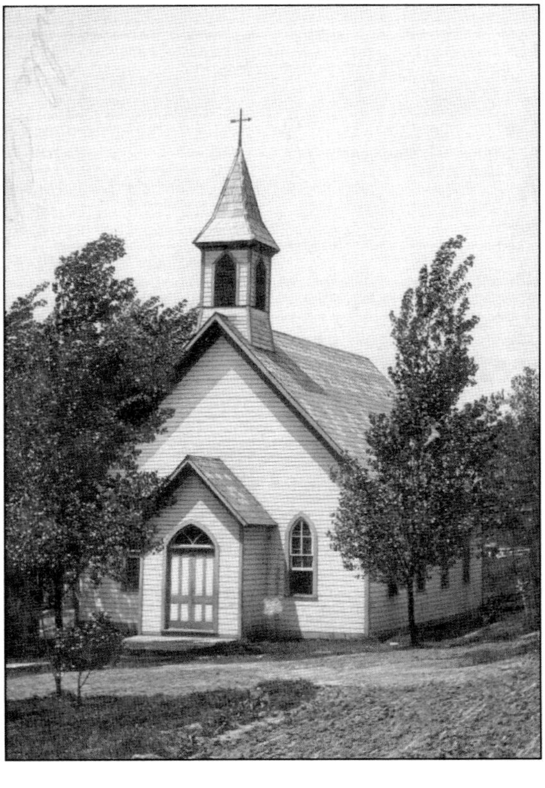

This picture of the Trimble Methodist Church dates to about 1914. Walker states that "the establishment of the Methodist church . . . [in Athens County] . . . antedates that of any other religious society." However, the Baptists and other Christian denominations have found their way into Trimble Township and the town of Trimble over the years.

Four

Athens County in Times of Trouble

Athens County, like every other place in the world, is vulnerable to the effects of time, Mother Nature's wrath, and man-made disasters.

The region has been particularly hard hit by flooding, a result of the Hocking River Valley's numerous hills force-feeding their runoff into creeks, streams, and the river. Great floods took place in 1832, 1847, 1858, 1873, 1907, and 1913. Though the channel of the Hocking River was moved by the Army Corps of Engineers around Athens to limit flooding in the 1960s, the county still suffers frequent spring flooding.

Fires have been caused by the misdeeds and carelessness of human beings and through the power of lightening. In 1854, fire destroyed the Eagle Hotel in Athens. In 1877, a blaze consumed a significant section of downtown Athens. Fires have taken buildings in Nelsonville, New Marshfield, Albany, and in many other parts of Athens County. Many structures and some lives have been lost to history as a result.

High winds occasionally cause problems as well. Though Athens County is nestled in the hills, tornadoes have struck several times. As recently as 2010, a tornado touched down in The Plains and in Athens destroying trees and property and costing insurance companies and taxpayers millions of dollars. The following pictures offer a quick glimpse into a few such events.

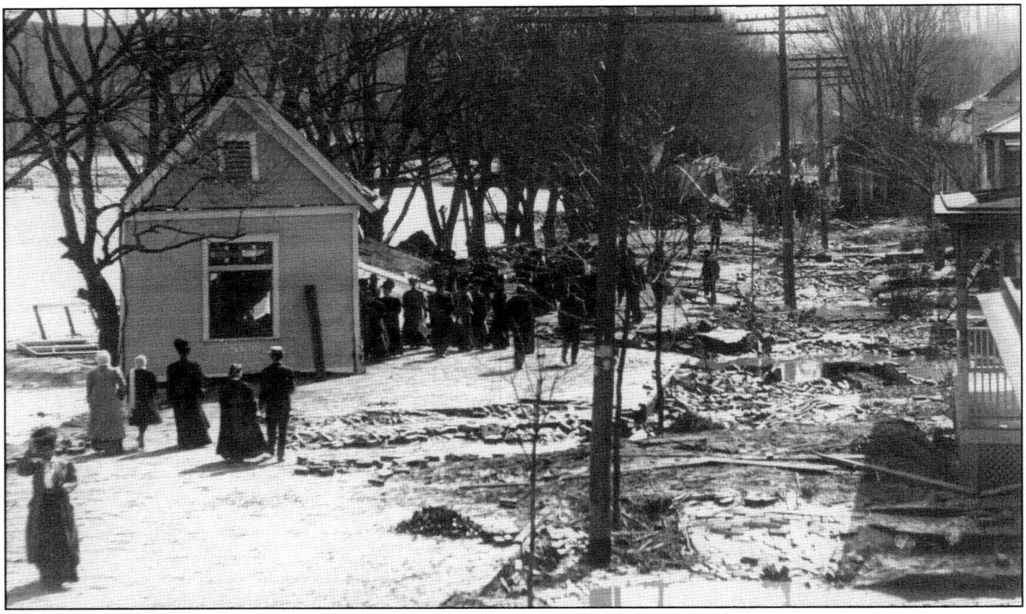

Here is Athens during the 1907 flood. Until the river was moved in the 1960s, flooding, like that of 1907, caused significant damage, particularly in the low-lying areas. Today, people drive down Richland Avenue not knowing that this area west of Athens met the kind of destruction shown here. Many homes, barns, animals, furniture, and irreplaceable personal items were lost.

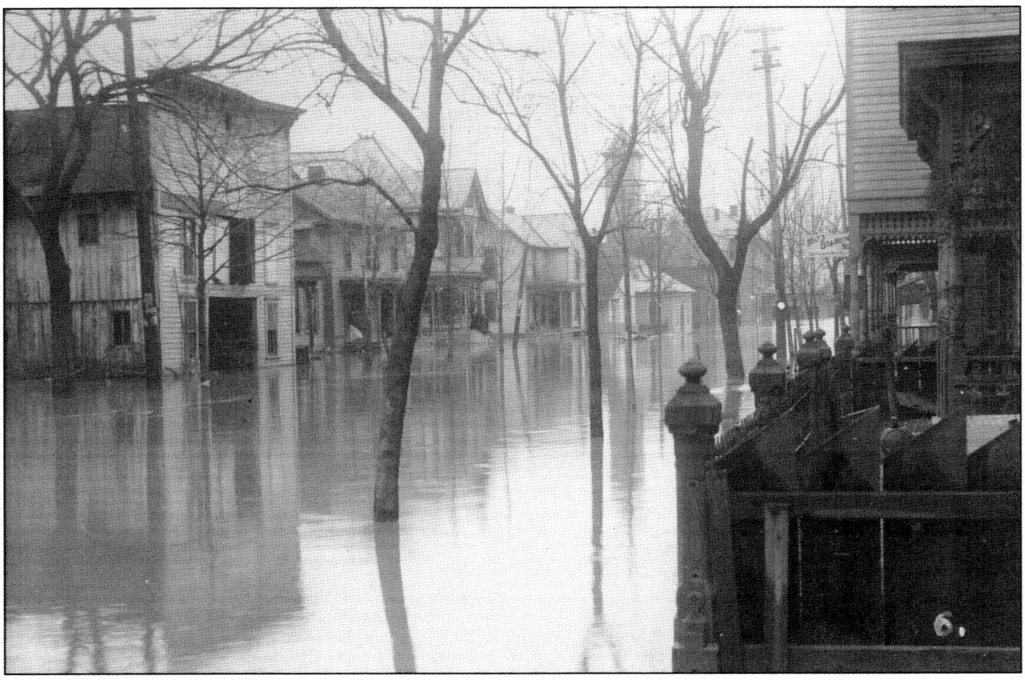

Here is Fayette Street, in Nelsonville, near Knights Livery Barn during the 1907 flood. Photographers seemed particularly drawn to Nelsonville during this great flood. The Athens County Historical Society and Museum has a good number of images of the city during that horrendous time. The author once owned a lovely old house that sits on Fayette Street, not far from where this picture was taken, and did not know it had once sat three to four feet deep in the floodwaters.

This image shows some of the rebuilding of the brick street at Robbins Big Store, in Nelsonville, after the 1907 flood. The store was located on Columbus Street at the end of the Public Square. The bricks have probably been heaved by the floodwaters. The workers, after making repairs on the building, would carefully lay the bricks back in place. Brick streets still exist throughout downtown Nelsonville and Athens.

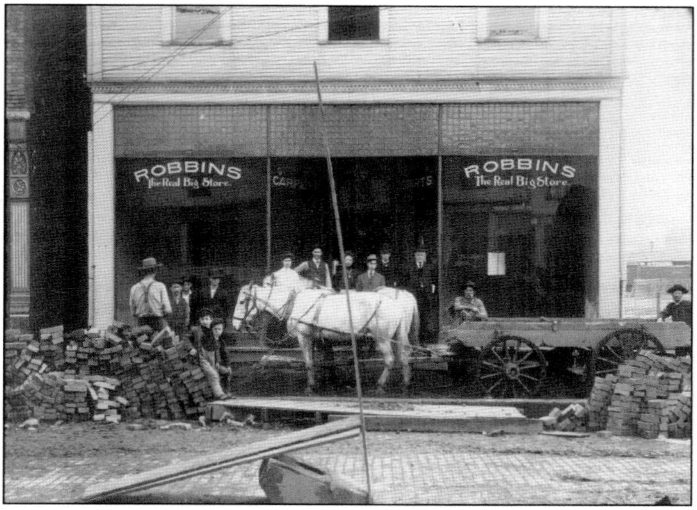

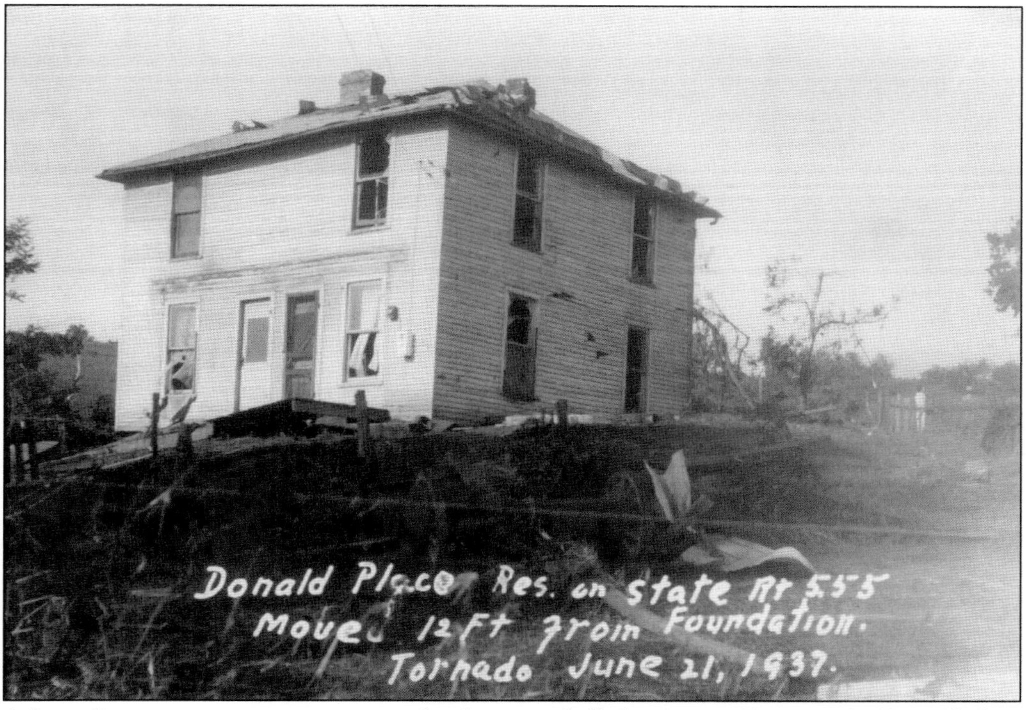

Athens County is not immune to tornados despite its hilly landscape. Shown is the Donald Place residence on Route 555, which was struck by a tornado in 1937; the house was moved 12 feet from its foundation. This tornado did tremendous damage (killing three people) and completely destroyed the area formerly known as Tablertown. It hit The Plains, Chauncey, Kilvert, and many rural areas of the county. This kind of destruction was experienced again in 2010 when numerous trees were uprooted, snapped like sticks, and thrown great distances, as were cars, mobile homes, parts of buildings, and so on. Numerous people were sent to nearby hospitals. Athens High School's Basil Rutter Field was completely destroyed, and the McKinstry Garage in Athens was completely lost. The field has been replaced, as has McKinstry's, but it will take years for people to let this episode become just another part of history.

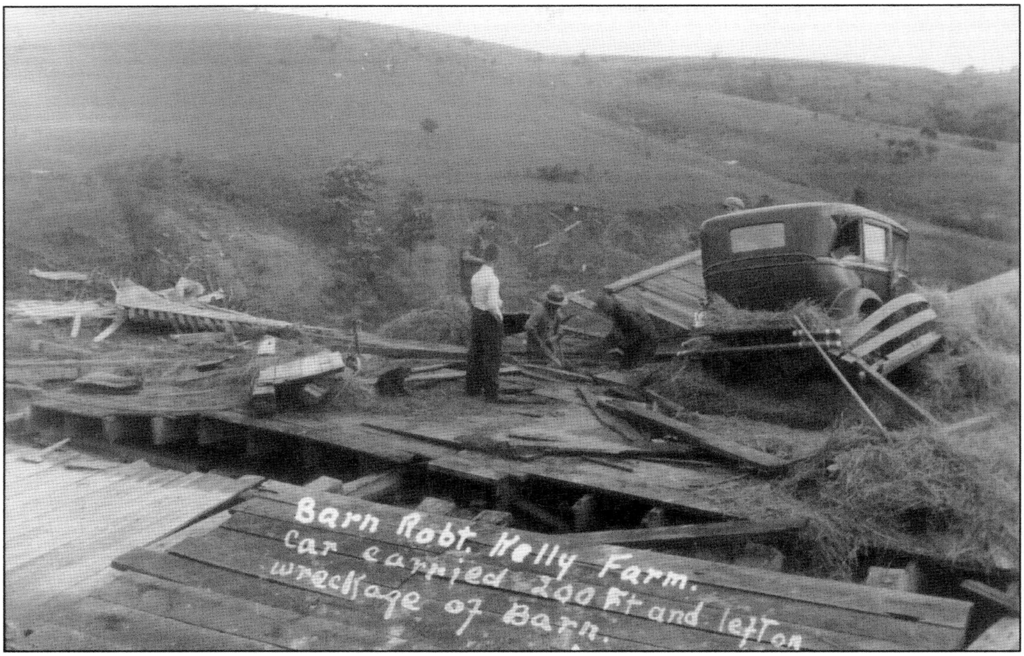

The Robert Kelly farm was hit during the 1937 tornado. The family car was carried 200 feet and dropped on what remained of the barn. This kind of destruction was to be seen in much of Athens County, including Nelsonville and The Plains, and caused numerous hardships. On the more positive side, local newspapers made money from insurance companies advertising to sell policies for tornado damage in case of future events.

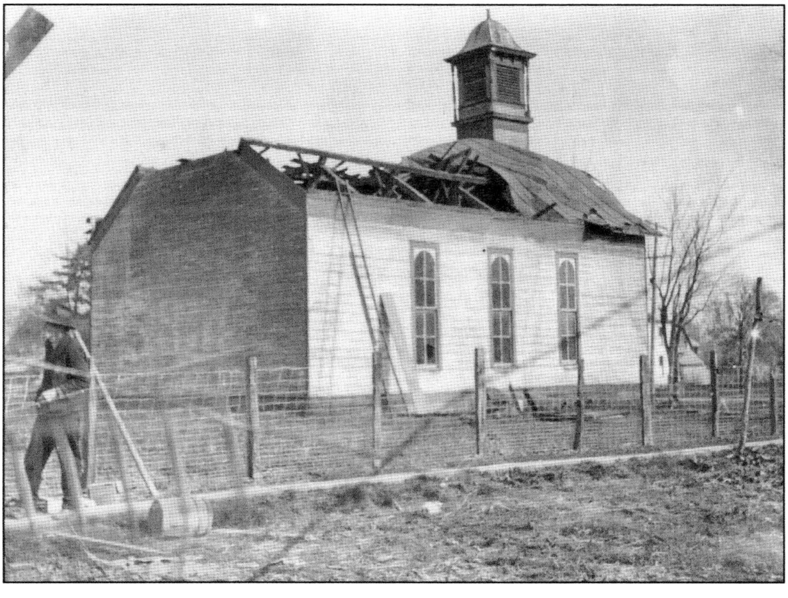

The Albany Baptist Church was hit by a cyclone on April 7, 1922. Writing on the back of the photograph states that a Mr. Rife is out front. The Free Will Baptist Church of Albany "is the oldest church society in the village." Ira Z. Haning founded the society about 1854, and the building was erected about 1857.

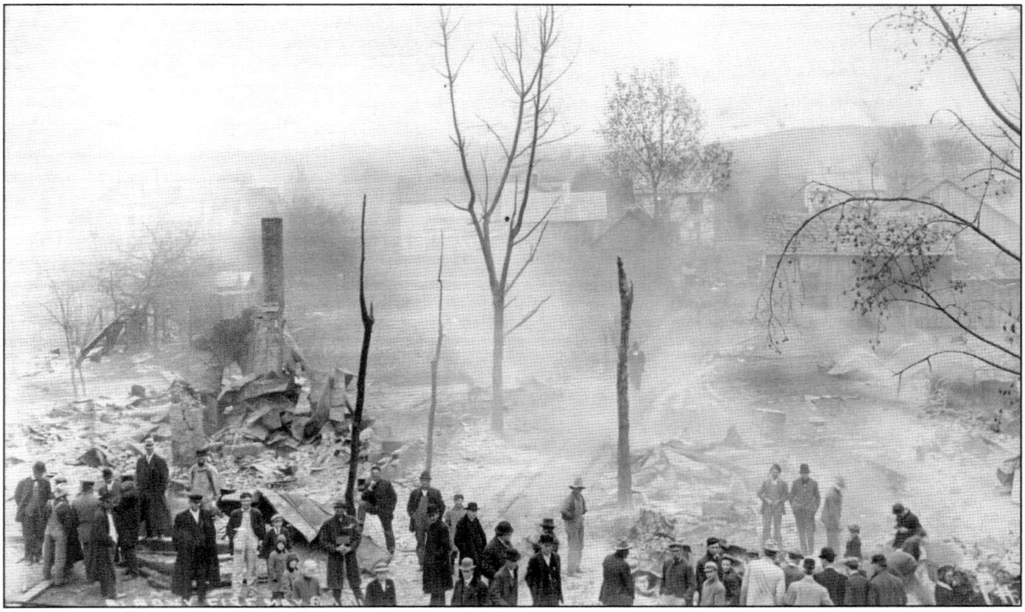

At approximately 5:00 a.m. on May 2, 1911, the town of Albany was struck by fire. The fire was first discovered in the Luster Fought wholesale and retail house. Six stores, a hotel, and residences were lost in the devastating blaze. Among the buildings lost was one containing the office of Dr. G.D. Swett with an apartment above it rented out to W.B. Rutherford.

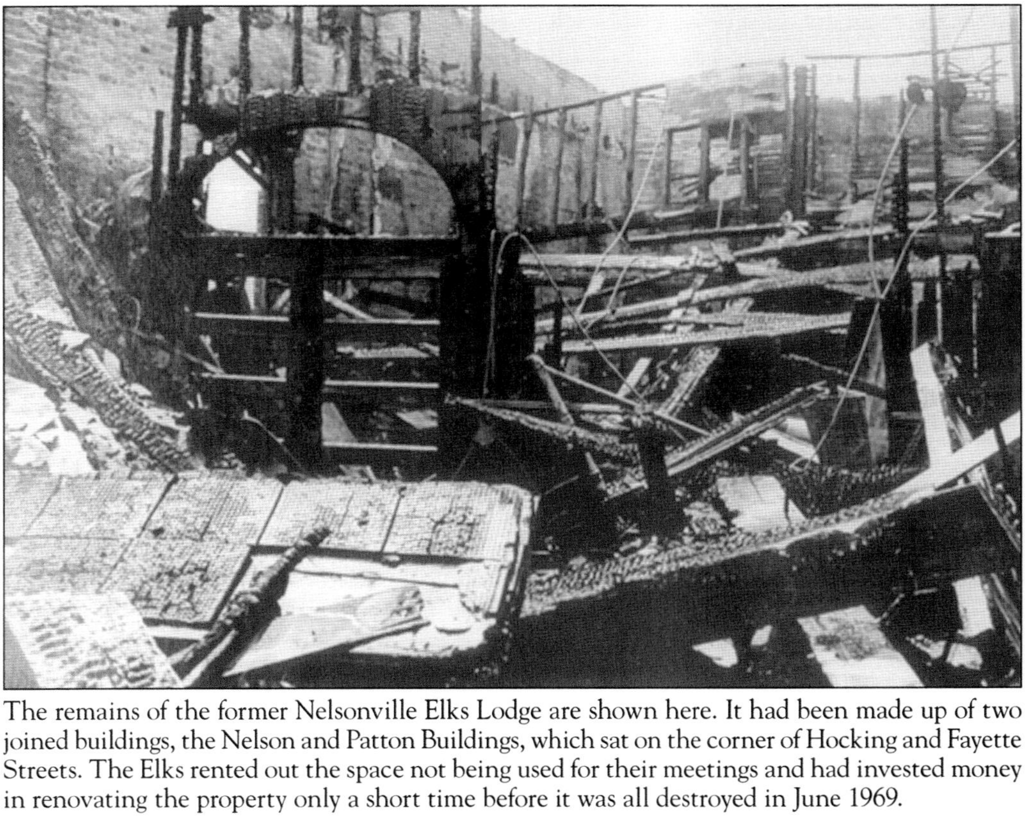

The remains of the former Nelsonville Elks Lodge are shown here. It had been made up of two joined buildings, the Nelson and Patton Buildings, which sat on the corner of Hocking and Fayette Streets. The Elks rented out the space not being used for their meetings and had invested money in renovating the property only a short time before it was all destroyed in June 1969.

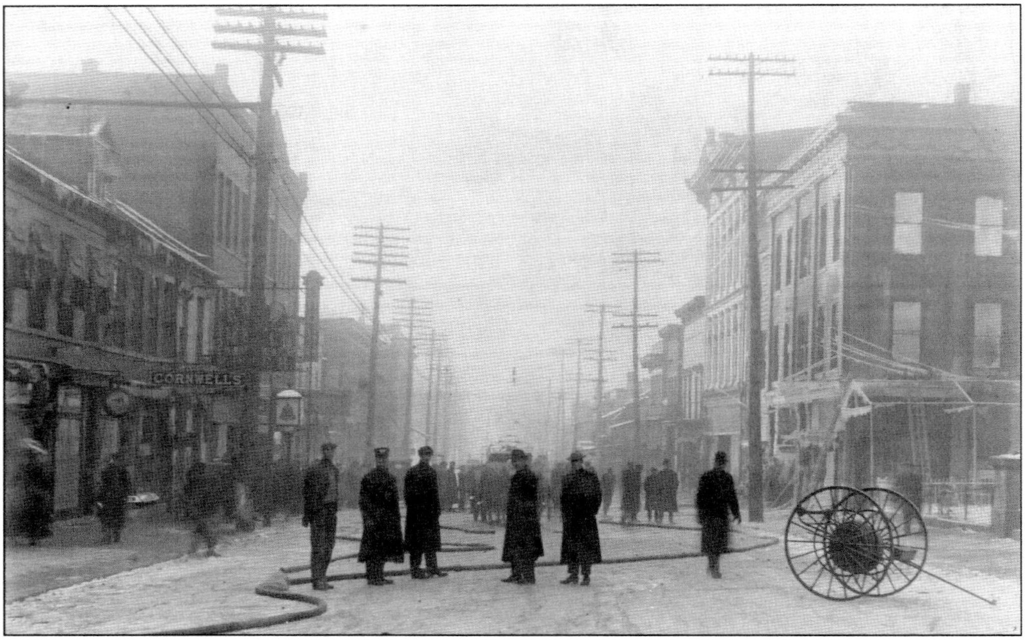

The Cline Building in Athens was severely damaged in February 1912. According to Robert Daniel, only the four outer walls were left after the fire. Thus, Cline "promptly cleared the site, then rebuilt." Included in the new building was an elegant soda fountain. This probably provided a great place for people to congregate and spend time over a delicious fountain drink.

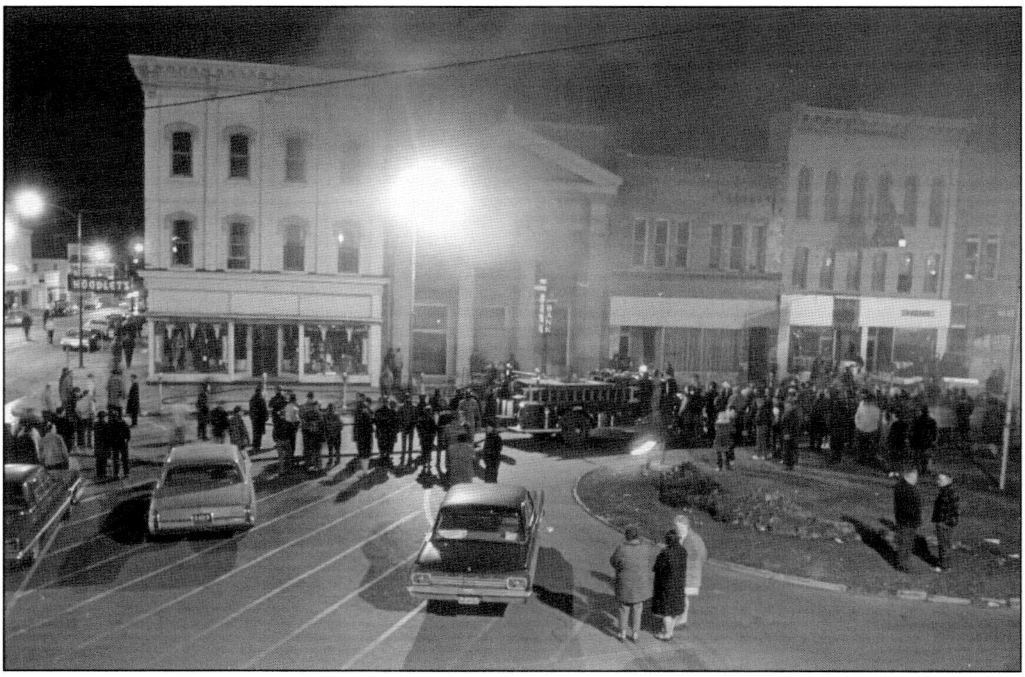

The First National Bank in Nelsonville caught fire on February 19, 1968. Fortunately, the building was saved and repaired. This bank was first the Merchant and Miners' Bank going back to the days of coal mining in Athens County. The bank took over the building on the corner (once Hoodlett's store) to the left and now uses that space for offices and loan transactions.

Five

Select Images of Athens County's Past

From its meager beginnings, Athens County has built a remarkable history worthy of entire books. Limiting that history to a single slim volume leaves much unsaid and much more to explore. The past holds many secrets, providing limitless opportunities for inquiry. We all have a stake in knowing where we came from, who our ancestors are, how we came to think as we do, and how we came to be who we are as members of a county-wide community. The following images touch upon facets of Athens County history that may spark further interest.

If you live in Athens County, I encourage you to get involved and work to preserve our history, not only for ourselves but for those who come after us. If you live outside of Athens County, I encourage you to learn as much about your own county as you can. You will quickly find that you are part of a history rich in colorful characters and events as well as ideas and traditions.

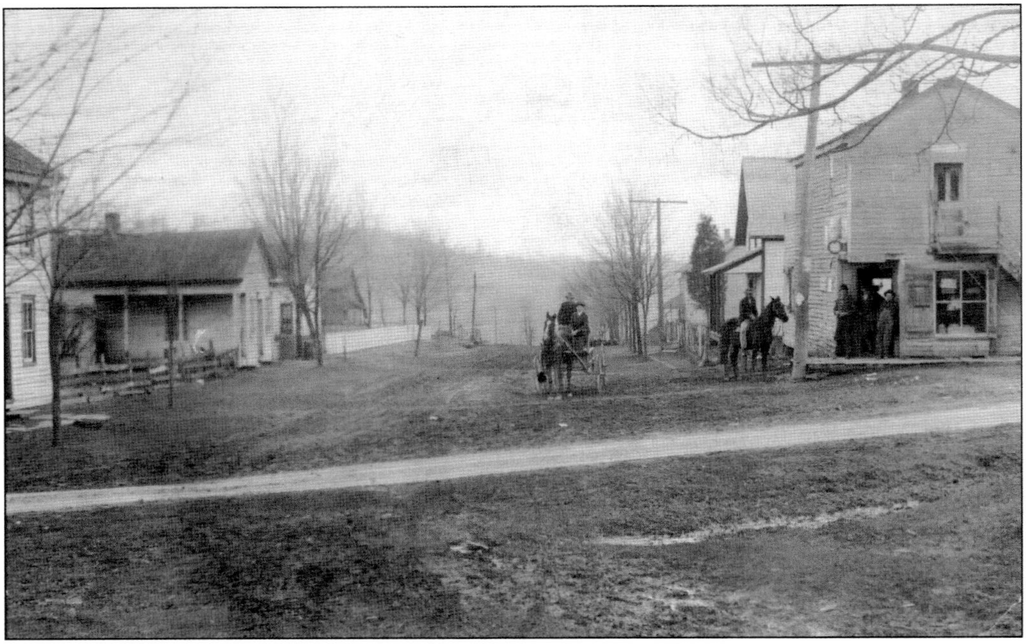

Shown here is the Hebbardsville Store in 1911. The town of Hebbardsville is located in the northwestern part of Alexander Township. The 1883 *History of Hocking Valley, Ohio*, mentions that there was a store and hotel kept by B. Bean, a blacksmith shop, a shoe shop, and a wagon shop. The principal cemetery is located by the Cumberland Presbyterian Church. (Courtesy of the Anastas Collection.)

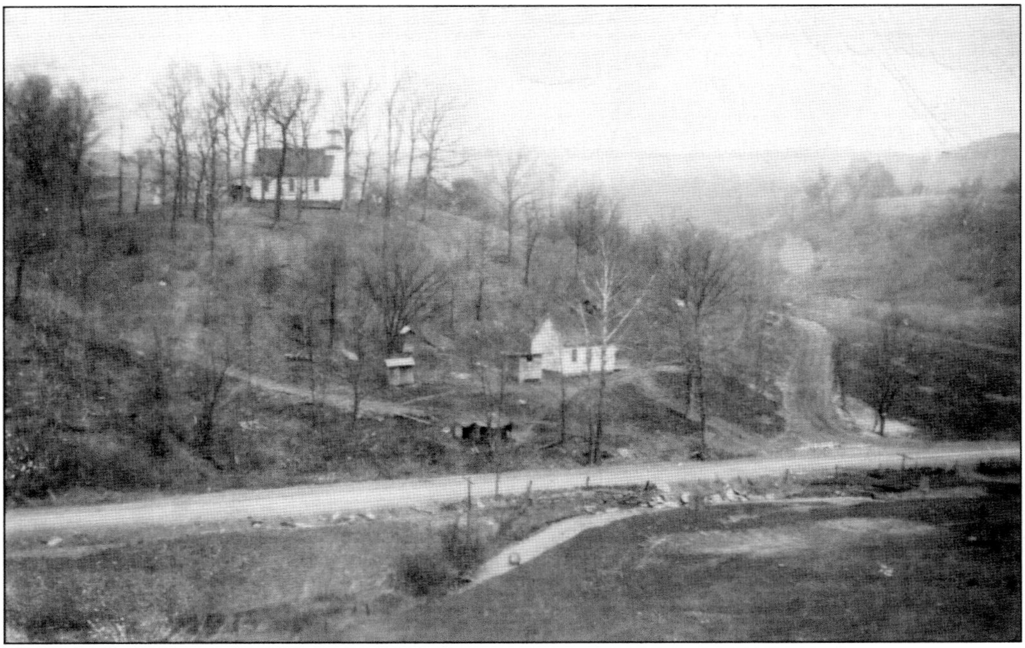

The McDougal Church and Hixon School stood on barren hills in 1942; today, the area is covered with trees. The church was built in 1883 by Harvey Wade Nye of Chauncey. Enoch Moore did the plastering, and Mr. McDougal donated the land. The first "settled" pastor was Rev. C.F. Matheny.

The Newsom and Brooks Undertakers business was located on West Union Street in Athens from 1906 to 1909. Mr. Newsom is standing in the doorway in this image, and Mr. Brooks is in the carriage. After 1909, the business moved to Court Street. The building to the left of the undertaker's business is the old Elk Hotel.

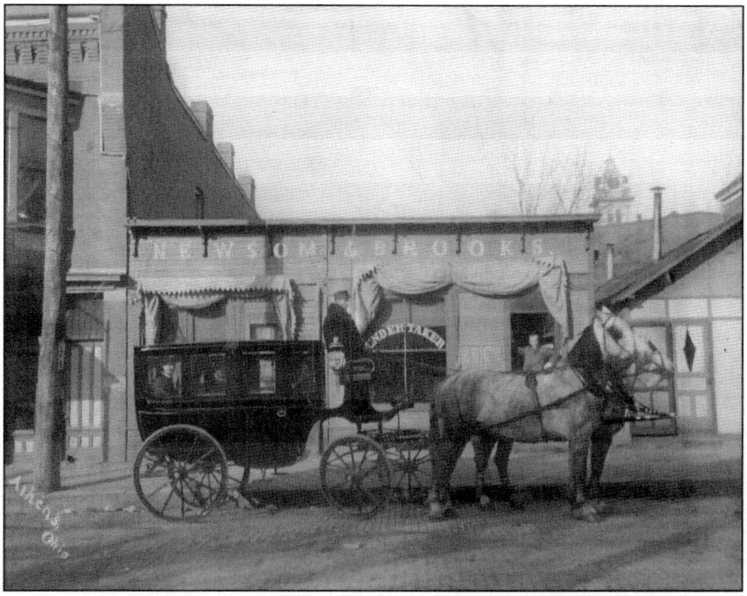

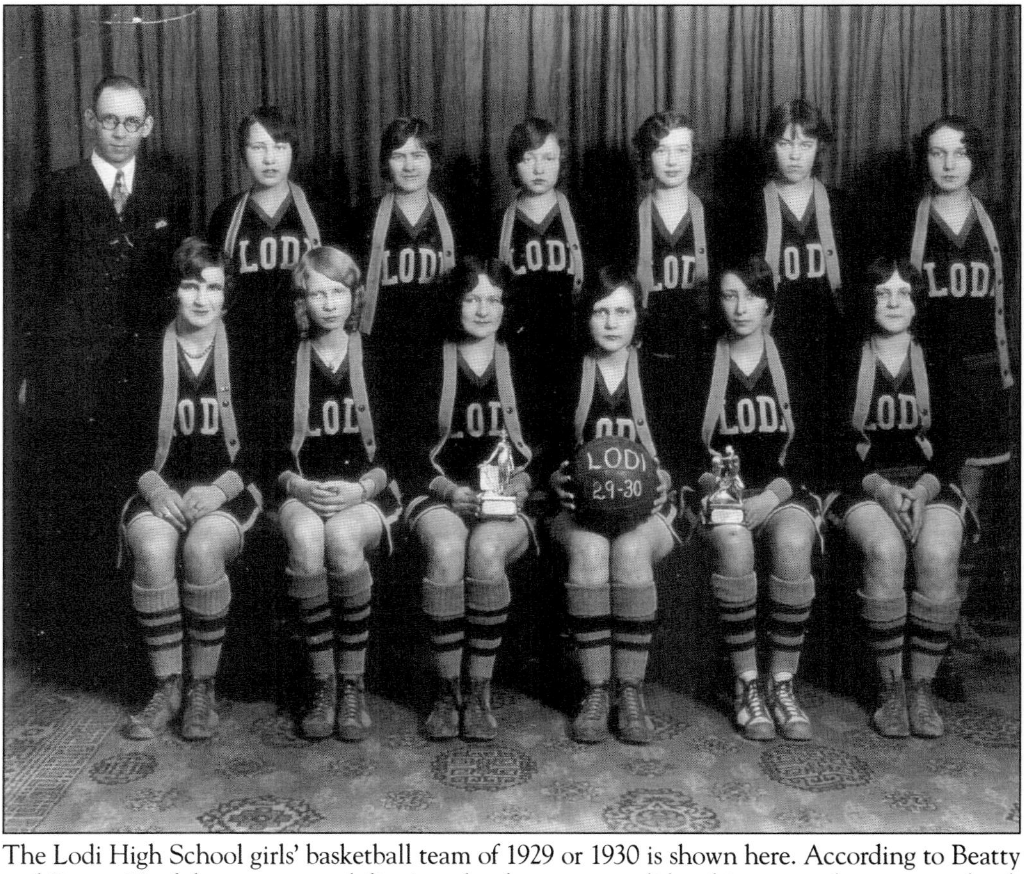

The Lodi High School girls' basketball team of 1929 or 1930 is shown here. According to Beatty and Stone, 10 of the common subdistrict schools were consolidated into one elementary school, and a high school was opened in 1922. Both elementary and high school levels were taught in a two-story building. A new school was built in 1936–1937, and the old school was abandoned.

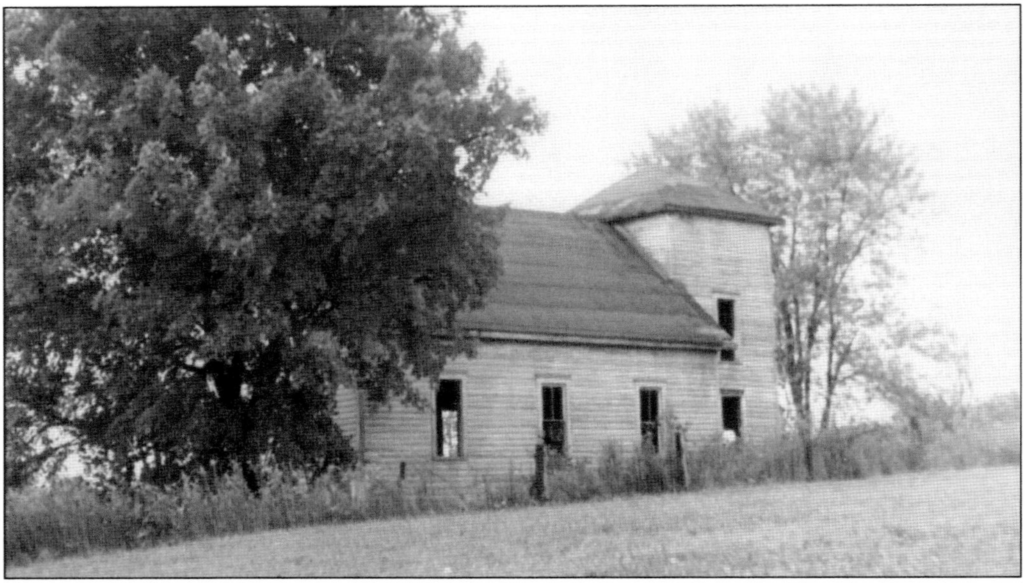

Pictured here is the Redtown Finnish Evangelical Lutheran Church. This building was first the main building of the Weethee Academy. When the academy closed, the building was removed to this site. The first "settled" clergyman was Kalle Salorvara (trained in Finland), serving from 1901 to 1910. The building was dedicated and consecrated in 1901. (Courtesy of the Anastas Collection.)

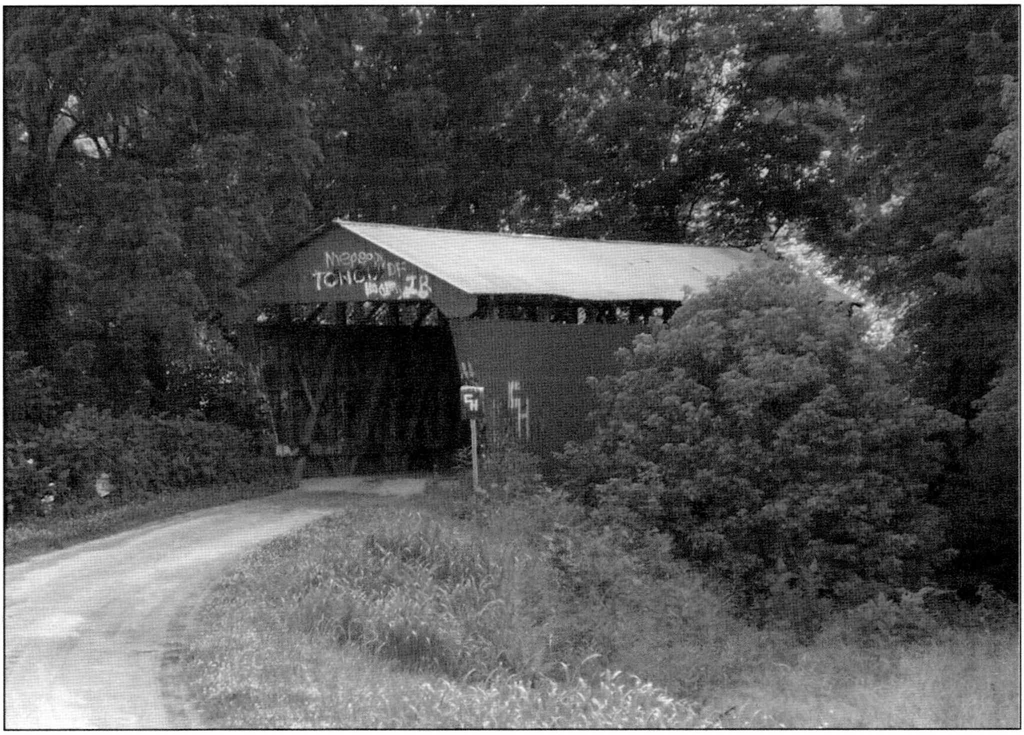

As of 2012, Athens County has only three covered bridges remaining: the Kidwell Bridge, the Palos Bridge, and the Blackwood Bridge; shown here is the Blackwood. At one time, covered bridges were commonplace, and very long covered bridges once spanned the Hocking River at Nelsonville and at Athens. This photograph was taken in 2011. (Author's collection.)

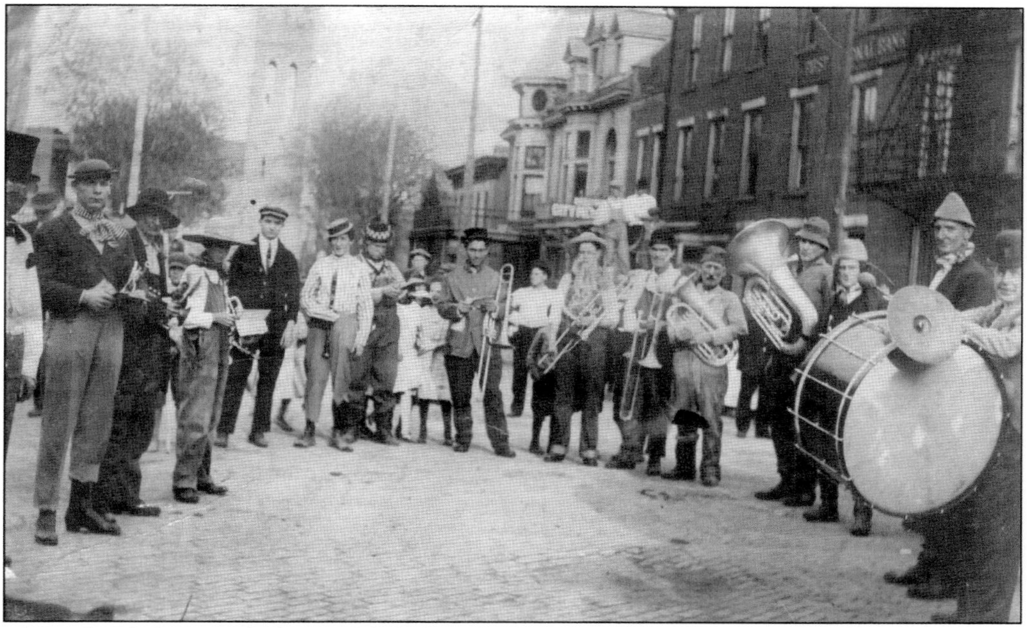

The undated photograph above is labeled "Old Athens City Band." The clothing would suggest that this group is having a fun time without a lot of formality standing in the middle of the intersection of Court and Washington Streets. The building to the right is the first version of three banks that have stood on that corner since the town's early history. The photograph below is of the Athens Band in 1915. Though others have not been identified, Clyde Mansfield has been named in the second row, second from the right. Bands appear to have been a great source of pleasure in the late 19th and early 20th centuries in Athens County. The Athens County Historical Society and Museum has pictures of bands in numerous townships, bands marching in parades, bands playing on the lawns of the Athens Asylum, men's bands and women's bands, and so on.

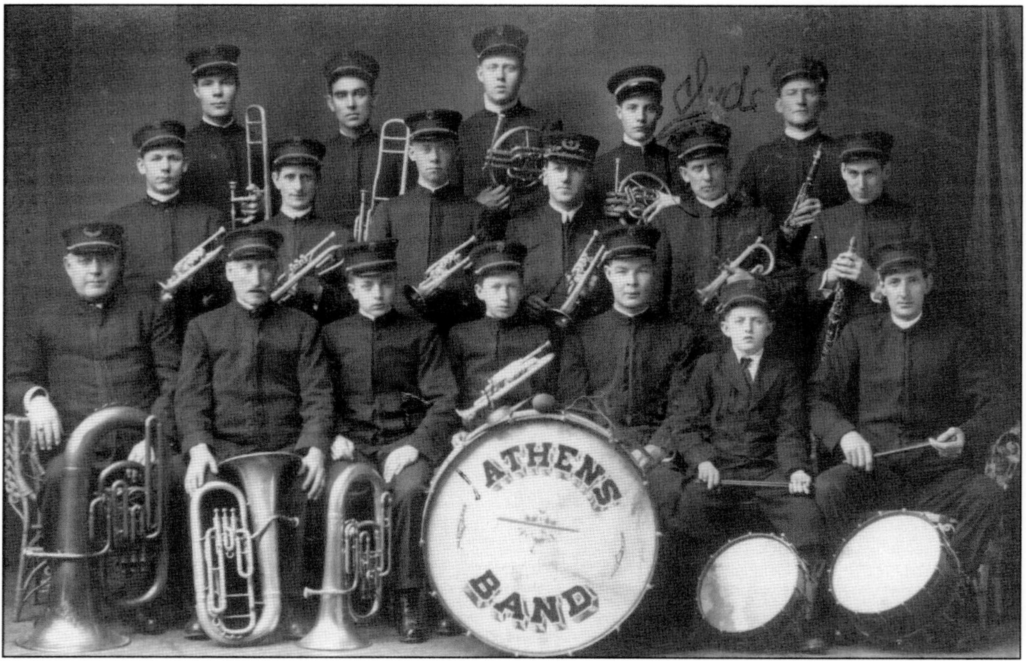

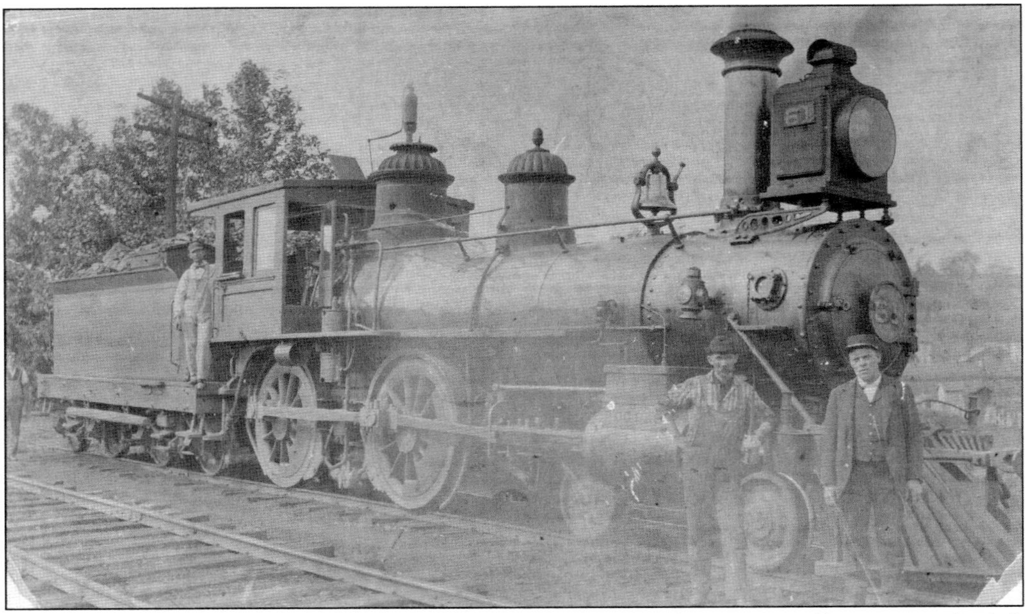

Shown here is the Hocking Valley Railroad Engine No. 61. Thomas R Mulligan is on the left (in foreground), and Marian Burnell Edgell is on the right. Plans for what would become the Hocking Valley Railroad began as early as 1852. A group of financiers (including Thomas Ewing) organized in 1864. By 1869, the trains were hauling coal out of Nelsonville.

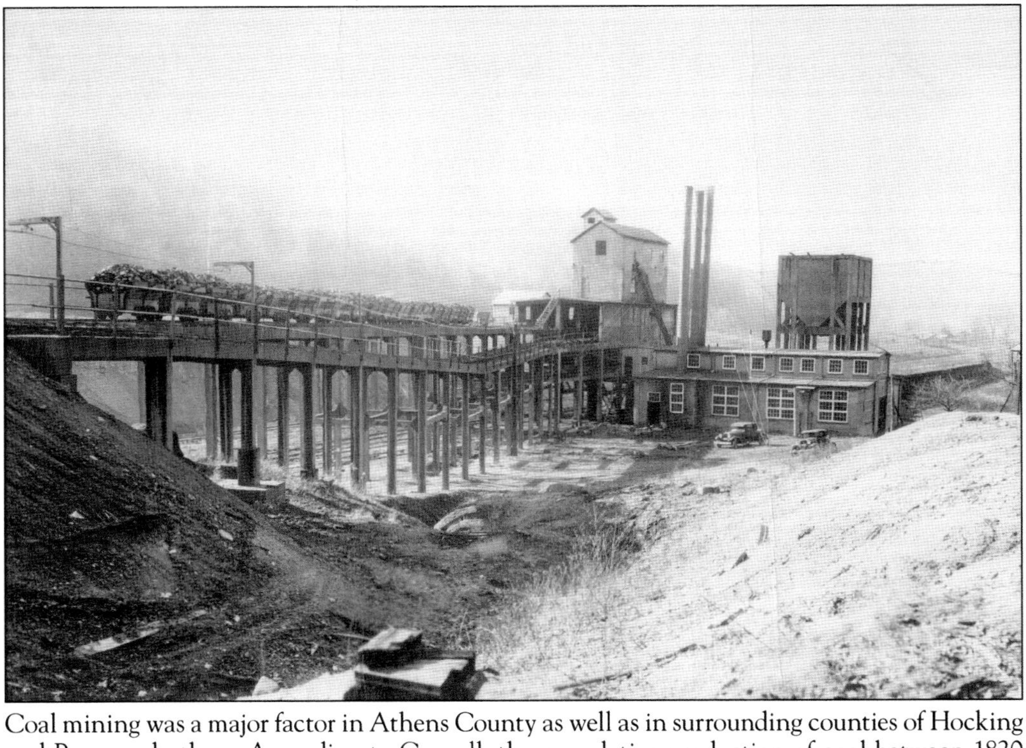

Coal mining was a major factor in Athens County as well as in surrounding counties of Hocking and Perry and others. According to Crowell, the cumulative production of coal between 1820 and 1993 in Athens County was 200,508,978 tons of coal; in all of Ohio between 1800 and 1993, 3,400,071,772 tons of coal were produced. This is Black Diamond Coal Mine No. 12.

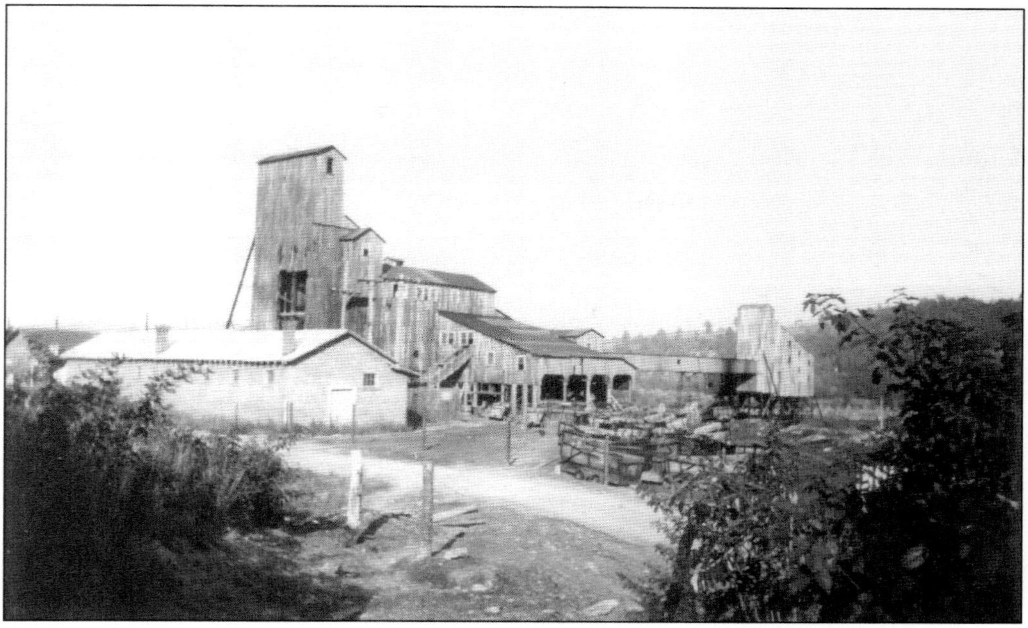

The Pittsburgh Coal Mine No. 9, seen here, was located west of Chauncey in Dover Township. Crowell states that the shaft was abandoned in 1925. He also states that the company store was in Nelsonville and was razed in the late 1920s or early 1930s, and its lumber was used to build the York Township Grange.

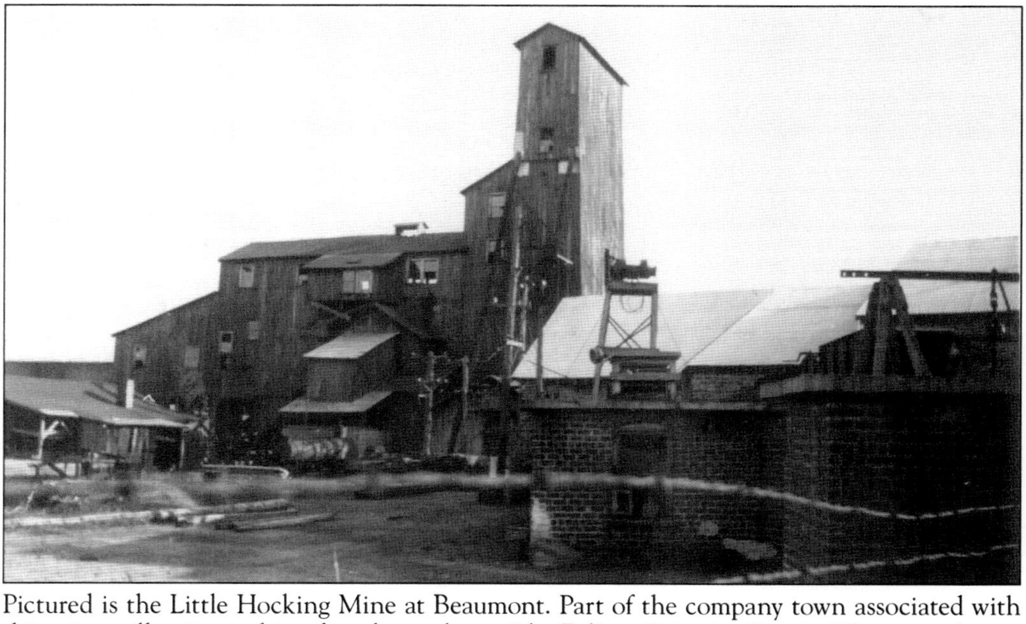

Pictured is the Little Hocking Mine at Beaumont. Part of the company town associated with this mine still exists and is referred to today as "the Eclipse Company" town. The general store has been renovated and is used for banquets and parties. The small company homes are used for both small businesses and dwellings. (Courtesy of the Anastas Collection.)

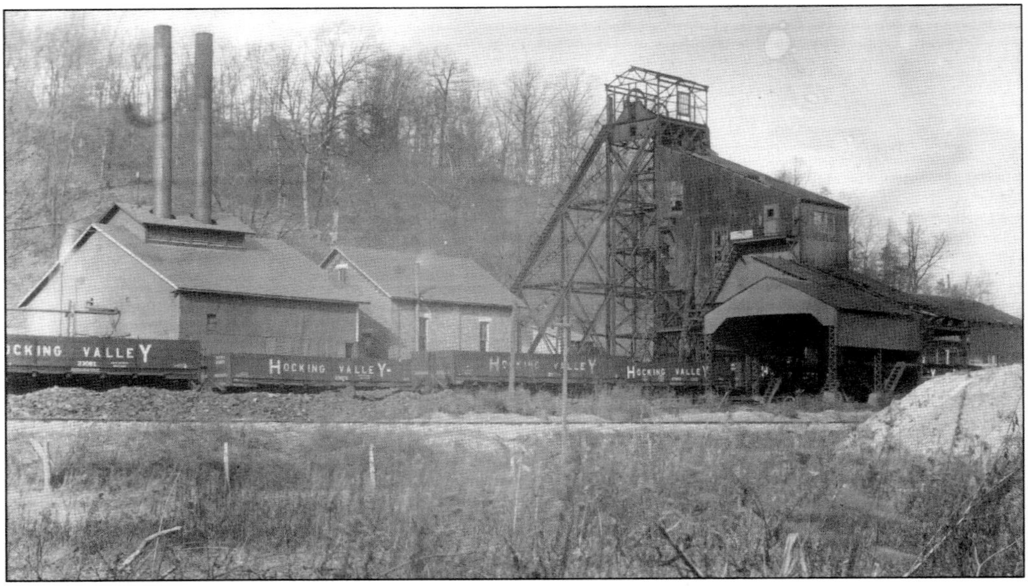

This image is of the Sugar Creek Mine No. 210 in 1910. Many of the old mines were named for the landscape nearby. The Sugar Creek comes in a southeasterly direction from Dover Township and curves back southeast to fall into the Hocking River. Route 550 from Athens curves and winds along about two-thirds of the lower portion of the creek before it veers off toward Amesville. (Courtesy of the Anastas Collection.)

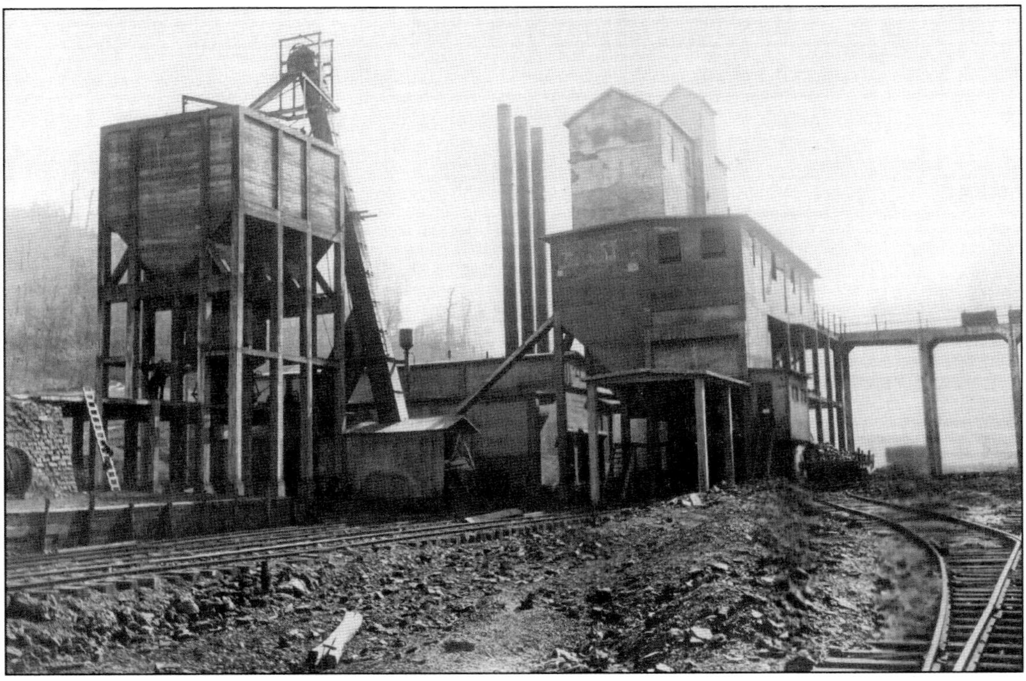

The Black Diamond Coal Company owned and/or operated several mines in Athens County. This mine (No. 2) was located in Lathrop in Bern Township. What is particularly interesting about this particular picture is that it shows one of the earliest uses of a cement tipple. According to Crowell, it was constructed in 1911 to replace a wooden tipple that caught fire and burned the previous year.

BIBLIOGRAPHY

Atlas of Athens Co. Ohio: From Actual Surveys by and Under the Directions of D.J. Lake, C.E. Philadelphia: Titus, Simmons & Titus, 1875.

Beatty, Elizabeth Grover and Marjorie S. Stone. *Getting to Know Athens County.* Athens, OH: self-published, 1984.

Blower, James G. *A Brief History of Trimble Township: Athens County, Ohio; Its Towns, Villages and People.*

Bush, Fred W. *The Centennial Atlas of Athens County, Ohio.* Athens, OH: The Centennial Atlas Association, 1905.

Crowell, Douglas L. *History of the Coal-Mining Industry in Ohio.* Bulletin 72, Department of Natural Resources. Columbus, OH: ODNR, 1995.

Downes, Randolph C. *Evolution of Ohio County Boundaries.* Columbus, OH: Ohio Historical Society, 1927.

Grabb, John R. *The Marietta & Cincinnati Railroad, and Its Successor—The Baltimore & Ohio: A Study of This Once Great Route across Ohio; 1851–1988.* Jackson, OH: Jackson Publishing Company, 1989.

History of Hocking Valley, Ohio: Together with Sketches of Its Cities, Villages and Townships, Educational, Religious, Civil, Military, and Political History, Portraits of Prominent Persons, and Biographies of Representative Citizens. Chicago: Inter-State Publishing Company, 1883.

Hollow, Betty. *Ohio University: The Spirit of a Singular Place; 1804–2004.* Athens, OH: Ohio University Press, 2003.

Howe, Henry. *Historical Collections of Ohio in Two Volumes: An Encyclopedia of the State.* Norwalk, OH: Laning Printing, 1896.

Peters, William E. *Athens County, Ohio,* Vol. 1. Athens, OH: self-published, 1947.

———. "Legal History of the Ohio University." *Ohio University Bulletin,* 7.4, July 1910.

Rose, Anna C. *Yesterdays of The Plains.* Shawnee Mission, KS: Inter-Collegiate Press, 1971.

Tribe, Ivan M. *Little Cities of Black Diamonds: Urban Development in the Hocking Coal Region 1870–1900.* Athens, OH: Athens Ancestree, 1986.

United States Post Offices Volume V—The Ohio Valley. Compiled by Richard W. Helbock. Scappoose, OR: La Posta, 2002.

Walker, Charles M. *History of Athens County, Ohio: And Incidentally of the Ohio Land Company and the First Settlement of the State at Marietta.* Ohio: 1869.

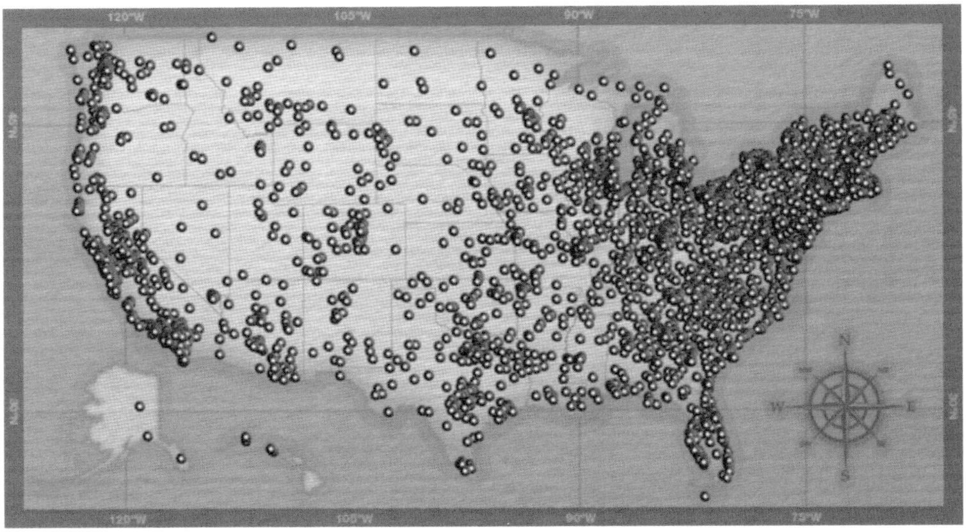